Fibromyalgia

Fibromyalgia

A Journey Toward Healing

Chanchal Cabrera

Contemporary Books

Chicago   New York   San Francisco   Lisbon   London   Madrid   Mexico City
Milan   New Delhi   San Juan   Seoul   Singapore   Sydney   Toronto

Library of Congress Cataloging-in-Publication Data
Cabrera, Chanchal.
   Fibromyalgia : a journey toward healing / Chanchal Cabrera.
     p. cm.
   Includes bibliographical references and index.
   ISBN 0-658-00305-4
   1. Fibromyalgia—Alternative treatment. 1. Title.

RC927-3 C337 2002
616.7'4—dc2l

2001055965

Contemporary Books

A *Division of The* **McGraw-Hill** *Companies*

1 2 3 4 5 6 7 8 9 0   AGM/AGM   1 0 9 8 7 6 5 4 3 2

ISBN 0-658-00305-4

This book was set in Minion by Robert S. Tinnon Design
Printed and bound by Quebecor Martinsburg

Cover design by Laurie Young
Cover illustration by Melissa McGill
Interior design by Robert S. Tinnon

McGraw-Hill books are available at special quantity discounts to use as premiums and sales promotions, or for use in corporate training programs. For more information, please write to the Director of Special Sales, Professional Publishing, McGraw-Hill, Two Penn Plaza, New York, NY 10121-2298. Or contact your local bookstore.

This book is printed on acid-free paper.

For my parents who always encouraged me
to do what felt right in my heart and for
Hein Zeylstra, my teacher and mentor.

CONTENTS

PREFACE

Millions of people are suffering from a strange new disease that many doctors don't recognize. The symptoms fit no familiar pattern, and drugs do not seem to help. Patients and practitioners alike are at a loss. The doctors scratch their heads and the patients' lives descend into a nightmare of recurrent muscle pain, fatigue, headaches, gastric upsets, genitourinary disturbances, and poor sleep. There are too many questions, but virtually no funding to do the research needed to provide the answers. But the prognosis is not entirely bleak. We can choose to take excellent care of our health to enhance our immunity to disease; moreover, once diagnosed, we can follow specific therapeutic protocols to ensure optimum health and well-being. This book is an exploration of the disease called *fibromyalgia*—what causes it, and how we can overcome the symptoms and regain quality of life.

I have written this book from my personal and professional experiences, both as an individual diagnosed with fibromyalgia and as a practitioner encountering it with increasing frequency in my clinical practice. I have often asked myself if I really want to be an "expert" on the subject of fibromyalgia. What does this focus on the disease have to do with healing, either my own or that of my patients? Does it, in fact, hold me back and keep me focused on disease instead of health? In some ways I hope that by writing this book I can finally lay the subject to rest. I consider this book the final stage of my personal healing journey. I hope that it will help you find your way, too.

There are many effective ways to manage and control fibromyalgia syndrome (FMS), to lessen symptoms and promote healing. Through my own healing journey, I have explored a number of them and found much relief.

Through discussions with other people living with FMS, and with health care providers treating the condition, I have come to know about many more therapeutic approaches as well.

Fibromyalgia is a "disease in progress." It has only relatively recently been recognized as a distinct entity, and we are far from understanding the entire picture. Even as I complete the writing of this book, new possible etiologies are being explored, including the involvement of interleukin 6 as a mediator of the energy balance, the likelihood of a viral or fungal component, and the possible significance of an enzyme recently found in the joints of people with FMS. Novel forms of treatment for connective tissue disorders are also being explored and some, such as pulsed signal therapy, are proving extremely effective.

I have described various pharmaceutical approaches, including guaifenesin, although I have not personally used them, because they are widely employed. I have also described the therapies and therapists who helped me, as an illustration of the holistic approach to healing FMS. The book speaks to a broad audience: to people diagnosed with fibromyalgia who seek to understand the condition better and find some solutions, and to professional health care providers who wish to broaden their clinical understanding of the disease and their therapeutic options. I have provided background material where appropriate, so as to better explain the pathophysiology of the disease. The more I researched, the more I realized that this disease is so complex that no one can easily understand all its many ramifications. I have tried to keep my language clear and concise, while also doing justice to the mass of science behind the disease's diagnosis and treatment.

The book is divided into two parts: Part I: "What Is Fibromyalgia?" and Part II: "Holistic Approaches to Fibromyalgia." Part I deals with the disease itself: how it presents (the signs and symptoms); what causes it (the pathophysiology); who gets fibromyalgia and why; and the application of modern, allopathic medicine to the condition. Part II covers the various natural treatment options: using food as medicine; herbal approaches to fibromyalgia; and adjunctive therapies and self-care. In Appendix One at the back of the book, you will find instructions on making herbal medicines. Appendix Two contains an extensive resource guide covering books, Web sites, organizations, and more. Appendix Three contains the herbal materia medica. More detailed information on this as well as text references can be found on my Web site: www.gaiagarden.com.

If you are a person with FMS, you may need to enlist the help of a qualified practitioner to help you decide on the right course of treatment. Don't feel that you have to undertake all these healing techniques at once. However, my clinical experience has shown me that the more healing practices you commit to, the more benefits you can expect. I recommend that you read the entire book before deciding where to start. Set realistic goals, stick to them, and track your progress.

During the course of my illness, I kept a diary, and I have included excerpts throughout the book to illustrate the process I went through as I learned to live with FMS. As I describe my own experience with this disease, I hope it will help you learn how to better manage FMS, either your own or that of a patient, friend, or family member.

ACKNOWLEDGMENTS

Fibromyalgia has been a long learning curve for me. This book has been nine years in gestation and nine months in writing. It could never have happened without some wonderful people helping me along the way. I have had technical support, and support in kind, from my colleagues, my patients, my students, and my family. I especially want to thank: Elena Orrego for spurring me on to leave the city, even though it doubled her workload; Paul Bergner, Jonathan Treasure, and Robert Crayhon for being so ruthlessly honest when reading the manuscript; Helen Kara for wielding that red pen so assiduously; Jan Kinzler for her Internet assistance; Liz McLeod for sharing the journey with me so closely; Ellen McCarthy for introducing me to Contemporary Books; and, last but not least, Robbie, who made it possible.

PART

I

What Is
Fibromyalgia?

Health is more than simply the absence
of illness. It is the active state of
physical, emotional, mental,
and social well-being.

WORLD HEALTH ORGANIZATION

CHAPTER ONE

FIBROMYALGIA
IN CONTEXT

The doctor of the future will give no medicine, but will interest
his patients in the care of the human frame, in diet and
in the cause and prevention of disease.
THOMAS EDISON

November 1991

Just been told officially that it's fibromyalgia. I guess I knew it anyway, but now

that I have a label, maybe I'll be taken seriously. Can't stand that no one sees

what's really going on. They all say I look well and have no idea of the effort it

takes to remain standing upright and talking with them. I have a flashing light

in my eye, but they can't see it; I have a burning and aching in my back, but

they can't feel it, so I must be imagining things. Don't they know I've got better

things to do with my life than to imagine illness? A hypochondriac I am not.

Now I have the whole insurance process to work out and it feels so weird

because I know I have to prove my "pain and suffering" to them, but I don't

know how to keep that from interfering with my healing process. If I am prov-

ing my disability, I am afraid it will warp my thinking and make it harder to

manage. I need to focus on being well, not being sick. My lawyer tells me that

now I can expect the insurance company to have me under video surveillance, trying to catch me doing things they think I shouldn't be able to, looking for

evidence to use against me. What a stupid situation. My doctors tell me to keep

active, that gardening and cycling are good for me, but the insurance company

will use this to deny my disability. Seems like a no-win situation to me.

Fibromyalgia syndrome (FMS) is one of the fastest-growing diagnoses in America today, with upward of six million people currently affected. It is also one of the most controversial conditions, with some doctors still denying its existence and others using it as an excuse for their inability to determine the actual cause of ill health. Some argue that it is vastly overdiagnosed and others that it is vastly underdiagnosed. Either way, it is causing significant suffering and costing many billions of dollars in health care and lost productivity; the condition is estimated to cost the American economy nearly $9.2 billion annually. Prevalence in the general population hovers around 2 percent, or one in fifty people, with 80 to 90 percent of these patients being women. In one study at Tufts University School of Medicine, 100 of 394 female patients (25.4 percent) with FMS and 12 of 44 males (27.3 percent) were so badly affected by the condition that they were unable to work. Estimates of the number of new patients presenting at rheumatology clinics with symptoms of FMS vary from 14.6 percent in 1983 to 25 percent in 1991. The reason for the difference lies partly in the decade-long gap between the estimates, with progressively more diagnoses of FMS being made today, and partly because misdiagnosis and confusion with other pathologies is very common.

As described by the Fibromyalgia Network (www.finnetnews.com), FMS is now considered by many authorities to be a complex of overlapping syndromes, each manifesting to a greater or lesser degree in different people at different times. It includes aspects of chronic fatigue syndrome, restless leg syndrome, irritable bowel, irritable bladder, multiple chemical sensitivities, primary dysmenorrhoea, migraines, periodic limb movement during sleep, tension headaches, temporomandibular joint dysfunction, and myofascial pain syndrome.

Fibromyalgia is chronic and debilitating. In a follow-up study of 530 people with FMS over seven years there was no significant improvement in pain, functional ability, fatigue, sleep, disturbance, or psychological status. Half the patients were dissatisfied with their health.

Fibromyalgia is misunderstood, misdiagnosed, and just plain missed. It manifests as muscle stiffness and pain, debilitating fatigue, tender points, brain fog, and a host of other symptoms. It is primarily a disease of young to midlife women, although it can affect children and the elderly as well. Patients are usually in the middle to upper earning brackets: ambitious, hard-working, perfectionists—what I call the "type AAA" personality. It occurs much less often in men, or so it appears; perhaps they just don't seek help for it as readily as do women.

Epidemiology

FMS is virtually unheard of in third-world and developing countries. Why? Is there something in our food or water or air that isn't in theirs? Is it that doctors outside the developed world are not trained or do not have the time and resources to recognize FMS? Is it a genetic trait found mainly in those of Caucasian origin? In the third world, where life is so much harsher and day-to-day survival more of an issue, could it be that chronic discomfort and disease become less urgent? Perhaps the preponderance of FMS in the developed world is more reflective of the high degree of urbanization in these countries, leading to greater exposure to electromagnetic radiation. Or is it possible that it is due to different exposures to industrial or agricultural pollution? Diet may well play a role, as quite clearly the diet in the West is very different from that of the rest of the world. In America we eat highly processed and refined foods, frequently devoid of nutrients and often laden with toxic residues.

While developing and third-world countries also have their share of toxic wastes, via herbicides and pesticides, the people tend to eat more traditional, natural foods and fewer packaged, processed foods. Or does the explanation lie somewhere else entirely?

Any of these are distinct possibilities and certainly worth researching in more depth. However, at the present level of knowledge, none of them can adequately explain the differences in diagnostic rates among various countries.

History

The symptoms of FMS were first described in the medical literature in 1904 and attributed to an inflammatory condition. Prior to that time, doctors had called the syndrome *muscular rheumatism* or *myalgia*. The condition was named *fibrositis* and later became *fibromyositis,* the *-itis* indicating the supposed inflammatory basis of the condition. When evidence of actual, overt inflammation was noted to be absent, and when the symptoms were associated with depression and stress, the disease was reclassified as *psychogenic rheumatism*.

Leon Chaitow, in his excellent book *Fibromyalgia Syndrome,* gives a detailed history of the development of understanding around FMS. The symptoms of FMS correspond closely with those of *neurasthenia* from one hundred years ago. Inexplicable muscle pain, anxiety, palpitations, dizziness, lassitude, and weakness were the symptoms then as they are now, and the condition was associated mostly with well-to-do young women. More recent research by Goldenberg in 1989 and Yunus in 1994 has identified that the stress and depression are more likely a result of, rather than a cause of, the symptoms, and it was renamed again *fibromyalgia,* meaning muscle pain and fibrosing without overt inflammation. As early as 1973 Hauri and Hawkins demonstrated intrusion of alpha waves into the delta phase of sleep in FMS patients, and in 1975 Moldofsky attributed the underlying cause to impaired sleep.

My Own Experience with Fibromyalgia

My own experience with FMS has been both personal and professional. I am glad to say that now, eleven years after the triggering event, I no longer have FMS. To get here I have had to question everything about myself and change my life and my lifestyle in many ways. I had to question what I had achieved and attained, what I had learned, my sense of self-worth and measurement, and what I really wanted for my life. I suppose you could call it a midlife crisis come early, or perhaps just an unlucky and tempestuous arrangement of the planets in the heavens, but whatever the cause, now, on the other side, I am amazed that I continued to function at all considering how lousy I felt most of the time. Now I wake up refreshed, I have loads of energy, and I do not have to visit the chiropractor every week. Now I can really enjoy every day and be grateful. It didn't used to be like this, believe me.

In 1991, I was a healthy and fit twenty-eight-year-old. I had graduated college in England in 1987, after almost four years of full-time schooling, with a Diploma of Herbal Medicine under my belt, and had worked for a year as a massage therapist in a ski resort before opening my own herbal clinic in Vancouver, British Columbia. I was very physically active, cycling all over the city, doing yoga, hiking, and walking. In July of that year I was a rear-seat passenger in a car sitting stationary in a line of traffic when we were nudged from behind by another car, so gently that the only damage to our car was a bent trailer hitch. That little nudge was to change my life.

At the moment of impact I was leaning forward and twisted through the front seats to give directions to the driver, and my seat belt was momentarily undone. Because of the angle of impact and direction of torsion of my body, the damage I suffered was out of all proportion to the severity of the accident, a fact not lost on the insurance adjuster, who later used it to cast doubt upon the validity of my claim for damages. Within minutes of the impact my neck and shoulders had seized up and a dull headache had consumed me. So began the slow descent into FMS. It took several months for a diagnosis to be made and then I began receiving appropriate treatment. As a health professional myself, it seemed natural to seek assistance far and wide. Some of this proved to be very useful and some was a waste of money. Along the way my understanding of the disease deepened. I talked about it with other health care providers, including the pain and rehabilitation specialists with whom I consulted for my own condition. Eventually they could see how helpful my herbal regimen was, and they began to send their patients to me until soon I was seeing as many as ten cases every week. This gave me a unique opportunity to learn about the condition both firsthand and as a health care provider.

Naturally, I couldn't advise people how to treat their FMS without undertaking such treatments myself. I was constantly confronted with the disease, and it was perhaps that, as much as anything else, that has enabled me to learn to control it rather than allowing it to control me. I believe that, in learning how to live with and through chronic disease, I have had a unique opportunity to grow and develop as a healer, and that I have learned many useful techniques and strategies for achieving and maintaining optimal health. It is these that I wish to share in this book.

In discussing this book as a work in progress with my friends, I laughingly said that I had figured out the cure for FMS and that it is as simple as changing your life. Although it was said in jest, there is a lot of truth to it. I believe that the fundamental problem in FMS, notwithstanding genetic, traumatic, and all sorts of other contributing factors, is that we are somehow out of balance with our world. We live and work in concrete boxes, and drive our air-conditioned cars from one to the other. We may join other urban dwellers for a walk in the park at lunch hour, but we rarely if ever experience Nature in all her might and glory, as our ancestors once did. We have lost touch with that essential, natural part of ourselves, and our rhythmic connection to the earth has been undermined. Frumkin has identified the therapeutic value of the wilderness experience and the critical importance to overall health of individual contact with the forces of nature. Many aspects of our urban life, from exposure to toxins and pollution to lack of sleep, yield a chronic pattern that our physical bodies can't handle. Prolonged adrenalin and glucocorticoid release as a stress response cannot be sustained by the adrenal glands, and they become exhausted. Thus begins the whole cascade of neuroendocrine dysregulation that characterizes FMS.

In a way I see FMS as a disease of the soul, a sort of psychic poisoning by the modern world. My preferred prescription for FMS is "move to the country." What is needed is a slower, more peaceful pace of life, a healthier environment, and the ability to absorb healing energies from the forest and field. Modern Western society does not honor, support, or encourage us to take the time to smell the roses. We are pressured through school, college, work, and family to do more, achieve more, produce more, be the first or the best. We are not taught to look after ourselves, to allow play time and recuperation time and quiet time for reflection and introspection. High levels of electromagnetic pollution, lack of contact with nature and the elements and seasons, excessively hectic and frenetic schedules, and more and more pressure on our time—these are all significant contributory factors in the development of FMS. I firmly believe that a more balanced lifestyle incorporating play, rest, and quiet time, as well as appropriate and pleasurable work, can ensure significant health improvements at every level.

If this sounds mystical and "New Agey," I offer no apologies but rather a challenge: try it and see. After struggling for seven years with FMS, attempting to maintain a clinical practice and a retail business, as well as a teaching schedule, I finally admitted defeat and took myself to live on a 150-acre organic herb farm in Virginia. Three years later I can honestly say that I don't have FMS anymore. This is not to say I don't get stiff or achy sometimes, or that my neck doesn't go out occasionally, but a couple of headaches in the past six months is nothing compared to the almost weekly, knockdown, drag-out headaches I used to get just a couple of years ago. Moreover, I now enjoy increased energy, deeper sleep, and an altogether greater *joie de vivre*.

These days I sleep an average of eight to nine hours a night, in a room that is absolutely dark. I go to bed much earlier than I have since I was a kid, and I sleep as long as I want in the morning. Even if I do occasionally waken in the night for a little while, knowing I don't have to get up in the morning allows me to relax and not fret; then I fall back to sleep much more quickly. My morning routine includes thirty minutes of stretching, which I do diligently an average of four days a week, and I walk thirty to forty-five minutes virtually every day. These days I can walk very fast and work up a good sweat, and I feel really good afterward. I am even able to do yard work quite comfortably now. I am exposed to less electromagnetic and airborne pollution. I still need chiropractic every few weeks, and I love a massage anytime, but I am no longer hooked into a cycle of treatment that sustained and maintained me but did not heal me. When I was ill, I did Pilates three times weekly, massage and craniosacral weekly, chiropractic fortnightly, and still felt lousy. I lurched from one appointment to the next and wondered why I wasn't getting any better. I couldn't have managed without those treatments in the past, but now they aren't a necessary part of my life support program.

I also eat differently now. For one thing, meals tend to be more regular and almost always at home. In the past I often ate in a hurry between meetings, or very late. Also, I have added fish to my diet, after years as a complete vegetarian, and I believe the additional protein has contributed to increased energy; improved health of skin, hair, and nails; and increased muscle endurance. I am taking specific supplements to balance my own biochemical individuality, which has also resulted in a significant increase in energy.

Through this whole experience, I have reached the conclusion that FMS is caused by a disharmonious lifestyle. Being out of balance or equilibrium at many levels, being disassociated from nature and natural cycles of the seasons, being disconnected from community and self—all of these will contribute to and predispose one toward ill health. People with full-blown FMS have usually been unwell for quite some time before they are diagnosed and, if questioned closely, will usually describe a sense of knowing that they were "out of balance" or "not in optimum health" for months or years before seeking help. Typically, they have ignored and suppressed messages from the body for years, messages saying "I am tired," "I am stressed," "I am nutritionally depleted," and so on. Instead of honoring these messages and paying attention, many people take more coffee or sugar, seek pharmaceutical relief, or simple ignore them. Years of stressing the body without giving it adequate exercise or sufficient rest, eating the wrong foods, smoking, drinking—eventually they exact their price.

I had been struggling with FMS for several years, denying the symptoms, surviving on herbs and vitamins and massage, pretending everything was fine, and trying to maintain a hectic schedule despite my declining health, when I had one of those epiphanies that changed my life. It happened in my clinic one day, with a patient called Ms. M who also had FMS. I had been treating her for some time, and we had achieved some successful management and coping strategies but were no nearer a cure than when she had commenced with herbal medicine. On the day in question she responded to my inquiries by saying that she felt lousy and wasn't sure the herbs were going to help. She was sitting on the floor—sitting in a chair was too uncomfortable—and she began to cry in frustration and pain. Without thinking about what I was doing, I found myself on the floor beside her, arms around her, and we wept together for about fifteen minutes. Once, for a moment I thought, "Whatever am I doing?! This is exactly what they told us in college to avoid doing, personalizing and empathizing with the patient, taking on her pain and fear." But it felt right, and I allowed myself to relax with the energy and to feel my own pain and weariness and fear. After a while we mopped our tears and began to talk. Ms. M said that this had been one of the most healing and beneficial sessions with a practitioner ever. She knew there were no magic answers to her problems, she appreciated that I did not try to fob her off with platitudes about how it was all going to be fine, and she appreciated knowing that I truly empathized with her and understood the frustration, fear, and pain she felt.

For myself, I felt as if I had undergone a revelation. I had stepped right outside the box, upended the nice, safe, familiar practitioner-patient relationship, and admitted that I did not have the solution to her health problems. I felt incredibly liberated. It was okay not to know how to help someone, okay just to feel her pain with her and to express my own to her, okay to be authentic. I knew from that moment that to heal myself I had to learn to "live outside the box." I had been so busy trying to live with and fix my health problems that I had never stopped to ask why I had become sick in the first place. I had never explored the fundamental imbalances that had lowered my resistance and made me vulnerable to FMS. I realized that I couldn't heal others until I had healed myself, and that to do that would require a complete change of lifestyle, stress patterns, and priorities. I believe that my healing journey started that day. I have come a long way toward health since then, and I believe that being true to myself, being authentic, honoring my own needs and desires, and placing health as a higher priority than income or career were all integral parts of the healing process.

The true challenge of fibromyalgia is to love and respect yourself enough to be willing to do whatever it takes to be well. Taking extraordinary care of your body and soul requires great sacrifices sometimes. For me it meant quitting my clinical practice, moving out of the city to live in the country, taking two years off to focus on healing and achieving balance, and, in the process, decreasing my income by more than half. Despite the difficulties of doing this, it has been worth every sacrifice to regain my health. Learning to take great care of my body; loving, honoring, and accepting myself exactly as I am right now—these, I learned, are the true secrets of achieving and maintaining good health of the body and soul.

Chapter Two

The Clinical Features of Fibromyalgia

*It is more important to know what kind of person has
a disease than what kind of disease a person has.*
HIPPOCRATES

January 1996

*Getting very fed up with this chronic fatigue and pain. I am functioning but at
a high price. I am having chiropractic twice a week because that is the only way
I can keep my neck in place, otherwise it goes out at the C2/C3 and I get blind-
ing right-sided headaches. Have had to cancel work and come home to lie down
several times. I feel weak, cold, shivery, and nauseous with the headache and
there are dancing spots and stripes in the right eye. Am also having weekly
massage which is a lifesaver. Costing me a fortune, but I have to do something or
I will just be in bed all day. Actually, that sounds like a terrific idea—I would
love to just sleep for about a year. I am so tired, so very tired and I never seem to
get enough sleep. Actually, my whole internal clock seems out of sync because
I get really tired after lunch, sometimes having to lie down between patients and
rest. If I'm at home, I try to take a nap. Then I get an energy surge around 9 or
10 P.M. and feel all lively and raring to go and unable to relax and sleep. When*

I do go to bed I lie awake awhile, wake several times in the night, and in the morning I am not refreshed at all. I am stiff and sore and aching. Thank God for the walk to work because it gets my blood flowing and makes me able to get through the day. God, what a litany of woes. Trying so hard to keep cheerful and positive; but sometimes I wonder why.

FMS is notoriously difficult to diagnose and many people are misdiagnosed (and consequently mistreated) for years before their wide range of apparently disparate symptoms finally gets recognized. On the other hand, many people are told they have FMS when in fact there is some other underlying pathology. It is both dismissed as being "all in the mind" and also used as a "garbage can" diagnosis when nothing else fits. The diagnosis is often one of exclusion—if the symptom picture doesn't fit any other recognized disease entity, then it must be FMS. This is compounded by the lack of clearly defined and consistently reliable diagnostic features for FMS and by the persistent lack of medical understanding of, or even belief in, the condition.

In 1990 the American College of Rheumatology (ACR) published criteria for the diagnosis of FMS based on clinical research drawn from all over the United States and Canada. The criteria are widespread aching and fatigue lasting more than three months and the presence of local tenderness at eleven of eighteen specified sites (tender points) in all four regional quadrants of the body (upper right, upper left, lower right, and lower left). Axial skeleton pain (in the cervical, thoracic, or lumbar spine, or the anterior chest) must also be present.

There is currently no blood test or other laboratory workup that definitively reveals FMS. This may change soon due to recent evidence pointing toward alterations in the neurotransmitters, Substance P, and serotonin levels in cerebrospinal fluid, as well as cerebrocirculatory abnormalities and possibly phosphate metabolism abnormalities. In the future perhaps we will test for these various disturbances and use them as diagnostic criteria. At present, though, accurate diagnosis relies upon a thorough case history plus careful palpation of tender points and exclusion of any other specific pathology. Over the years doctors have come to recognize a variety of distinctive clinical features of FMS, any or all of which may be present at various times through the duration of the illness in any individual. They may wax and wane over time, but the muscle fatigue, stiffness, and tender points are always present.

(*Note:* The "Natural Remedies" offered throughout this chapter are aimed at symptomatic improvement; they do not necessarily address the whole condition. For details on how to apply these remedies and how to customize and personalize a treatment protocol, refer to Chapter 7.)

Major Symptoms of Fibromyalgia

The following are the major symptoms of fibromyalgia:

- Muscle stiffness and aching
- Muscle fatigue
- Tender points
- Disturbed sleep
- Fatigue
- Sensitivity to cold
- Bruxism (tooth grinding)
- Digestive disturbance
- Genitourinary disturbance
- Sensory overload
- Brain fog
- Depression
- Dry eyes and mouth
- Headaches
- Rhinitis (sinus disturbance)
- Skin, hair, and nail problems

Widespread Aching and Diffuse Stiffness

Deep aching and stiffness in the muscles is the universal symptom of FMS. It is often worse in the morning and may ease up as the day progresses. It may affect any or all muscle groups. Medical diagnosis requires the stiffness and pain to be present in all four quadrants of the body, to have been present for more than three months, and to be unrelated to any other known disease process. Muscle stiffness may be so severe that ligaments and tendons are involved. This will cause a "crunching" sound with certain movements as tight tendons and ligaments move over joints. The stiffness is frequently worse in the mornings, easing somewhat as the day goes on, is aggravated by strenuous exercise, and is made much worse by cold. Gentle stretching exercises, heat applications, and physical therapy such as massage can reduce the stiffness temporarily.

Natural Remedies

- Stretching, yoga, massage, heat applications
- Mustard oil massage
- Warming and stimulating essential oils such as black pepper, juniper, rosemary, and niouli
- Epsom salt bath
- Cramp-Ease liniment
- Circulatory stimulants such as prickly ash, ginger, and cayenne
- Muscle relaxants such as lobelia, cramp bark, and kava

Easy Fatiguing of Muscles

People with FMS have a low tolerance to repetitive movements or to strenuous exercise. Such common daily activities as chopping vegetables, scrubbing the bathtub, or carrying shopping bags may cause extreme muscle pain and fatigue.

The fatigue may be mild or severe, even disabling. It may be eased somewhat by stretching exercises and mild to moderate aerobic activity. This improvement after moderate exercise is one of the diagnostic differences between FMS and chronic fatigue syndrome.

Natural Remedies

- Learn to pace yourself.
- Set realistic goals and don't overdo it.
- Get plenty of sleep and take naps when you can.
- Circulatory tonics such as prickly ash, ginger, and cayenne
- Adrenal tonic herbs such as licorice, verbena, and Siberian ginseng
- Coenzyme Q10, spirulina, royal jelly, and bee pollen
- Get outside and enjoy nature as often as possible.
- Practice breathing exercises and really oxygenate the body.

Trigger Points and Tender Points

There is much confusion in the literature between these two closely related muscle symptoms. Essentially, they are brought about by various muscle stressors, and both manifest as palpable sore spots felt in the muscles of the arms, legs, back, and chest; the muscles themselves are often ropy and fibrous as well. The difference is that while trigger points refer their pain to distant sites, tender points do not. It has been suggested that tender points are in fact latent trigger points.[1]

Trigger points and tender points are thought to occur when chronic tension and contraction of muscle fibers impairs the local circulation to the muscle and the microcirculation to the affected area. This causes accumulation of metabolic waste materials from the affected cells, chiefly lactic acid due to ischemia or lack of oxygen, and impairs the body's self-healing ability. This initial impairment of local and microcirculation will occur when a muscle is chronically stressed through overuse or misuse, when the body is kept in a state of chronic stress (hyperadrenalism), or when there is chronic sleep disturbance and consequent impairment of tissue healing. In some cases it is possible to actually feel the trigger and tender points as hard, granular accretions that may "crunch" under the fingers.

Pressure on a tender or trigger point may initially cause symptoms varying in degree from mild discomfort through soreness to acute pain according to intensity of the pressure and the level of conditioning of the muscle. Sustained pressure on a trigger point may cause some temporary easing of the soreness, but also causes referral of pain to nearby areas served by related nerves.

In the medical diagnosis of FMS much has been made of the importance of tender points, which are clinically different from trigger points in that they don't refer pain to distant sites. The tender points of FMS also tend to contribute to a widespread muscle tension and aching that is not so prevalent in myofascial pain syndrome (MPS). There are eighteen different tender points (nine pairs) that occur with some regularity in FMS patients. For a medical diagnosis of FMS to be made, eleven of the eighteen must be present in the expected sites. (See Figure 2.1.) Using moderate pressure (about 4 kg, or enough to whiten the thumbnail when pressing), actual pain should be elicited, not just a tenderness or the sensation of the pressure. The drawbacks to this diagnostic criteria are that awareness of pain is very subjective and that the tender points tend to migrate and to wax and wane in severity over time. On a good day only three or four tender points may be really troublesome, whereas on a bad day it could be twenty or more. Despite current medical opinion to the contrary, I believe that absence of the classical tender points does not mean one doesn't have FMS. The entire symptom picture must be taken into account and a diagnosis should not be made on the presence or absence of one symptom alone. (See Figure 2.2.)

Occasionally a nerve will pass between a tender point and a bone. When this occurs a nerve may become entrapped, causing numbness and burning, tingling, and crawling sensations. Ice will usually relieve this sensation temporarily.

The sternocleidomastoid muscle (SCM) runs from behind the ear (the mastoid process) to the clavicle (collarbone) and sternum. It serves many purposes, including turning the head and keeping the head upright. Nerve endings in the muscle transmit signals that tell the brain the spatial position of the head and consequently the rest of the body. When tender points are

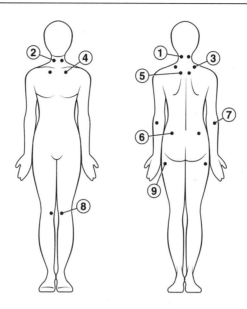

1. The insertion of the suboccipital muscles at the base of the skull
2. Anterior aspect of lower neck—intertranverse spaces between C5 and C7 vertebrae.
3. The trapezius muscle in the midpoint of the upper border
4. The costochondral junctions, of the second ribs
5. At the origins of the supraspinatus muscles above the scapular spine
6. The gluteus medius muscle, upper outer area of the buttock
7. 1 to 2 cm distal of the epicondyles of the elbow (tennis elbow)
8. The medial, upper knee, proximal to the joint line
9. The greater trochanter (top of the thighbone)

Figure 2.1 Tender Points Typically Found in Fibromyalgia

Myofascial Pain Syndrome	Fibromyalgia Syndrome
• Trigger points refer pain to distant sites	• Tender points do not refer pain
• Usually caused by trauma or misuse	• Multiple structural and functional causes
• Men and women affected equally	• More women affected than men
• About 30 percent have fibrous, ropy muscles	• About 60 percent have fibrous, ropy muscles
• Little impairment of muscle stamina or endurance	• Significant impairment of muscle stamina or endurance
• May cause sleep disturbance	• Caused in part by and causes chronic sleep disturbance
• No morning stiffness	• Noticeable morning stiffness
• No fatigue, memory loss, confusion	• Chronic fatigue, memory loss, confusion
• No associated digestive or urinary symptoms	• Associated with irritable bowel syndrome, vulvodynia, and interstitial cystitis
• No associated cardiac abnormalities	• High correlation with mitral valve prolapse
• Usually localized to a specific area	• Widespread and generalized; occurs in all four quadrants of the body
• Exercise is not particularly helpful	• Moderate exercise is helpful and beneficial
• Physical therapy, massage, chiropractic, and acupuncture can be very helpful	• No cure known; management strategies can help
• Prognosis and clinical outlook is good	• Prognosis and clinical outlook is chronic

Figure 2.2 A Comparison of Myofascial Pain Syndrome and
       Fibromyalgia Syndrome

present in the SCM, which is common in FMS, the nerve messages sent to the brain may be disrupted or disturbed. When the head moves, for example with turning or standing up, the brain may compute the location of the body according to the impulses it receives, but in fact the body may not be quite there. This may cause dizziness or a sensation that the walls or floor are tilting. Because of this people with FMS often seem clumsy; they walk into doors, drop things, and trip. This is probably aggravated by circulatory abnormalities in the brain, especially in the thalamus, which is a relay station for all sensory and motor impulses.

Disturbed Sleep and Chronic Fatigue

Sleep disturbance is almost universal in people with FMS. Problems may include difficulty falling asleep; waking in the night, sometimes for an hour or more at a time; or waking early and being unable to sleep again. Some unlucky people have elements of all three types of disturbances. People with FMS tend to be light sleepers, with sensitivity to noise, light, or other distractions. They often get sleepy at inappropriate times (in the middle of the morning or right after dinner). If they refuse to give in to the urge to rest and push on, they will often get a second wind and may even start to feel "wired." Later, when they do want to rest, this surge of adrenaline may disrupt sleep even further.

One of the most common complaints in FMS is nonrestorative sleep. Even after eight or ten hours in bed, one still wakes feeling exhausted and no amount of resting seems to help. Sleep is essential to healing and without it you may enter a vicious cycle where healing and recuperation become progressively harder to attain. Pituitary hormones released during deep sleep trigger the healing of microtrauma in the muscles. In addition, a host of other positive neuroendocrine and neuromuscular events occur. Studies of people with FMS in sleep laboratories have shown repeated intrusions of alpha wave (waking) brain patterns into the delta (deepest) sleep phase. Thus, the body does not stay in the deep, healing, restorative sleep phase long enough. To compound the problem, chronic sleep deprivation will worsen the perception of pain, and all other symptoms of FMS are aggravated when sleep is disturbed. As many as 25 percent of people with FMS suffer from sleep apnea, meaning they momentarily stop breathing many times during the night. As many as 16 percent of people with FMS have "restless leg syndrome," which means they cannot keep still in bed. This can seriously disrupt sleep, as can bruxism, or teeth grinding, which also affects many people with FMS.

Natural Remedies

- Go to bed and get up at regular times.
- Exercise daily.
- Take melatonin before bed.
- Sleep in the dark.
- Practice stress reduction.
- Use sedative and hypnotic herbs such as passionflower, kava, wild lettuce, and Jamaican dogwood.
- Avoid caffeine.

Sensitivity to Cold

Almost all people with FMS experience a worsening of their symptoms when they are in cold or wet weather. They prefer sunny climates and generally feel better in the summer. This is probably due to reduced peripheral circulation when the body is cold, leading to impaired perfusion of muscles and waste removal, with consequent buildup of lactic and uric acid, and hence aggravation of stiffness and pain in the muscles. Almost 40 percent of people with FMS also experience some degree of Raynaud's phenomenon. This is a condition in which the microvasculature of the hands goes into spasms in cold weather, causing impaired circulation and ischemia. Initially the hand will be white and cold, then blue and numb. A rebound response will then cause overdilation, and blood rushes back, causing reddening along with tingling and burning. People with FMS should always be sure to dress warmly and wear gloves in the winter. Recent research has suggested that sensory receptors in the skin that register cold are unusually sensitive and cold and pain thresholds were lowered in people with FMS.

Natural Remedies

- Ginger tea
- Exercise
- Spicy foods
- Circulatory stimulant herbs such as prickly ash, cayenne, and rosemary

Bruxism and Temporomandibular Joint Pain

Teeth clenching and teeth grinding (bruxism) are very common in people with FMS. This typically leads to some degree of temporomandibular joint dysfunction (TMJ), manifesting as stiffness and pain in the muscles of the jaw, as well as clicking or popping sounds on opening the jaw and difficulty in opening wide. This is certainly aggravated by misalignments of the cervical spine and by spasming of tender points in the muscles of the neck and throat. Chiropractors believe there is a connection between TMJ and misalignments of the sacroiliac joints. Because clenching and grinding may cause damage to the teeth, it is important to wear a splint or guard. These are made of plastic and fit over the teeth to prevent grinding tooth on tooth. A splint should be made for the lower, not the upper, jaw. This is because the bony plates of the skull, which meet in

the bony palate of the upper jaw, exert a rhythmic pulsation that pumps cerebrospinal fluid around the central nervous system. Wearing a splint on the
upper teeth would lock the bones into one position and prevent this essential
pumping action. In addition, a splint is more comfortable to wear on the lower
jaw, although slightly harder for the dentist to fit. Chiropractic and craniosacral
therapy can be particularly helpful for this condition.

Digestive Disturbance

When the body is in chronic or acute stress, the sympathetic component of
the nervous system predominates, with the catecholamines, chiefly adrenaline and noradrenaline (epinephrine and norepinephrine), as the predomi-
nant neurotransmitters. These cause diversion of blood supply from the
digestive, eliminative, and reproductive organs to the limbs, brain, and lungs.
Reduced blood supply causes impaired oxygenation of the tissues. Glands
that are not adequately perfused are unable to produce their normal secretions, including hydrochloric acid, digestive enzymes, sodium bicarbonate,
and mucus. People with FMS are known to exhibit excessive sympathetic
dominance, and this predisposes to symptoms of impaired appetite, indigestion, gas, bloating, and alternating constipation and diarrhea.

Some people also experience abdominal cramping to varying degrees. This
suggests that spasming and tension may be occurring in smooth muscle as
well as in skeletal muscle. This gastrointestinal component of FMS closely
resembles irritable bowel syndrome (IBS), a condition known to be associated
with stress. Many people with FMS note that they experienced some digestive
disturbance long before developing full-blown FMS. Indeed, some researchers
are suggesting that IBS is a form of FMS. Many people with FMS experience
episodic or alternating bouts of constipation and diarrhea, which again mim-
ics IBS. Reduced secretion of digestive juices due to chronic stress allows partially digested food particles to pass down the gut, where they may cause

irritation of the mucous membrane. This is compounded by the reduction in protective mucus, and the end result can be the formation of microlesions in the gut wall through which improperly digested food particles may enter the bloodstream. This phenomenon is called "leaky gut syndrome" and may lead to food allergies and possibly autoimmune disease. Adding to this problem is the fact that improperly digested sugars tend to ferment in the gut and provide a good growth medium for the *Candida albicans* yeast and other fungal growth. Filaments from *Candida* can penetrate the gut wall and provide an easy passage of partially digested food particles into the bloodstream. In addition, the fermentation of sugars and the metabolic processes of *Candida* tend to cause accumulation of gas, which may lead to abdominal bloating and cramping. Other well-known symptoms of *Candida* include fatigue, disturbance of memory and concentration, and brain fog. Obviously it is important to differentiate between the presence of *Candida* in the system and the occurrence of FMS. Overlapping of symptoms and concurrent existence of the two conditions can lead to much confusion. In clinical practice it is wise to test for and treat *Candida* before commencing treatment for FMS; otherwise it may be impossible to assess the benefits and efficacy of the FMS treatment.

Natural Remedies

- Digestive enzymes such as papain, bromelain, and betaine HC1
- Acidophilus and probiotics
- Slippery elm gruel
- Demulcents such as marshmallow and plantain
- Carminatives such as peppermint, chamomile, and ginger
- Tannins such as tormentil and red raspberry
- N-acetylglucosamine
- Quercitin
- Glutamine

Genitourinary Disturbance

Genitourinary symptoms commonly associated with FMS include inflammation of the bladder (cystitis) and urethra (urethritis), stinging or burning pain on urination (dysuria), spasmodic cramping of the urinary tract manifesting as sharp pains in the loin or groin, sharp or dull pains in the reproductive organs of women (vulvodynia), and inflammation of the vaginal glands and lowest part of the vaginal canal (vestibulitis). Many people with FMS experience frequency of urination and a sensation of being unable to empty the bladder completely. In the absence of bacterial infections or *Candida* in the bladder this may be diagnosed as interstitial cystitis (IC). This is a condition of unknown etiology that may also have autoimmune implications. It appears likely that many women with IC probably also have FMS. Possibly IC is another example of generalized and widespread muscle spasms rather than another, separate condition, or they may be one and the same condition manifesting in different forms. Just as with irritable bowel syndrome and chronic fatigue syndrome, there are too many correlations and overlaps for convenient categorization and classification of distinct disease entities. Both the Interstitial Cystitis Network and the Interstitial Cystitis Association have acknowledged in their newsletters and Web sites that FMS, IBS, and vulvodynia are the conditions most commonly coexisting with IC. Some relief may be obtained by using the pharmaceutical *Pyridium*, which numbs the bladder. In very severe situations a qualified herbalist may use a plant called *Hyoscyamus niger* or henbane. A toxic plant when improperly prepared, it can be used to relax bladder spasms. A new drug called Pentosan polysulphate (Elmiron) coats the bladder lining and provides a soothing effect. The same effect can be obtained by the use of demulcent herbs.

Dr. R. Paul St. Amand claims the situation is exacerbated by irritation of the delicate urethral mucosal lining by calcium phosphate, calcium oxalate, and other crystals that accumulate in the neck of the bladder.[3] Muscle wall biopsies have so far failed to confirm this. Vulvodynia, or vulvar pain syndrome, is a condition of sometimes acute and severe pain, with or without itching, in the female genitalia. There may be varying degrees of visible inflammation or lesions, sometimes self-induced through uncontrollable scratching. Urination over inflamed tissue is painful, intercourse is impossible, and even wearing tight clothing such as jeans can create incredible pain. Research by Dr. Clive Solomons, a biochemist, suggests that urinary oxalates are the culprit, serving as a chemical irritant. He has found disproportionate amounts of excreted oxalates in the urine of women with vulvodynia. He has devised a treatment plan based on a low-oxalate diet. See Chapter 5 for details of a low-oxalate diet.

Natural Remedies

- Mix ½ teaspoon bicarbonate of soda in a glass of water and drink. Do *not* do this daily to avoid overalkalizing the body.
- Avoid cranberries, which acidify the urine. This is not an infection so cranberry is not warranted.
- Avoid caffeine, hot spicy foods, alcohol, and soda pop.
- Use soothing diuretic herbs such as couch grass, corn silk, and marshmallow.
- Drink lots of water.
- Place castor oil packs over the bladder.

Sensory Overload

This is not an objective finding but a subjective experience. People with FMS may experience anxiety, hyperventilation, and palpitations when exposed to loud sounds, bright or flashing lights, or crowds of people. On a bad day even seeing a striped or spotted fabric is painful, and watching television or viewing a computer screen becomes impossible. People with FMS appear to be

, sensitive to electromagnetic frequencies (EMF). Often they suf-
_rbation of their symptoms when around power lines, computers,
mi͝ ͵wave ovens, and fluorescent lights. Many people experience improvement of their symptoms in the countryside, and it is possible that this might
be due to the relative absence of EMF.

With sensory overload, the ability to cope with stress is reduced. It feels as
though the normal protective barrier between oneself and the rest of the
world has worn thin. Pacing oneself is essential in learning to cope with this
symptom. You might be able to go to the meeting *or* the party, but not both;
maybe you can only stay an hour at either before you need to go home and
rest. This extreme sensitivity to sensory stimulus may be associated with
chronic stress patterns. Under sympathetic dominance, such as occurs with
chronic stress, there is impaired circulation to the adrenal glands and this
may exacerbate the problem by inhibiting adrenal function and reducing the
stress-coping hormones.

Natural Remedies

- Lie down and rest at intervals throughout the day.
- Don't try to do more than one thing at a time.
- Make sure you get outside, ideally into nature, every day.
- Sedative and relaxing herbs such as chamomile, valerian, passion-
  flower, and verbena
- Nerve tonic herbs such as St. John's wort, oats, damiana, and
  borage
- Avoid undue exposure to EMF—electric blankets, heating pads, hair
  dryers, microwave ovens, computers, cell phones, clock radios,
  and televisions.
- Avoid perfumes and other artificial scents and chemicals.

Brain Fog

Technically referred to as cognitive dysfunction, this is a common complaint in FMS. Inability to remember names or dates or words, confusion, difficulty forming coherent sentences, difficulty telling left from right, and poor concentration are frequent features of FMS. Children with FMS may be misdiagnosed as being dyslexic. Brain fog is known to happen to people deprived of sleep for several nights and is presumably due to neurotransmitter and cerebral circulatory abnormalities. Brain fog is often compounded by the side effects of various medications, specifically antidepressant drugs.

Natural Remedies

- Get plenty of sleep.
- Walk in the fresh air daily.
- Cerebrocirculatory stimulants such as rosemary, ginkgo, and gotu kola
- Periwinkle to improve uptake of oxygen and glucose by the brain
- Phosphatidyl serine and choline
- S-adenosyl-methionine (SAMe)
- Peppermint, basil, pine, black pepper, and essential oils

Depression

Certainly people with FMS will be depressed. Their lives are often shattered by chronic pain, they may lose relationships and jobs, and their quality of life is seriously impaired. And yet, as we are seeing in so many diseases, from allergies to cancer, the attitude that we adopt toward our current condition dictates much about how the experience will be perceived. As Fritzjof Capra says in *The Tao of Physics,* "the observer influences the outcome." All sufferers of chronic disease, including FMS, would benefit from some form of meditation or spiritual practice to help them cultivate a positive attitude toward the healing process and prevent the tendency to become a victim of the condition.

However, there are some people with FMS for whom stronger medicine is needed. Chronic pain is known to cause depression. It exhausts the body's ability to produce endorphins, the hormones that modulate pain and provide a natural antidepressant and mood-elevating effect. Serotonin deficiency may compound this situation and worsen both the sensation of pain and depression. The noticeable improvement of symptoms of FMS in the summer months gives rise to speculation that people with FMS may be more

---

Major Clinical Signs of Depression

- Depressed mood most of the time and for days at a time
- Diminished interest or lack of pleasure in almost all activities of the day or nearly every day
- Unexplained, significant weight loss or gain, and decreased or increased appetite nearly every day
- Insomnia or hypersomnia (excessive sleep) nearly every day
- Abnormal restlessness or drop in physical activity
- Fatigue or loss of energy nearly every day
- Feelings of worthlessness or inappropriate guilt nearly every day
- Diminished ability to think, concentrate, or make decisions nearly every day
- Recurrent thoughts of death, or recurrent suicidal thoughts

From the American Psychiatric Association, *The Diagnostic and Statistical Manual of Mental Disorders* (1987).

susceptible than others to seasonal affective disorder (SAD), a type of depression induced by lack of sunlight. There is no doubt that mild antidepressants, especially the tricyclics and selective serotonin reuptake inhibitors (SSRIs), often reduce the symptoms of FMS and aid sleeping. However, the sleep they induce is usually nonrestorative because the alpha wave interruptions are not inhibited, and delta phase 4 sleep is reached less easily and for shorter durations with these medications. Furthermore, they induce habituation and may cause a morning hangover.

Natural Remedies

- Nerve tonic herbs such as St. John's Wort, oats verbena, skullcap, passionflower
- Exercise and sunshine
- Meditation and prayer
- Counseling or psychotherapy

Dry Eyes and Dry Mouth

A significant number of people with FMS have a tendency to dryness and irritation of the eyes and mouth. The chronically elevated level of catecholamines circulating in the bloodstream of people with FMS are probably responsible for causing a general reduction in bodily secretions. This is often first felt as dry eyes and/or a dry mouth and may progress to cause hyposecretion of digestive juices causing digestive disturbances, hyposecretion of hormones causing menstrual disruption and possibly infertility, hyposecretion of adrenal hormones causing impaired ability to manage stress, hyposecretion of mucus in the lungs causing reduced resistance to disease, and hyposecretion of serous fluids into the joints causing or aggravating arthritic pain.

Natural Remedies

- Avoid astringent foods and herbs (tannins).
- Drink lots of water.
- Demulcents such as marshmallow, plantain, and slippery elm internally
- Plantain or eyebright as an eyewash
- Suck on slippery elm lozenges.

Headaches

Headaches are common in FMS. Sometimes they are oppressive and viselike, possibly due to impaired circulation to the scalp; at other times they may be needle sharp and lancing, possibly due to impingement of nerves in the neck if there is excessive muscle tension. Vision may be affected, frequently with a sensitivity to light not unlike that found in migraines. Indeed, if neck tension is predominantly on one side, the headache may be unilateral and mimic a classic migraine. A classic migraine is a unilateral headache associated with light sensitivity and digestive disturbance. The most common type of true migraine is the "hot" type where the headache is bursting and throbbing; there may be redness of the face or distention of superficial blood vessels, and the person feels warm and craves cold drinks and ice packs. This is the type of true migraine best treated by feverfew, a markedly cooling herb. However, in the "cool" type of migraine, and commonly in FMS, the headache is constrictive and the person will feel chilly and crave a warm bath or a hot water bottle. This type of headache is best treated with warming herbs such as ginger, cinnamon, and cramp bark. Although a person with FMS may also have concurrent migraines, the classic headaches of FMS are not true migraines of vascular and inflammatory origin, but are usually due to nervous and muscular tension, and spinal or TMJ misalignments.

Natural Remedies for Hot, Congestive, Throbbing Headaches

- Ice packs on neck or forehead
- Iced peppermint or plantain tea
- Feverfew

Natural Remedies for Cold, Constrictive Headaches

- Warm packs or hot water bottle on neck and feet
- Hot ginger and catnip tea
- Warming and stimulating herbs such as cinnamon, prickly ash, and cayenne

Rhinitis

Rhinitis refers to a runny nose and postnasal drip in the absence of overt infection or allergy. It is a common problem for people with FMS. Whether they actually have allergies is not clear but seems probable. This symptom is especially interesting in the light of guaifenesin, the most recent drug treatment discovery, which is a common mucolytic ingredient in cough and sinusitis medicines and which may be effective in some cases of FMS. Although it is prescribed in FMS for a different reason, it may provide an incidental benefit to this particular symptom as well.

Natural Remedies

- Anticatarrhal herbs such as plantain, goldenrod, and bayberry
- Quercitin
- N-acetylglucosamine

- Inhalation of essential oils such as ravensara, eucalyptus, peppermint, and sage
- Avoid dairy foods and cold, watery foods.

Skin, Hair, and Nail Problems

Many people with FMS complain of thin or fine hair, lacking in luster; breaking nails; assorted skin rashes; and dryness, itching, flaking, and poor healing of the skin. Dr. R. Paul St. Amand attributes these disparate symptoms to impaired cellular metabolism and lack of energy in the cells. Because these are all cell lines that multiply readily, they have a relatively high requirement of energy, and impaired energy production would result in cell death and tissue breakdown. Additionally, phosphate is a key constituent of these tissues and their health may be adversely affected by phosphate metabolic dysfunction.

Natural Remedies

- Horsetail capsules or homeopathic silica
- Calcium and magnesium
- Peripheral circulatory stimulants such as rosemary and prickly ash
- Gelatin (if not a vegetarian)
- Chickweed, calendula, and plantain in creams or infused oils for skin applications
- Lavender, benzoin, and Peru balsam essential oils

Conditions Commonly Associated with Fibromyalgia

The following are conditions often associated with fibromyalgia:

- Myofascial pain syndrome
- Chronic fatigue immune dysfunction syndrome (CFIDS)
- Mitral valve prolapse syndrome
- Irritable bowel syndrome
- Autoimmune diseases, notably rheumatoid arthritis and lupus
- Hypoglycemia
- Closed head injuries
- Thyroid deficiency

Because FMS is clearly a multifactorial condition, and because it isn't always the only condition affecting a person, it is often difficult to sort out the threads of a person's health history. Determining which disease occurred first can help to identify the causes and the aggravating factors that can keep a person sick. A careful case history and differential diagnosis is required to ensure that the right conditions are being addressed and in the right sequence. This approach of elucidating the causal chain of disease is explored in more detail in Chapter 6.

Myofascial Pain Syndrome (MPS)

Acute trauma or injury to an area, or repeated stress on a single muscle or set of muscles, may result in MPS. It is characterized by a persistent aching in a localized area with trigger points some distance away. Patterns of referred pain are frequently different from those expected on the basis of nerve root innervation. Prolonged shortening (contraction) of the affected muscle worsens the pain, as does overuse. Like FMS, the discomfort of MPS is worsened by exposure to cold and probably involves some degree of increased sympathetic nervous activity. However, as described in the section on trigger and tender points, MPS is functionally different from FMS and generally responds well to physical treatment.

Chronic Fatigue Immune Dysfunction Syndrome (CFIDS or CFS)

Some people use the terms FMS and CFIDS almost interchangeably, and yet they are two distinct and different diseases, albeit with some significant overlaps. CFIDS mostly affects young, upwardly mobile women, much like FMS, and is similarly associated with great fatigue, clumsiness, brain fog, and impairment of memory and concentration, all being worse when under stress. However, CFIDS does not exhibit the tender points and muscle changes that are diagnostic of FMS. Additionally, CFIDS is associated with specific immune dysfunctions, including probable viral infections, chronic sore throats, and lymph gland swelling, as well as fevers and generally impaired resistance to infection. In CFIDS there is very poor exercise tolerance and antidepressant drugs are not helpful.

Over the last couple of decades of medical research, several authorities have referred to chronic fatigue immune dysfunction syndrome as the "canary syndrome": CFIDS patients seem to be universal reactors, sensitive to multiple foods, chemicals, and drugs. They are supersensitive to environmental stressors and are made sick by the modern world. Their immune systems are so off-kilter that they can no longer distinguish self from nonself and have lost most semblance of control over the immune response. Just like the canary in the coal mine that succumbed to the lethal effects of carbon monoxide before the men and so gave them some warning and hopefully time to get out, it is suggested that the person with CFIDS might be an indicator of the extent of toxic pollution in the modern world. We are all adversely affected, but these individuals are more sensitive and succumb first. Practitioners who treat FMS suggest this may be equally true for both conditions.

Mitral Valve Prolapse (MVP) Syndrome

The mitral valve is the largest of the four heart valves with an opening of almost 5 square cm. It separates the left atrium from the left ventricle and prevents the retrograde flow of oxygenated blood during cardiac contraction. If the valve prolapses, then oxygenated blood flows backward from the ventricle to the atrium.

This results in engorgement and eventual enlargement of the left atrium, predisposing to atrial fibrillation (rapid heartbeat) and reduced flow of blood into the aorta and hence the systemic circulation. This reduced cardiac output results in less than optimal oxygen delivery to the tissues, causing fatigue, pallor, dizziness, chilliness, and fainting. These are similar symptoms to anemia, with which it is often confused.

Other associated symptoms include a variety of autonomic nervous disturbances, including impaired temperature control (sweating and chills as well as sensitivity to cold), urinary urgency, dizziness and spacey feelings, impaired concentration, vertigo, poor balance and spatial awareness, insomnia and sleep disturbance, palpitations and arrhythmias, numbness and tingling in the hands and feet, bowel urgency, constipation and/or diarrhea, sensitivity to stimulants such as caffeine and amphetamines, poor stress management, unstable blood sugar with frequent hypoglycemic episodes, hypothyroidism, chemical and food sensitivities, severe PMS, breathlessness, and anxiety or full-blown panic attacks.

It appears as though people with MVP have an inappropriately heightened response to low-grade stress and the catecholamines flood out, causing sympathetic overload. The symptom picture is remarkably similar to that of FMS and a surprising 75 percent of people with FMS are found to have concurrent MVP, although the significance of this finding is not yet understood.

MVP is probably congenital and is often asymptomatic until the person enters his or her thirties. It is most common in women, and often the first time they learn of it is when they have a prenatal physical exam. It is estimated that around 5 percent of the population has this condition, making it the most widespread valvular disease. It is exacerbated by magnesium deficiency, and treatment with high doses of magnesium (up to 1,500 mg daily) can provide significant symptomatic relief. Use of L-carnitine and coenzyme Q10 may also be beneficial.

Irritable Bowel Syndrome (IBS)

This is the most common gastrointestinal disorder reported to general practitioners and up to 50 percent of referrals to gastrointestinal specialists are for this complaint. It presents as recurrent abdominal pain and distention with diarrhea and/or constipation, in the absence of any demonstrable organic pathology. It is more common in women, especially between the ages of twenty and forty. There is commonly a multifactorial etiology, including stress, food intolerance, antibiotic therapy, or food poisoning. Lactose (milk sugar) intolerance is common among people with IBS. Symptoms include pain in the right and/or left iliac fossae, "flitting" pain that is typically increased with food and reduced by defecation, variable bowel habits, diarrhea (especially in the morning), pelletlike stools alternating with bouts of constipation, bloating and abdominal distention, excessive flatus and loud bowel sounds, nausea, weight loss, headache, lassitude, and lack of energy.

The association of IBS with FMS is not well understood. Chronic catecholamine overload leading to reduced digestive function and the smooth muscle spasms of FMS may cause the bowel symptoms, or at least exacerbate an underlying bowel pathology.

Autoimmunity

Some of the symptoms of FMS may mimic those of certain autoimmune conditions. The dry eyes and mouth of FMS may mimic sicca or Sjogren's syndromes, joint pain and swelling may mimic rheumatic and arthritic disorders, and muscle fatigue may mimic multiple sclerosis. The exact interrelationships among these various disorders is unclear, but to date no autoantibodies have been identified specifically in people with FMS that would explain the widespread and varied symptom picture. Various researchers have found between 22 and 25 percent prevalence of FMS in patients with systemic lupus erythematosus (SLE). Symptoms of SLE did not appear to be worse in these patients than in those without concurrent FMS, although the presence of FMS added significantly to the feeling of general unwellness. Additionally, around 25 percent of patients diagnosed with rheumatoid arthritis and 50 percent of patients with Sjogren's syndrome have concurrent FMS.

Hypoglycemia

Hypoglycemia refers to blood sugar level less than 50 mg per deciliter of blood. The symptoms include hunger, irritability, headaches (usually viselike and constrictive), tremors, weakness, chills, memory lapses and confusion, loss of concentration, palpitations, anxiety attacks, muscle cramps, and diarrhea. If this sounds familiar, that's because it is. The symptoms overlap significantly with FMS and both conditions must frequently be treated simultaneously for optimum health benefits. The details of blood sugar balancing and the consequences of cycling from times of hyperglycemia through hypoglycemia and back again, which is common with the modern junk food diet, are described in detail in Chapter 5, along with a dietary plan for managing the condition and stabilizing the blood sugar. Here let us just say that as long as hypoglycemia remains undiagnosed and untreated, no other treatment for FMS will be entirely successful. Additionally, for people with FMS, it is significant that insulin serves to encourage renal reabsorption of phosphate. If, as has been suggested FMS is a phosphate excess condition, then repeatedly elevating the insulin levels by eating refined sugars and carbohydrates is extremely unwise. Even in the absence of overt hypoglycemia, people with FMS will benefit from a low-carbohydrate diet.

Closed Head Injuries

A closed head injury involves a blow to the head resulting in localized brain damage and swelling in the absence of a visible surface lesion. It may be caused by a fall or being struck by a blunt object, but the most common cause is whiplash sustained during a car accident. In this type of injury (combined acceleration/deceleration injury), the frontal lobes are especially affected. It is important to note that in this type of injury, impact of the skull with a hard and immobile object does not have to occur. Acceleration/deceleration and rotational movement, such as are common in minor whiplash incidents, are sufficient to produce symptomatic brain injury. Numerous studies have investigated the type of impact required to produce brain injury. Denny-Brown and Russell demonstrated that less force is needed to produce concussion if the head is free to move, as is the case in a car, than if it is fixed. Holbourne demonstrated that shear forces occur in relation to acceleration/deceleration as opposed to impact itself. Several researchers have demonstrated loss of nerve cells and structural alteration, including axonal degeneration, following mild head injuries.

Symptoms of closed head injury include vertigo, dizziness, headaches, tinnitus, impaired memory, reduced attention span, deterioration of logical and analytical thinking, insomnia, apathy, lethargy, easy fatigability, irritability, anxiety, mood swings, personality changes, and depression. With injury to the frontal lobes due to collision of the brain with the skull, planning, organization, learning, attention, concentration, emotional control, and memory will be particularly impaired. Depending on the exact location and severity of the injury, sensory-motor coordination, manual dexterity, fine motor coordination, and the sense of balance may be impaired. Persons suffering from the effects of a closed head injury may have reduced speed and capacity for processing information and may suffer from a sensation of sensory or information overload leading to anxiety or panic attacks. They may become unable to split their attention and think of more than one thing at a time. Abstract and cognitive thought processes may be impaired. CAT scans and EEGs may fail to identify a closed head injury and neuropsychological examinations are usually required to make this diagnosis. Clearly, some of these symptoms overlap with FMS and, given the propensity for FMS to be triggered by a car accident or other physical trauma, it is reasonable to assume that there is a close patho-

Differential Diagnoses of Fibromyalgia

- Chronic fatigue syndrome
- Epstein-Barr viral infection
- Systemic lupus erythematosus
- Lyme disease
- Myofascial pain syndrome
- Multiple chemical sensitivity
- Chronic candidiasis
- Mitral valve prolapse
- Nonarticular (soft tissue), multifocal rheumatism
- Polymyalgia rheumatica
- Polymyositis
- Multiple sclerosis
- Dermatomyositis
- Reflex sympathetic dystrophy
- Neuroses (psychosis, depression)
- Metastatic carcinoma
- Closed head injury

Endocrine myopathies:

- Hypothyroidism
- Hyperthyroidism
- Hypoparathyroidism
- Hyperparathyroidism
- Adrenal insufficiency/Addison's metabolic myopathy

Adapted from P. Ahler Hench, M.D., "Evaluation and Differential Diagnosis of Fibromyalgia," *Rheumatic Disease Clinics of North America*, Vol. 15, No. 1, February 1989.

physiological link between the conditions. While FMS does entail the presence of other symptoms, and while neuroendocrine and myofascial components are significant in FMS, perhaps at least some of the symptoms are due to or aggravated by an undiagnosed closed head injury as well.

Thyroid Deficiency

The clinical presentation of hypothyroidism is very similar to that of FMS. The most common FMS symptoms, including pain, fatigue, stiffness, sleep disturbance, bowel disturbance, depression, poor memory, low concentration, and cold intolerance are also classical symptoms of hypothyroidism. Additionally, low thyroid measurements are found in many people with FMS. The incidence of hypothyroidism in the general population is about 1 percent, while the incidence in FMS patients is between 10 and 13 percent according to different authorities.

Chaitow presents a strong argument for the actual problem being an inherited or acquired cellular resistance to thyroid hormone. He suggests that many patients with symptoms of FMS/hypothyroidism but with normal blood titers of the hormone are actually exhibiting the symptoms of thyroid resistance. These patients would not normally be treated for thyroid deficiency, but in fact may benefit significantly from elevation of T3 (the active form of thyroid hormone). The interplay of hormones and releasing factors is complex and easily disturbed. Thyrotropic-releasing hormone (TRH), which triggers the pituitary gland to release thyroid-stimulating hormone (TSH), is released from storage in the pineal gland in association with melatonin. At the same time growth hormone (GH) is released from the pituitary and triggers tissue repair. Deficiency of GH reduces the conversion of T4 (inactive thyroid hormone) to T3 (active hormone) and hence contributes to functional hypothyroidism. It is important to note that simple TSH tests may not be adequate to identify these problems, and more sophisticated T3, T4, free T3, and free T4 tests are recommended.

CHAPTER THREE

WHO GETS FIBROMYALGIA AND WHY?

Not everything that counts can be counted.
Not everything that can be counted counts.
ALBERT EINSTEIN

June 1996

*Saw a rheumatologist, a so-called independent medical examiner. I don't know
how anyone can think he is independent when he is paid by the insurance company. Very fancy office, all primitive art and glass doors leading to a garden and
pool. Charming doctor, very good at putting me at ease. Reasonably thorough
examination but didn't really ask about diet, exercise, or lifestyle. I think he
was surprised by how flexible I am. I told him it was the yoga and that I try to
exercise daily. Now comes the letter from his office, his report, stating that I had
many tender points but only nine in the places he was measuring, and that I
was physically active and consequently couldn't have FMS. Never mind the
other two dozen tender points. I can feel the muscle stiffness, the headaches, the
fatigue, the brain fog; if I don't have the right eleven points then I cannot have
fibromyalgia, and nothing else adequately defines my symptoms, therefore they
must all be in my head and I am not eligible for insurance payments. Most*

insulting of all, he referred to my "professed level of disability," as if I am lying and making the whole thing up! I am furious but completely powerless. If we ever get to court then I might be able to prove my case, but in the meantime this stupid little doctor is virtually libeling me and there is nothing I can do.

There are so many theories about the etiology of FMS that it can become quite baffling trying to make sense of it all. We are still groping in the dark and exploring a multitude of options. Of course, what we are really discovering is that FMS is multifactorial. Just as cancer is now recognized as being due to many correlating factors, including genetic predisposition, dietary and environmental factors, stress patterns, etc., so clinicians and researchers are now seeing that multiple triggers are required to develop full-blown FMS. There is no single unifying theory, although many interactions and interdependencies are apparent. In this chapter I will identify the key or central dysfunctions and their ramifications, as well as describe the layering or interconnections of the pathophysiology and symptomatology. Some of these key dysfunctions we have extensive information about, and some remain speculative at best. The analytical study of FMS is a new phenomenon and much work remains to be done before we truly understand the nature of the beast.*

Genetic Causes

To date, although FMS clearly does run in families, there is no strong evidence linking FMS to any specific genetic abnormality. Dr. R. Paul St. Amand suggests a genetic dysfunction causing accumulation of phosphate in the muscles that results in the musculoskeletal abnormalities of FMS. He suggests that the preponderance of female patients with FMS indicates that it is carried on the X chromosome. This is, however, purely speculative and much

* Concepts presented in this chapter are complex. For explanatory diagrams to accompany the text, please see www.gaiagarden.com.

research remains to be done. It is also possible that single-generation genetic malfunctioning may make an individual more susceptible to chronic stress, less able to recover from injury, or more likely to exhibit various neurotransmitter abnormalities.

In a study of seventeen patients drawn from a regional support group and their close family members (parents and siblings), 52 percent of relatives also exhibited signs and symptoms of FMS. This finding suggested an autosomal dominance inheritance, but the very small sample size and the failure to repeat the research cast some doubt on the results. Another study randomly selected thirty people with FMS and assessed ninety-one of their parents, siblings, or children for FMS, finding it in 26 percent. Interestingly, the incidence was 14 percent among male relatives and 41 percent among female relatives. Given that the prevalence of FMS in the general population is around 2 to 3 percent, this high rate of concurrence is significant. However, again, the small sample size is a drawback to the study. It is important to remember that even in the absence of any specific genetic abnormality, familial tendencies may also be due to learned behavior patterns, including stress reactions; attitude; dietary, exercise, and lifestyle habits; or to other as yet unknown factors.

Psychogenic and Social Causes

The likelihood of clinical depression coexisting with and contributing to FMS is quite high. It is hard not to get depressed when you are in chronic pain and unable to lead a normal life. However, I challenge the idea that FMS is just a subset of depression and that all people with FMS are, de facto, also depressed. Many people with FMS do not exhibit classical signs and symptoms for depression. Research suggests that people with FMS cope with stressful events through cognitive processing and restructuring rather than active behavioral coping, such as relaxation or distraction. This tends to make them "control freaks." It also means that well-conducted cognitive therapy can be very helpful. Research into perceived quality of life, as measured by physical, social, and emotional criteria, demonstrated significantly less perceived quality for people with FMS when compared to matched controls with other chronic rheumatic diseases. This does not mean that people with FMS imagine or create their disease, but rather that their chances of being overwhelmed by pain and suffering are higher than for the person without FMS. The good news here is that by employing the power of positive thinking and specific stress management strategies, it is possible to significantly down-regulate the symptoms and manifestations.

The issues of age, social status, and gender are interesting, especially because they overlap so closely with chronic fatigue syndrome. As mentioned, the high number of women with FMS may be explained by some as yet unidentified genetic defect on the X chromosome. Alternatively, it may be that there are many men out there with all the symptoms, but not officially diagnosed. Certainly, women make up 60 to 70 percent of the average medical practice, and women are generally more comfortable asking for medical care and assistance, but this is unlikely to be sufficient to explain the markedly higher number of women with FMS than men. I wonder sometimes if perhaps when men present to their physician with symptoms, they are more likely to be taken seriously and assigned a "respectable" diagnosis, such as arthritis, thyroid dysfunction, or lupus, while women patients may be treated more dismissively. Women are traditionally the "weaker sex," so perhaps are simply more vulnerable; more akin, if you like, to the environmentally sensitive "canary" than are the tougher, more resilient males. Maybe all of these are factors, and others yet unnamed.

The issue of age is confusing as well. While the majority of patients getting diagnosed are between the ages of thirty and forty-five, patients can range from young children to seniors. In my own practice the youngest was diagnosed at thirteen and the oldest at seventy-three. Clearly, chronology is not the only or most significant factor. Perhaps women in the thirty- to forty-five age range are more frequently in the doctor's office because of obstetrical, pediatric, and gynecological problems and consequently have more opportunity to discuss their symptoms. Perhaps it is because they are trying to do too much—juggling home, kids, career—and they "burn out" (although why this wouldn't also happen to lots of men isn't clear).

Professional women, with challenging careers and very busy lives, tend to be more commonly affected than unskilled workers. This may be because they are more capable of describing their symptoms and asking for help, or more empowered generally in asking for medical intervention. They may also have higher expectations of their quality of life, or possibly FMS is a consequence of specific emotional or environmental stressors. Obviously there are many unanswered questions about the gender and age distribution of FMS.

For many years now in my clinical practice I have guided my patients toward using the disease as an opportunity to go deep within themselves and really explore their personal space. I have been lucky to have shared my consulting room for eight years with Joanne Fallow, a gifted and insightful therapist to whom I have referred many patients, and she has greatly helped their journey toward health. See Chapter 7 for a discussion on using the power of the mind to initiate true healing.

Nutritional Causes

Nutritional imbalances may underlie much of the manifestation of FMS. While no one vitamin or mineral deficiency is sufficient to cause FMS, a chronic imbalance may make the body more vulnerable to stress, less able to carry out normal cellular and tissue functions—especially hepatic detoxification and muscle energy production, less able to heal and repair itself, and less able to resist disease. This topic is explored in some detail in Chapter 5 but can be easily summarized: Too much refined food, especially carbohydrate and sugar, coupled with inadequate intake of fruits, vegetables, and high-quality protein creates a nutritional imbalance.

Magnesium, calcium, zinc, B vitamins, essential fatty acids, vitamin C, vitamin E, and many other essential nutrients are commonly deficient in the average Western diet today. These nutrients are critical and essential cofactors in many metabolic processes, including the manufacture of neurotransmitters and detoxification processes in the liver. Deficiencies can seriously disrupt the body chemistry.

Food allergies may mimic some of the symptoms of FMS, such as fatigue, brain fog, and irritability. Long-term disruption of bacterial balance and yeast overgrowth may also predispose to parasitic infections, further compounding the symptom picture. Many of the symptoms of chronic candidiasis overlap with FMS and this may be aggravated by blood sugar disturbances due to high sugar intake. A wildly fluctuating blood sugar level can cause fatigue, irritability, brain fog, headaches, and chilliness.

Toxins and Environmental Stress

Many people with FMS experience exacerbation of symptoms when they eat certain foods or are exposed to certain chemicals. How many of the symptoms can be attributed to as yet unidentified chemical sensitivities we can only guess at. There are so many toxic residues in our air, water, and food from city, industrial, and agricultural pollution that we will probably never be able to separate the strands and define the extent of harm done by each individually. Many food additives, such as monosodium glutamate (MSG) and aspartame, are known to cause FMS–like symptoms in otherwise healthy subjects, and many pesticides are neurotoxins. All of the artificial chemicals we are subjected to must be eliminated by the liver, using the enzymes that carry out degradation and conjugation, which renders them unavailable for normal metabolic processes. If they cannot be eliminated by an existing biochemical pathway, then they will accumulate in the body, tending to be stored in fat (adipose) tissue, which is relatively metabolically inactive. As noted below, people with FMS accumulate lactic acid in the muscles, indicating a ketogenic or fat-burning tendency that may serve to keep more toxins in circulation and hence make them more available to disrupt health.

People with chronic fatigue immune dysfunction syndrome and with FMS frequently report feeling improvement when they are in the country.

Fresh air, sunshine, exposure to nature, quiet, reduced light pollution—all of these probably play a part, and a recommendation to live in the country is often part of the ideal prescription for these conditions.

Neuroendocrine Causes

This area of research has yielded fascinating evidence of the close involvement of the entire endocrine (hormonal) system and the central nervous system (CNS) in the cause and perpetuation of FMS. The CNS consists of the brain and spinal cord. It manufactures and responds to myriad electrochemical messengers called neurotransmitters. Some of these do double duty in the endocrine system, where they act as hormones, influencing distant tissues and organs. This is a vast and complex network, intimately connected and finely calibrated. It responds to negative feedback loops that control contrasting sets of chemicals, such as glucagon and insulin or noradrenaline and acetylcholine. It is the great integrator of all bodily functions, and disturbances of the neuroendocrine system cause dysregulation of many bodily processes and multiple health problems.

One of the key control elements of the neuroendocrine system is the pineal gland. Back when our primeval ancestors crawled around in the mud, there was a light-sensitive organ on top of the head, still found today in a few reptiles. In time it was covered over by the cerebral cortex and we now call it the vestigial third eye, or pineal gland. Melatonin hormone, released at night from the pineal gland, sets the diurnal rhythms of the body, including the sleep-wake cycle, the cyclical activities of all endocrine glands, and the production of neurotransmitters.

The pineal gland is tiny and located deep within the brain, attached to the roof of the third ventricle. It is wrapped in a capsule of meningeal tissue and is composed of connective tissue in the form of neuroglial cells, providing a supportive role to secretory parenchymal cells called pinealocytes. Sympathetic nerve fibers surround the pinealocytes, so that as well as receiving hormonal feedback information in the bloodstream, the functional cells of the pineal gland receive direct innervation for more rapid response to changing situations.

The pineal gland responds to intensity and duration of light. Light entering the eyes and falling on the retina generates a nerve impulse that transmits up the optic nerve to the middle brain and a cluster of nerve cells in the hypothalamus called the superchiasmic nuclei, where the light intensity is recorded. At night, in the absence of light, the superchiasmic nuclei send an impulse, proportionate to the light intensity, to the pineal gland. This stimulates production and release of melatonin, the major hormone of the pineal gland. Several other substances have been identified in the pineal gland, including norepinephrine, serotonin, histamine, gonadotropin-releasing hormone, and gamma-aminobutyric acid. These have been delivered to the gland by the bloodstream and nerve fibers and are not manufactured in the pineal gland.

Melatonin has been called the "regulator hormone" because it sets the rhythmic release of most other hormones in the body. It has evolved to enable appropriate and continuous adaptation to the environment, and governs such things as hibernation, migration, estrus, and conception in animals; sleep-wake cycles; and the human female menstrual cycle. The pineal gland is believed to be sensitive to electromagnetic frequencies and this helps birds find their way across thousands of miles to return to the very same breeding and feeding sites each year. Melatonin is passed to infants through breast milk and it is possible that formula feeding may cause sleep disturbances and possibly widespread endocrine abnormalities. Some clinicians are even asking themselves if the high rates of FMS today could be due to a widespread reduction in breast-feeding since the 1960s leading to chronic melatonin disturbance. Additionally, melatonin is manufactured from tryptophan and serotonin, both of which have been shown to be in short supply in people with FMS.

The pineal gland is largest in children and gradually calcifies and atrophies with age. Some researchers believe that it controls biological aging, and as it degenerates and produces progressively less melatonin, the cells of the body deteriorate and aging occurs. Given that growth hormone, the hormone of tissue repair, is produced during delta phase sleep under the influence of melatonin, perhaps there is truth in this assertion. Certainly mouse studies have unquestionably demonstrated the antiaging effects of melatonin extracts and even of pineal transplants from young to old mice.

Melatonin also plays a significant role in the availability and activation of thyroid hormone, and hence the level of physical energy available to the body. Thyrotropin-releasing hormone (TRH), probably manufactured elsewhere and stored in the pineal gland, is released into the bloodstream when more cellular energy is required. Receptor sites for TRH in the pituitary gland respond to the rising blood level and cause the production and release of thyroid-stimulating hormone (TSH). This, in turn causes the thyroid gland to release stored thyroid hormone. In adults it facilitates muscle repair.

So it is possible to infer that:

Light pollution +
Electromagnetic pollution +
Impaired sleep +
Tryptophan deficiency +
Serotonin deficiency +
Meningeal torsion +
Disturbed cerebral circulation
$\downarrow$
Reduced
melatonin $\rightarrow$ reduced growth hormone $\rightarrow$ impaired tissue healing
$\rightarrow$reduced thyroid hormone $\rightarrow$ impaired energy production
$\rightarrow$ impaired conversion of T_4 to T_3 $\rightarrow$ impaired energy production

The Issue of Stress

Probably the fundamental problem or disturbance facing the neuroendocrine system today is the chronicity of the stress that we feel in the modern world. Early on in the evolutionary process we developed adrenaline (epinephrine) to help us handle sudden and acute, life-threatening stress. If the saber-toothed tiger jumped out of the cave, our primitive ancestors had to react fast—by either running or fighting. Thus adrenaline came to be called the hormone of "fright, flight, or fight." It is released in the brain in response to acute stress in the form of a neurotransmitter that causes activation of the sympathetic nervous system, and as a hormone from the adrenal medulla in response to chronic stress. The sympathetic nervous system operates involuntarily and is designed for survival and safety. It causes almost instantaneous dilation of the pupils to allow better vision, dilates the airways, increases the depth and rate of breathing, and diverts blood from the abdomen and pelvis toward the muscles for running and the brain for thinking. Faced with a life-or-death situation, you don't need to stop to eat and digest food, urinate, or procreate, so blood is diverted from the gut, urinary system, and reproductive system to the muscles for improved stamina and strength, and to the brain for faster thought processing. This is excellent as a survival strategy, allowing rapid response to danger, but it is not designed for sustained operation. Chronic stress destabilizes the control mechanisms, we become stuck in sympathetic mode, and eventually become exhausted and drained.

By running from danger or struggling physically to overcome it, by exerting the body and using the muscular energy produced under adrenaline surge, we produce endorphins, natural opiates that reduce sensitivity to pain and create a feeling of well-being. They have a balancing effect upon adrenaline and damp it down after the danger is past. When we relax, we operate in parasympathetic mode, utilizing acetylcholine as the neurotransmitter. This causes slowing of the respiratory and heart rates, activation of the gut and the digestive process, and a calming of brain-wave pattern.

In the modern world the metaphoric saber-toothed tiger is all around. The boss gives you a hard time at work because you are not producing your quota, your spouse is angry at you, the kids are fighting, and the dog throws up on the rug. No wonder your adrenaline surges! Most people today live with chronic stress, operating in the sympathetic mode all day, and then having trouble winding down and entering the parasympathetic mode after work. This is especially true where there isn't enough exercise to counterbalance the adrenaline.

The convolutions of the biochemistry in the neuroendocrine system can become confounding, but underlying it all is chronic stress. Added to chronic stress in our modern world are the so-called excitotoxins. These are substances that up-regulate the adrenal glands or mimic adrenaline in the body and so aggravate the sympathetic response. They include caffeine, nicotine, sugar, and allergens—the very things we so often turn to when we are feeling stressed!

The Hypothalamic-Pituitary-Adrenal Axis

Correct functioning of the hypothalamic-pituitary-adrenal (HPA) axis is critical to the coordinated physiological response to physical or emotional stress. Pituitary and adrenal hormones are secreted in a diurnal rhythm closely approximating the sleep-wake cycles. Thus in a healthy individual the pituitary gland is most active very early in the morning, then the adrenals and other effector organs are active from about dawn until later in the day. For example, the cortisol level would normally be highest in the morning and lowest at the end of the day. Several negative feedback loops, primarily mediated by Type I and Type II glucocorticoid receptors, terminate activity of the HPA axis. When they register a certain level of cortisol they will inhibit production and release of the hormone, thus regulating the optimum blood levels within precisely calibrated parameters. Disturbance of the cortisol levels will cause widespread disruption of the HPA axis.

Chronic stress causes the hypothalamus to release corticotropic-releasing hormone (CRH) and arginine vasopressin (AVP). These in turn cause the pituitary gland to release adrenocorticotropic hormone (ACTH), which stimulates the adrenal glands to produce adrenaline as a hormone, thus sparing the nervous system from having to produce it all the time. ACTH also stimulates the adrenal cortex to manufacture cortisol, which mediates the activity of the immune system and damps down the activity of the HPA axis. If stress is not reduced, then eventually the adrenal glands become exhausted and depleted, resulting in reduced cortisol production, disruption to the diurnal rhythms, sleep disturbance, immune dysfunction, and loss of energy. This may be the early stage of FMS.

Griep, Boersma, and de Kloet showed that people with FMS secreted higher-than-normal levels of ACTH when administered a specified amount of CRH. This suggests that in FMS, the pituitary may be abnormally sensitive to stimulating hormones. Crofford et al. reported that the adrenal glands of people with FMS produced diminished levels of cortisol when administered CRH. This may indicate that their adrenal functions are depressed. This same study showed a reduced level of urinary cortisol excretion, confirming the finding that people with FMS have disrupted HPA–axis function. Other studies have suggested that, while people with FMS have lower morning cortisol levels, they may also exhibit abnormal evening elevation. This would contribute to the commonly observed disturbance of the sleep-wake cycles in people with FMS.

People with FMS usually have normal levels of adrenaline and noradrenaline in the plasma and urine. However, Crofford et al. reported that people with FMS have markedly lower plasma levels of *neuropeptide Y.* This neuropeptide is known to be released under sympathetic stimulation and in response to exercise, and it is postulated that it serves to down-regulate the HPA axis. Its absence, especially in conjunction with reduced cortisol production, may therefore indicate progressive activation of the HPA axis and a loss of the normal negative-feedback loops.

It is worth noting here that certain types of depression have been identified that correlate with HPA-axis dysregulation, specifically increased or diminished CRH production, and also that post-traumatic stress disorder is associated with reduced cortisol levels due to enhanced glucocorticoid negative feedback. Clearly the brain biochemistry is intimately connected to mood and well-being, although what all the pathways are remains to be elucidated.

The Sleep Connection

As many as 75 percent of people with FMS report difficulty with sleeping and a tendency to waken not feeling refreshed or rejuvenated. Most of them report not having had such problems prior to the onset of FMS. Interrupting sleep repeatedly, specifically phase 4 or delta phase sleep, in healthy individuals will generate fatigue, widespread muscle aching, and trigger-point tenderness virtually indistinguishable from FMS. Interestingly, when the same sleep disruption was applied to long-distance runners, no such symptoms occurred, suggesting that muscle can be conditioned by regular exercise to respond differently to sleep deprivation. This suggests that sleep impairment may be a cause or at least a contributing factor in FMS, as well as being caused by it. What is certain is that getting a good night's sleep makes the individual with FMS feel like a new person and that sleep impairment is one of the most distressing subjective symptoms of the condition.

In normal, healthy sleep, one cycles regularly through five sleep stages each sleeping period. Waking is often considered the sixth stage. Dreaming occurs during the REM sleep stage which recurs about every ninety minutes throughout the night. Non-REM (NREM) sleep—stages 1 through 4—lasts from 90 to 120 minutes. Each stage from lasts 5 to 15 minutes. Stages 2 and 3 repeat backwards before REM sleep is attained. So, normal sleep has this pattern: waking, stage 1, 2, 3, 4, 3, 2, REM. Usually REM sleep occurs 90 minutes after sleep onset. REM sleep is distinguishable from NREM sleep by changes in physiological states and is characterized by rapid eye movements and is associated with reduced muscle tone, increased body temperature, increased oxygen consumption, and variable cardiac rate. Deprivation of REM sleep results in profound psychological changes, including moodiness and irritability. Alpha, beta, gamma, and delta are progressively deeper sleep phases, with progressively higher-amplitude and slower-frequency EEG waves. In delta phase sleep, the deepest sleep, specific endocrine and immune activities occur, including release of melatonin and the release of growth hormone (GH) from the anterior pituitary gland, which stimulates tissue repair.

Repeated studies of the sleep patterns of people with FMS show alpha waves interrupting the delta phase of sleep and preventing deep and restful sleep from occurring. Lack of restorative sleep will lead to morning grogginess, brain fog, impaired memory and concentration, clumsiness, cognitive dysfunction, and irritability. Physiological disturbance may be more subtle but no less significant. Probably the single biggest factor here is reduced output of GH.

GH is produced by the anterior pituitary under the influence of melatonin during delta phase sleep and in response to exercise. It causes the liver to produce insulin-like growth factor 1, or IGF1, which stimulates the growth of muscle and bone. In children, IGF1 increases height and muscle bulk. In adults it is concerned with stimulating repair of microtrauma in muscle tissues as a result of normal daily wear and tear, as well as regulating immune self-repair. GH occurs only transiently in the bloodstream, and measurement of IGF1 gives a more accurate reading of GH activity in the body. This should be highest early in the morning; it is known to decline progressively in persons over the age of twenty-five. Bennet et al. found that people with FMS are deficient in GH and IGF1.

Other research suggests that GH, IGF1, and dihydroepiandrosterone (DHEA) deficiencies may be aggravated in FMS by elevated corticotropic-releasing hormone from the hypothalamus in response to chronic stress. CRH enhances production of somatostatin, the counterbalance hormone to IGF1, which in turn inhibits the secretion of GH by the pituitary gland. People with FMS failed to secrete GH after injection with clonidine or L-dopa, both of which initiate GH production in normal control subjects. People with FMS given GH injections can achieve normal plasma IGF1 levels, indicating that there is no defective GH receptor function. Additionally, people with FMS who exercised were unable to achieve a marked elevation of GH as occurred in normal control subjects. Injection of pyridostigmine, a cholinergic stimulant that down-regulates somatostatin, resulted in achievement of normal exercise-induced GH elevation, indicating a possible excess receptor sensitivity to somatostatin. Some reports suggest success treating people with FMS using GH and this may become a treatment of choice in the future.

The Immune Response

Deficiency of GH has profound effects on the immune system and the muscles. Although FMS is not, per se, an immune dysfunction, it commonly coexists with and is diagnostically confused with several autoimmune disorders, including rheumatoid arthritis, polymyalgia rheumatica, systemic lupus erythematosus (SLE), Sjogren's syndrome, and sicca syndrome. FMS does not exhibit any specific autoantibodies, nor is there a focal inflammatory site. Unlike people with chronic fatigue syndrome, those with FMS do not have a notably reduced resistance to infectious disease, but they do seem to be more prone to chronic, low-grade inflammatory conditions, especially the autoimmune diseases. For this reason FMS can be considered to be, at least in part, an immune dysfunction.

Peter and Wallace reported that people with FMS exhibit elevated levels of interleukin-2, alpha interferon, and helper T cells, all of which are regulators of the immune response. They postulated that alterations in cortisol and serotonin may contribute to these imbalances as well. Other research suggests that interleukin-1 beta deficiency may be significant. This immune fraction increases secretion of GH, CRH, serotonin, beta-endorphins, and catecholamines (adrenaline). Recent evidence suggests interleukin-6 is also critical.

Relaxin Deficiency

Relaxin is a polypeptide hormone, structurally similar to insulin and related growth-promoting hormones. In women it is manufactured in the ovaries and found in the ovaries, uterus, and blood, as well as in the placenta during pregnancy. It is highest during the first trimester of pregnancy, where it serves to relax the anterior joint of the pubic bones. In the third trimester, it aids dilation of the cervix, preparatory to labor. In nonpregnant women, there is a relaxin surge immediately following the preovulatory luteinizing hormone surge, and again during menstruation, indicating that it probably serves to ease spasms or muscle cramps during ovulation and menstruation. Additionally, relaxin has breast-enlarging effects and increases glycogen synthesis and water uptake of the uterine muscles while reducing their contractility. In men it is not detectable in the bloodstream, but occurs in the seminal fluid. Its role in men is more ambiguous and direct effects on reproductive organs have not yet been demonstrated. In both men and women it appears to affect smooth, skeletal, and cardiac muscles; tendons; ligaments; bones; cartilage; nervous tissue; and all connective tissue, including fascia, meninges, and skin. It exerts a relaxing effect on connective tissue fibers and may contribute to the regulation of the relative viscosity of ground substance, the gel in which are embedded all the fibers and organelles of connective tissue.

According to Dr. Samuel Yue of the Minnesota Pain Center in St. Paul, Minnesota, diminished levels of relaxin may cause or contribute to symptoms of FMS. (See Figure 3.1.) He suggests that women during the perimenopausal

Striated Muscle FMS Myofascial pain Muscle dysenergism	*Autonomic Nervous System* Visual disturbance Reduced secretions Irritable bowel Irritable bladder
Smooth Muscle Irritable bladder Irritable bowel Cold extremities	*Connective Tissue* Joint pain TMJ Brittle hair and nails Dry, scaly, or itching skin Fascial dysfunction
Cardiac Muscle Dizziness Arrhythmias Shortness of breath	*Central Nervous System* Cognitive dysfunction Emotional distress Poor coping mechanisms Headaches

Figure 3.1 Symptoms of Relaxin Deficiency According to Dr. Yue.

years (forty to fifty) and those who are postmenopausal, or who have had a hysterectomy, oophorectomy, or tubal ligation, or used oral birth control pills (which suppress ovarian function) for an extended period may be at higher risk of relaxin deficiency and consequent FMS–like disease. Dr. Yue points out that there are receptor sites for relaxin in smooth and cardiac muscles, as well as in connective tissue and the autonomic and central nervous systems, and suggests that easy fatiguing and spasmodic pain in these tissues may be treated by supplementation with relaxin extracted from pigs. He makes no secret of the fact that he is financially associated with this product, which certainly raises questions about the authority with which he speaks, and yet we must be careful not to dismiss his claims out of hand. Relaxin does cause muscle relaxation, so at least on that basis it is worthy of careful assessment.

Dr. Yue suggests that either a deficiency of relaxin itself or a receptor site defect could cause inhibited relaxin function. He further postulates that this might be due to autoimmune destruction as is known to happen in other receptor site dysfunctions, such as myasthenia gravis. At the present time antibodies to relaxin receptors have not been identified, but that doesn't necessarily mean they don't exist. He points out that a high percentage of women in his clinic presenting with FMS have a history of gynecological disturbances over many years, and that many males in his practice with FMS had a history of testicular problems, including mumps, undescended testicles, trauma, or surgery. He states that up to 70 percent of the male patients with FMS had reduced testosterone, which leads to reduced relaxin. Testosterone is also essential in women, albeit in lesser amounts, but nothing is yet known about the relationship of this hormone to FMS. Clearly, more research is required, as with so many aspects of this elusive disease. In the meantime, relaxin is available as a nonprescription item from Dr. Yue's Web site. A blood test to determine your clinical needs is recommended before commencing treatment.

Dr. Yue prescribes relaxin therapeutically for many conditions associated with FMS, including cognitive dysfunction, memory loss, confusion, depression, anxiety, panic, sleep disturbance, muscle tension, muscle spasm, muscle fatigue, tender points, hyperadrenalism, and chronic sympathetic dominance. According to Dr. Yue's research, relaxin will regulate the force and rhythmicity of cardiac muscle contraction, restore elasticity to smooth muscle, and promote healing and remodeling of skeletal muscle and all other connective tissue that is in a process of constant turnover. He suggests that it can be used to promote strong, healthy hair, nails, and skin.

I have not used relaxin in my clinical practice, partly because the information is only newly available and I am not currently seeing many patients. Additionally, I am aware that it is a hormone and that tinkering with the endocrine system is strong medicine and not to be undertaken lightly. As when prescribing melatonin and DHEA, I would prefer to see a blood test to confirm the deficiency. Even that, of course, isn't entirely reliable because if there is receptor site damage the blood levels may be normal or even elevated due to a lack of negative feedback from the receptor site. Until an antibody is found for these receptors, that idea remains unproven.

Summary

For all this talk of the neuroendocrine and the neuromuscular system, most of it is speculation and much research must be done if we are ever to understand the threads. At the present time research on the multitudinous neuroendocrine causes of FMS is lacking and information is scanty. Our understanding of the interdependencies and interrelationships among hormones and with the nervous system is growing daily, and sometimes it seems that the more we learn the less we know. Clearly, great complexity exists, and analyzing the pathological process is a bit like determining which came first, the chicken or the egg. In truth, probably all are coexistent and we may never know a single, ultimate cause. There are even other hormones that have not yet been explored for their potential to influence FMS. They are all interconnected and when one is imbalanced they all are affected. It is no wonder that intervention with hormone therapy is rarely really effective in any condition, let alone one such as FMS, about which we still know so little. (See Table 3.1.)

Table 3.1 Summary of Hormones Known to Be Significant in Fibromyalgia

Production Site	Hormone	Target Tissue	Action
Pineal gland	Melatonin	Bodywide effects	Sleep-wake cycle Cyclical functions Release of GH Thyroid activation
	Thyroid-releasing hormone (TRH)	Pituitary	Release of thyroid-stimulating hormone (TSH)
Hypothalamus	Corticotropic-releasing hormone (CRH)	Pituitary	Release of adrenocorticotropic hormone (ACTH) Increases sympathetic tone Stimulates somatostatin
	TRH	Pituitary	Release of TSH
Pituitary	TSH	Bodywide effects	Stimulates metabolism and energy production
	ACTH	Adrenal cortex	Release of cortisol and adrenaline (epinephrine)
	Growth hormone (GH)	Liver	Release of insulin-like growth factor 1 (ILGF1)
Brain	Neuropeptide Y	Central nervous system	Down-regulation of HPA axis
Liver	ILGF1, also known as somatomedin C	Bodywide effects	Growth and development in children Tissue repair and immune support in adults
	Somatostatin	Pituitary	Inhibition of GH

Continued overleaf

Table 3.1 Summary of Hormones, *continued*

Production Site	Hormone	Target Tissue	Action
Ovary & testes	Relaxin	Smooth, skeletal, and cardiac muscles	Regulates mood, sleep, cognitive functions
		Autonomic and central nervous systems	Increases parasympathetic tone
		Connective tissue	Increases elasticity of connective tissue and stimulates healing and remodeling Partus preparartor
Adrenal gland	Dihydroepi-androsterone (DHEA)	Bodywide effects	Precursor to progesterone, estrogen, testosterone, cortisol
	Adrenaline (epinephrine)	Bodywide effects	Increases sympathetic tone, Stimulates metabolic rate
	Cortisol	Bodywide effects	Increases protein catabolism, gluconeogenesis, anti-inflammatory

The Perception of Pain

Muscle pain, aching, and stiffness are the most commonly reported symptoms in FMS and the currently accepted clinical diagnostic criteria is the presence of tender points in the muscles. But doesn't everyone feel achy and stiff sometimes? Of course they do. The difference is that in FMS, not only is the symptom picture more prevalent and more persistent, but there is pathophysiological change in the muscles themselves, as well as in both the peripheral and central nervous systems. People with FMS suffer from a reduction in pain threshold, an increased response to painful stimuli, and persistence of pain after cessation of the stimulus. As with the complexity of the neuroendocrine interrelationships, in the interaction of the muscle tissue and the nervous control system there are many interdependent processes that feed back upon one another in a perfectly designed system of checks and balances. Disturbance or disruption of any part of the system will have profound and far-reaching consequences.

The sensation of pain is registered by nociceptors in tissues throughout the body and is transmitted via specialized nerve fibers to the spinal cord. In muscle tissue the free nerve endings that act as nociceptors are concentrated around small arterioles and capillaries between the muscle fibers. The nucleus of these cells is located in the dorsal horn ganglion of the spinal cord and this cell forms the first order neuron in the sensory pathway. Muscle pain travels in myelinated A delta fibers and in unmyelinated Type C fibers. In the spinal cord they synapse, or meet, at the level of entry to the cord with the second order neuron. The second order neuron crosses over at that level and pain sensation ascends the spinal cord in the lateral spinothalamic tract on the opposite side to the occurence of pain in the body. Another synapse occurs with the third order neuron in an area of the brain called the thalamus. This structure, deep within the brain, serves as a relay station for all sensory stimuli except smell as they move up to the cerebral cortex for processing, sorting, and responding. All motor impulses descending from the motor cortex to the muscles also pass through the thalamus. The thalamus interprets information about pain and interposes it directly with emotion and memory, another example of an old survival strategy in case pain required quick recognition and response. Muscle nociceptors are activated by unusual stretching or pressure, during inflammation, or by serotonin and potassium ions. They are not activated by normal muscle use.

Substance P Excess and Serotonin Deficiency

The key neurotransmitters used by the lateral spinothalamic tract to transmit information about pain upward to the brain are Substance P and calcitonin-gene-related peptide (CGRP). Increased density of Substance P receptors has been found on the postsynaptic membrane after a noxious stimulus, which has the effect of up-regulating the response to pain. The cerebrospinal fluid of people with FMS has been found to be as much as three times higher in Substance P than the spinal fluid of healthy controls. Animal research has shown that persistent pathological pain is associated with an increased expression of the c-fos proto-oncogene, which up-regulates the production of pain neurotransmitters. Substance P is also known to flow from the nociceptors into the surrounding tissue, which sensitizes the tissue, making it more responsive to sensory stimulus.

Recent research suggests that people with FMS experience pain differently from healthy people. Not only do they have elevated Substance P in the cerebrospinal fluid, but they also have reduced serum concentrations of serotonin and reduced serotonin metabolites in the cerebrospinal fluid. Serotonin is manufactured by the body from the amino acid tryptophan and decreased levels of this amino acid are associated with symptoms resembling FMS. Serotonin is also known to interact with the HPA axis, so deficiencies of this neurotransmitter may interfere with the neuroendocrine system.

Research into the search of reduced serotonin has pointed to tryptophan deficiency as the most likely cause. This may be due to dietary deficiency or possibly to enzyme imbalances at the cellular level. If tryptophan does not convert to serotonin, then it may enter the kynurenine pathway for degradation. John Russell, M.D., has identified elevated kynurenine in the cerebrospinal fluid of people with FMS, while kynurenine metabolites were lower than in control subjects. The conversion of tryptophan to kynurenine is mediated by the enzyme indole-2,3-dioxygenase (IDO), and the onward conversion of kynurenine to 3-hydroxy-kynurenine is mediated by the enzyme kynurenine-3-oxygenase (K3O). An immune fraction called gamma interferon is known to up-regulate IDO, which may tend to divert tryptophan away from the serotonin-forming pathway; it also down-regulates K3O by depletion of a critical enzyme cofactor called *nicotinamide-adenine-dinucleotide* (NADP) that provides the energy for enzyme function. The NADP level in the blood of people with FMS is significantly lower than in healthy individuals. The pathophysiological and clinical significance of down-regulating K3O and hence prolonging the presence of kynurenine has not yet been determined. Research has so far failed to confirm that gamma interferon is elevated in people with FMS, but recent German research has suggested the presence of circulating antibodies to serotonin receptors that, if found to be true, would further explain a complex situation.

Common biochemical and functional features of FMS include low levels of tryptophan, low serum serotonin, low NADP in red blood cells, low 3-hydroxykynurenine in the cerebrospinal fluid, increased kynurenine in the cerebrospinal fluid, and increased Substance P in the cerebrospinal fluid. 5-hydroxytryptophan or 5-HT, and analogs of it, are known to mediate the nociceptive influence of Substance P in animals. Thus, deficiency of tryptophan results in heightened awareness of and sensitivity to pain overall. Activation of NDMA (N-methyl D-aspartate) pain receptors in the central nervous system by elevated Substance P will further aggravate the problem. NDMA receptor blockade by a drug called *Ketamine* is showing some promise in relieving the pain of FMS.

Several FMS drug therapies, especially some of the antidepressants (selective serotonin reuptake inhibitors), are predicated on the assumption that elevating serotonin levels will alleviate symptoms. While this may be true in the strictest sense, it should be noted that any interference with this delicate and complex system of checks and balances must be approached with great caution. Using selective serotonin reuptake inhibitors, which prolong the effective life of serotonin, whether they be Prozac or St. John's wort, may have far-reaching physiological effects.

Cerebral Circulation

Another change seen in the nervous system of people with FMS is disruption and disturbance of normal cerebral circulation. Mountz et al. have shown that in people with FMS, most especially in those people with increased sensitivity to pain, there was reduced blood flow to the thalamus, which regulates transmission of sensory and motor impulses, and to the caudate nuclei, which regulate pain responses and are involved in memory and concentration. It is suggested that reduced oxygen supply induces pathological change in the tissues, causing amplified transmission of nervous impulses and hence a heightened awareness of pain sensations. Positron emission topography (PET) scanning has indicated a reduction in the utilization of glucose in the brains of people with chronic fatigue syndrome and a reduced level of temporal and frontal lobe circulation and neuronal activity, which may correlate to impaired cognitive function.

Neuroplasticity

A further complication for people with FMS is that chronic, persistent nociception tends to up-regulate or sensitize all the central nervous structures involved in pain perception. This is called neuroplasticity and refers to a rewiring of the synapses such that pain may be felt in the absence of a sensory stimulus. The most extreme example of this is the person who feels agonizing pain in a phantom limb after amputation. In people with FMS the increased production of pain neurotransmitters and the elevated cerebrospinal levels of Substance P, along with reduced serum serotonin, are all significant contributing factors. But yet more neuronal disruption is required for chronic sensitization to occur. Connecting nerve fibers linking the cell bodies of the first order nociceptive neurons in the dorsal horn ganglia may become activated by chronic stimulation of an adjacent cell body, thus spreading the sensation of pain beyond the original site of the stimulus. This is called an expansion of the receptive field and results in a widespread sensation of pain from a focal stimulus. It partially explains the referral of trigger-point pain to distant areas and why peripheral tissues, where the pain is felt, are largely normal in histological and biochemical examinations. The mechanism of sensitization is believed to be via Substance P, which is known to be markedly elevated in people with FMS. Substance P causes depolarization of spinal and interspinal neurons by reducing or inhibiting the naturally occurring magnesium block in the calcium channel of the neuron. This allows entry of calcium into the neuron and transmission of the nervous impulse. The unusually elevated intracellular calcium then initiates a variety of secondary messengers, which cause early expression of c-fos-proto-oncogene and hence up-regulation of algesic neurotransmitters.

The normally inactive interspinal synapses are modulated by descending antinociceptive fibers, which use endogenous opioids (endorphins) as the neurotransmitter within the brain and serotonin as the neurotransmitter in the spinal cord. Thus defects in the descending antinociceptive pathways or reduced levels of neurotransmitters, specifically serotonin, may result in increased perception of pain. The antinociception mechanism is normally active only under significant psychological stress, and may even result in complete relief of pain in extreme cases. It is this mechanism that allows the football player to finish the game with a broken clavicle or the severely injured person to walk a mile to get help.

The question that remains is, to what extent is neuroplasticity reversible? Most of the research on these biochemical pathways has been done on animals and for only a few minutes or hours. We cannot yet be certain that this is exactly what is occurring to humans, nor how the chronicity of the stimulus can be significant. It is entirely possible that a certain critical mass is reached in which a self-perpetuating state occurs. If negative feedback is impaired, then a positive feedback loop may ensue, causing a descending spiral of symptoms, each one causing the next. This, of course, may be complicated by the fact that FMS is not only a physical but also an emotional experience. Given that mood is known to alter pain perception and that chronic pain causes depression, we cannot ignore the mental-emotional input to neuroplasticity.

Cellular Metabolic Disturbance

For a long time FMS was classified exclusively as a muscular disease, based on stiffness, pain, and tender points. Musculoskeletal disease is traditionally treated by natural health practitioners through cleansing and detoxification. For as long as natural health practitioners have been treating FMS, and even when we treated a patient with all the symptoms and no diagnosis, we have focused on the presence of tender points as an indicator of metabolic disruption and accumulation of toxic wastes. Allopathic physicians have scoffed at these ideas and only very recently have we been somewhat vindicated in this view by the theories of Dr. R. Paul St. Amand in California.

Dr. St. Amand postulates that an inherited genetic defect causes the kidneys to inadequately excrete phosphates. Eighty to 90 percent of dietary phosphates are absorbed and they are readily taken up from the extracellular fluids into the cell. There they exist in equilibrium in the cytosol (cell matrix) and the outer mitochondrial chamber (the space between the outer and the inner mitchondrial membranes). Adenosine tri-phosphate (ATP) is the energy currency of the cell. Energy-rich phosphate bonds are released to yield energy for the cell to fuel metabolic functions. The Krebs cycle and the generation of energy in the form of ATP occur in the inner chamber or matrix of the mitochondria. If inorganic phosphate accumulates in the outer mitchondrial chamber it will form a dynamic equilibrium with phosphoric acid. Release of hydrogen ions from the acid prevents the egress of hydrogen ions from the matrix to the outer chamber, a process which is required for ATP formation. Additionally, it is suggested that the accumulation of inorganic phosphate in the outer chamber might in some way interfere with entry of phosphate into the matrix for use in forming ATP. The end result of these metabolic imbalances is lack of ATP to power muscle relaxation, and this may be the underlying problem in FMS.

Because muscles and the brain have the highest and most immediate energy requirements, the symptoms of insufficient energy are felt there first. Dr. St. Amand further suggests that the accumulation of phosphate is followed by the accumulation of calcium for electroneutrality and that this contributes to muscle contraction as well. It has been estimated that 40 percent of the energy used by a muscle fiber is required for pumping calcium in and out of storage and thus regulating muscle contraction. Lack of cellular energy will result in impaired movement of calcium back into storage and prolonged stimulation of muscle contraction.

Dr. St. Amand's groundbreaking work in treating FMS has centered on this phosphate metabolism defect. He calls FMS a *dysynergism syndrome* and describes a host of metabolic markers that can be used to identify and differentiate FMS.

He uses a generic drug called guaifenesin, which is commonly sold as a mucolytic to reduce phlegm and chest congestion. With this drug he claims increase in urinary phosphate excretion, along with an increase in calcium and oxalate excretion, and no appreciable increase in uric acid excretion. Significant reduction in symptom severity and frequency appears to confirm his theories.

Neuromuscular Causes

The process of muscle contraction requires calcium ions to be released from storage to initiate the movement. When the muscle relaxes, the calcium is taken up again into storage in the cell. Under normal, healthy feedback control, the release and later reuptake of calcium ions is precisely calibrated through specific, active transport pumping processes that require energy to function. A failure to generate sufficient energy to remove the calcium after contraction will result in progressive contraction and stiffness. The most extreme example of this is rigor mortis, when cell death results in no energy at all being produced and consequent rigidity of the muscles.

Stimulation by substance P as well as injury to the muscle fiber may allow calcium ions from the interstitial fluid to enter the cell and this promotes contraction. Elevated calcium levels within muscle cells may also lead to the activation of calcium-dependent enzymes such as phospholipase and certain muscle proteases. These may then cause progressive muscle fiber damage, sometimes initiating an inflammatory response. This will usually be healed eventually, but may form fibrous scar tissue, with possible permanent shortening of the muscle. In FMS, where growth hormone is decreased, there is poor repair of microtrauma to the muscle tissue, allowing calcium influx and consequent increased muscle tension or even cramping. This is why you really are more stiff and sore after a poor night's sleep; your muscles haven't repaired and calcium is flooding in, triggering contraction. The more this occurs, the more likely it is that the resolution will be fibrous tissue with a slow, progressive decline in muscle functioning and worsening stiffness. This is why many researchers suggest that muscle deconditioning is a significant factor in FMS, and why moderate exercise is very beneficial to reduce muscle tightening. Conversely, overexercising can be very harmful to muscle health because of the impaired microtrauma repair mechanisms.

A muscle always has a few fibers actively contracting at any given moment, and this provides "tone." In muscle tissue, interspersed among the muscle fibers are many tiny muscle "spindles" that transmit information about the degree of tone in a muscle. Each spindle consists of three to ten specialized, noncontractile muscle fibers enclosed in a connective tissue capsule filled with lymph. Wrapped around the spindle fibers are sensory nerve endings, the Type I and Type II fibers that rapidly transmit information about muscle activity to the nervous system. In many different neuromuscular diseases, such as disuse atrophy, corticospinal damage, or prolonged steroid use, Type II fibers atrophy, and this is also apparent in some people with FMS. Additionally, in FMS there is an increase in the lipid (fat) droplets and a slight proliferation of mitochondria in the Type I fibers, indicating increased workload for the Type I fibers and increased fuel requirements. Why the Type II fibers atrophy and the clinical significance of increased workload for the Type I fibers are issues still requiring further research.

A recent study in the Netherlands suggests that certain amino acids (valine, leucoine, isoleucine, and phenylalanine) are deficient in patients with FMS and that this may contribute to the pathology by reducing energy production and protein synthesis in muscle tissue.

Disintegration of the sarcomere, the functional unit of the muscle fiber, is evident in FMS, and is especially apparent in those muscle fibers that are the most mechanically active. Electron microscopy of people with FMS shows a tendency for muscle mitochondria abnormalities, including accumulation of creatine kinase. This is the enzyme that liberates energy from phosphocreatine, a molecule with energy-rich bonds that is formed in the muscle in times of abundant fuel. Excessive creatine kinase generally may cause exhaustion of phosphocreatine stores and consequent energy disruptions and a feeling of muscle fatigue. Bengtsson and Henricksen found that muscle lesion biopsies from patients with FMS demonstrated a 20 percent reduction in adenosine triphosphate (ATP) and creatine phosphate when compared to tissue biopsied from adjacent but unaffected muscle.

Both James Daley, M.D., and Robert Bennet, M.D., have found that the muscles of people with FMS produce excessive quantities of lactic acid. This causes cramping and rapid fatiguing of the muscles. Lactic acid may also contribute to microtrauma. Lactic acid is more likely to accumulate in people who do not properly utilize glucose in the Krebs cycle. Glycolysis and the use of proteins and fats as an energy source leads to accumulation of lactic acid and a ketogenic tendency.

There has been much debate about the actual physical changes in the muscles that we identify as tender points. Many authorities suggest that these are accumulations of lactic and possibly uric acid, probably in the region of the muscle spindles. This chronic chemical irritation of the spindle may cause inappropriate nerve impulse generation and send a message to the brain that the muscle is contracting when in fact it is not. This could account for the sensation of tightness or cramping in the muscles. Evidence also points toward a chronic shortening of the sarcomere (the unit of contraction within muscle fibers). This would mean that the muscle is tight and contracted in the absence of motor impulses from the brain telling it to shorten. The result of this would be impaired circulation to the muscle and hence lactic acid accumulation from anaerobic respiration in the muscle, and uric acid accumulation from impaired waste removal. Additionally, muscle contraction may impair the flow of lymphatic fluid around the sarcomere and reduce metabolic waste removal.

Fascia and Fibromyalgia

Fascia is functionally divided into the deep and superficial types. Superficial fascia lies under the skin and is relatively fatty and loose. It stores water and fat, it provides insulation against heat loss, it provides mechanical protection from injury, and it carries nerves and blood vessels. Deep fascia wraps the muscles and organs. It is a denser tissue and has a more structural role in the body. Deep fascia wraps and penetrates all tissues and forms a continuous sheath connecting all parts of the body with the rest.

Fascia is composed of layers of connective tissue. It consists predominantly of collagen fibers, providing strength and resilience, with some elastic fibers, supplying elasticity and tensile strength. These are held in a ground substance, which is a type of gel that can become more or less viscous according to varying factors, including levels of hydration, nutrition, oxygenation, the influence of growth hormone, and so on. Fascia carries the blood, nerve, and lymph vessels and sometimes provides a point of attachment for the underlying muscle fibers. It merges into tendons, ligaments, and muscles. Extensions of the fascia extend around each muscle within a group, around the bundles of muscle fibers within a muscle, and finally, around the individual muscle fibers themselves. Muscle is wrapped, held together, and separated into functional groups by fascia. It binds everything together and keeps it discretely compartmentalized. In the fascia are macrophages (phagocytic white blood cells), which have a defensive action; plasma cells, which give rise to antibodies; and mast cells, which produce histamine and mediate the allergic response.

Production and repair of collagen fibers and ground substance is under the regulation of growth hormone (GH). Although it has not been proven conclusively yet, it appears likely that FMS might be, at least in part, a disorder of fascia and connective tissue repair. Specifically, deficiency of GH could cause reduced fluidity of the ground substance with consequent stiffness in the fascia, extending from the subcutaneous to the interstitial level. Additionally, tension or torsion of the fascia could lead to nerve entrapment, impaired local circulation, reduced oxygen delivery and hence reduced energy production and muscle fatigue, muscle pain, and tender points. Interestingly, the brain and nervous tissue are technically a type of connective tissue, as are muscles, joints, the skin, the heart valves, and other tissues commonly involved in FMS.

Is this part of the puzzle? Can connective tissue disrepair and dysfunction contribute to FMS? The likely answer is "yes," but the truth is we just don't know for sure yet. What we do know is that certain types of bodywork may help and that getting plenty of vitamin C and bioflavonoids will promote connective tissue repair and are probably worth taking as supplements. Connective tissue tonic herbs may also be used to advantage here, including hawthorn, gotu kola, and horsetail.

Physical Trauma as a Causative Agent

Despite a lack of discussion in the literature, anecdotal evidence strongly suggests that physical trauma is a significant part of the etiology of FMS. A majority of patients report exacerbation of symptoms after a blow or an injury and this is commonly the trigger for finally seeking medical help. In other words, probably a great many people walk around with some of the symptoms of FMS, but are coping and managing until an accident of some sort finally tips them over the edge into full-blown FMS. Sometimes it can even be from emotional or health trauma such as the breakup of a relation-ship, death of a loved one, or undergoing surgery.

Professor Dan Buskila and Greenfield et al., among others, have suggested that as many as 23 percent of people with FMS identify a specific precipitat-ing event.[1] In my clinical practice I have seen a patient who developed FMS after falling off a garden swing, another who developed it after slipping on some ice, and yet another in which it was triggered by her diving into a shal-low pool and hitting her head. One patient correlated the onset of symptoms to losing his job. By far the majority of injuries, though, are from car acci-dents, which no doubt says something about the frequency with which we ride in cars. Occasionally the accident is serious and injuries are severe, with FMS becoming apparent after the initial injuries have healed and sometimes impossible to differentiate from normal healing responses. In many cases, though, the accident is a fairly minor rear-ender type, or "fender bender." The patient may be no worse than shaken and bruised, but weeks or months later the symptoms of FMS become apparent.

How and why this occurs is still open to speculation. Perhaps the person is already stressed and has excessive sympathetic dominance. The physical and emotional stress of the accident may trigger overloading of the system and a breakdown of health. But if this is the case, why doesn't it happen to every stressed person who has an accident? What makes some people more suscep-tible than others?

Whiplash Injury

Physical therapists suggest that part of the problem lies in the nature of the impact. The disproportionate number of rear-end accidents that trigger FMS leads to a high number of whiplash injuries. Properly called a cervical accel-eration/deceleration (CAD) injury, this is probably the most common type of injury preceding a diagnosis of FMS. In this type of accident, the head is thrust first in the direction of the impact, then in the opposite direction.

Thus, for example, in a car stopped at a traffic light that is rammed from behind, the heads of the driver and passengers will move rapidly backward toward the striking car. At the moment of impact, while the heads are thrust backward, the vehicle itself and the bodies inside are propelled forward. When the struck car comes to rest the bodies still have forward momentum, which continues until arrested by a seat belt, steering wheel, or windshield, and this causes the heads to be thrust sharply forward. Thus the necks are said to be cracked like a whip, first backward, then forward. This is a key cause of closed head injuries.

One immediate repercussion of a whiplash injury is that, during the backward and forward movements of the neck, inertia causes a fractional delay in the following movement of the mandible, or jawbone, which is suspended below the skull. This causes first an anterior mandibular displacement, immediately followed by a posterior mandibular displacement. This stretching and possibly tearing of the ligaments and connective tissue, even sometimes dislocation of the articular disc, of the temporomandibular joint (TMJ) will commonly give rise to TMJ problems, a notable feature of FMS.

Matthew Avery, a researcher at the Motor Insurance Repair Research Centre in England, has reported that whiplash injuries are more common now than in previous decades due to changes in car design and impact resilience of car materials.

Meningeal Tension and Cerebrospinal Fluid Disturbance

Surrounding the entire brain and spinal cord are three layers of tissue called the meninges. The outer layer, called the dura mater, is made of dense connective tissue and forms a complete tube around the spinal cord and wraps all around the brain. Below this layer is the arachnoid mater, which comprises thin and delicate connective tissue. Between the two layers is the subdural space, which contains serous fluid for lubrication and friction-free movement of the brain and spinal cord within the protective capsule. The inner layer is called the *pia mater*; it comprises a very fine sheet of connective tissue that adheres to the surfaces of the spinal cord and the brain, and carries many blood vessels. Between the pia mater and the arachnoid mater is the subarachnoid space, which contains the cerebrospinal fluid (CSF), in which the brain and spinal cord actually float. CSF circulates all around the brain and spinal cord, as well as through the ventricles (cavities) of the brain. It is pumped through the subarachnoid space by rhythmic contractions of the skull. It acts as a shock absorber to cushion the brain and spinal cord, and also delivers nutritive substances that are filtered from the blood and removes wastes and toxic substances produced by the brain and spinal cord. It is composed of water with dissolved glucose, salts, protein, and urea, and it also contains some lymphocytes for immune functioning. CSF is produced by filtration from the blood vessels in the ventricles of the brain. After circulation around the brain and spinal cord, the fluid is reabsorbed into the blood stream.

During any sudden, sharp impact, such as a whiplash injury, there is a reflex tightening or constriction of the meninges that wrap around and protect the entire central nervous system, and possibly of the fascia, too. Of course the meninges themselves are not muscular, but they contain some scattered contractile elastic fibers and are surrounded by fascia and connective tissue, which may become more or less viscous according to circumstance. Tension of these tissues is a reflex protective mechanism with profound adverse consequences if allowed to persist. Some physical therapists suggest that a whiplash injury may stress the neck so greatly that there is chronic protective tightening of the meninges with consequent impairment of CSF circulation. This may be aggravated by any torsion in the meninges if the head was turned or the body twisted at the moment of impact.

It is interesting to note that the pineal gland is surrounded by a layer of pia mater and is nourished and cleansed by the circulation of CSF. Perhaps blockage of the CSF flow could have a detrimental impact in pineal function and this could explain why physical trauma is often the trigger for the development of full-blown FMS.

This theory is supported by the fact that craniosacral therapy is often very helpful in FMS. This is a type of physical therapy in which the practitioner endeavors to reestablish the rhythmic contractile pulsations of the skull that promote CSF flow. Parasympathetic fibers exit the spinal cord in the cervical and sacral areas, and craniosacral therapy also promotes parasympathetic dominance and reduced sympathetic stimulation. (See Chapter 7 for details on craniosacral therapy.)

Clearly, much research is required before we properly understand the connection between physical trauma and FMS, but there is little doubt that impact injuries are a common denominator in many cases and a significant causative agent.

CHAPTER FOUR

MODERN MEDICINE AND FIBROMYALGIA

*Physicians pour drugs of which they know little,
to cure diseases of which they know less,
into patients of which they know nothing.*
VOLTAIRE

December 1994

Tried a sleeping pill last night—10 mg of Elavil—and was knocked out this morning. I mean I always wake feeling rough, but this was much worse. My normal waking thought is that I've been hit by a bus, and this morning it felt like a train! I am used to popping ibuprofen occasionally when the headaches are truly disabling and haven't noticed any ill effects so I never expected so much from such a low dose of this supposedly mild sleeping pill. I have some patients that take 50 or 75 mg nightly. How do they do it? Anyway, I cannot really believe that any drug can offer much help to so complex and multi-factorial a condition. Maybe drugs can handle symptoms, make you feel a bit better for a little while, but you would have to take so many different things to treat so many different symptoms that you would become a walking pharmacy. Come to think of it, that is exactly what some of my patients are like! They take one thing to treat A, another to treat B, and yet another to treat the side effects

of A and B. This is crazy-making—just swapping one problem for another and

in the meantime distracting them from addressing the real core of the problem

which is stress and unhappiness and overwork and poor diet and lack of bal-

ance or harmony in their lives.

To date there is no drug that cures FMS, although many pharmaceutical agents are used to address the symptoms. Only guaifenesin so far shows real benefit in FMS and it is still in an experimental phase. Given the multifactorial, mutable, and entirely individualistic nature of the condition, it is doubtful if there ever will be a specific drug protocol that actually overcomes it. At the present time drugs are used to alleviate symptoms, which does not prevent them from recurring, nor does it mitigate the pathophysiological process. This may be appropriate where natural remedies and lifestyle adjustment are either inadequate or are too slow, and acute care is required. If you are in severe pain, then by all means take a painkiller, but do not to confuse alleviation of symptoms with attainment of true well-being. Pharmaceutical drugs are exceptionally good for crisis care and acute intervention. They are powerful and effective, but at a price. The list of side effects is long and they should be reserved for extreme situations where natural therapies have not worked. For chronic care situations such as with FMS, where sleeping agents, muscle relaxants, and painkillers are commonly prescribed, many drugs can be replaced from the herbal pharmacy, and usually without marked side effects or habituation.

Allopathic drugs, by masking symptoms and reducing discomfort, may enable a person to overcome pain and difficulty to achieve a reasonable quality of life. This provides an opportunity for the patient to learn and practice the general principles of a healthy lifestyle that can aid in full recovery and maintenance of health. Alternatively, drugs can be used to mask symptoms and enable the patient to ignore the dietary, lifestyle and attitudinal changes that are fundamental to healing. One of the jobs of the holistic therapist is to help the patient determine which drugs may actually be helpful and appropriate and which are less than useful. This may require a certain amount of trial and error—drugs that sedate some people may stimulate others, and individual biochemistry and pathophysiology play a strong role in determining drug efficacy. A particular problem for the FMS patient is that if you express depression and mental exhaustion from chronic pain and disability, then you risk being dismissed as suffering from psychogenic pain and being treated as a mental health case. On the other hand, if you consistently put a brave face on it and try not to complain, then you risk being dismissed as not really having tangible symptoms and not needing treatment. It is imperative that health care professionals remember that having an emotional reaction to pain does not mean that the pain is caused by an emotional state. Pain tolerance tends to diminish over time as chronic pain persists—perhaps due to exhaustion of endorphins and disruption of the endogenous (internal) pain control mechanisms. Eventually even slight stimulation can generate intolerable pain and this is frequently compounded by habituation to analgesics—a vicious cycle that is very hard to break. I have found that it is not very useful to inquire how severe pain is. Everybody's tolerance level is different and what may be mild pain to one person may be excruciating to another. More useful is to inquire as to the degree of disability. Can patients dress themselves, prepare meals, do the shopping or laundry, hold down a job? This gives a useful scale against which to measure patient progress.

Helpful Pointers When Taking Prescription Medication

- When taking any medication, you should aim for the smallest effective dose, even if this means going below what your doctor prescribed. When trying a new drug myself, I always take half the prescribed dose and monitor my reactions for a few days. You may wish to buy a tablet cutter at the local health food store or drugstore, or simply use a razor blade.

- Consider using drugs only during acute flare-ups when natural remedies just aren't working, and resist the urge to take progressively more
  drugs as they become progressively less effective.
- Beware of mixing medications because they may summate and have a
  stronger effect than you expect.
- Try to introduce only one new medication at a time so that you can
  more easily monitor the results.
- Keep a written record of your medications and your reactions. Refer
  back to it as needed and learn to listen to the messages that your body
  is trying to tell you.
- If you wish to reduce a medication you should go about this slowly,
  shaving down the tablet a little more each day with a razor blade. Do
  not shock the body by stopping a drug suddenly after long-term usage.
- Research every drug, herb, nutrient, or other medication you are taking
  and become familiar with the side effects and contraindications of each.
- Make sure you tell each health care practitioner all the products and
  medications you are currently using.
- Most prescription drugs are metabolized in the liver, utilizing existing
  detoxification pathways and sometimes compromising normal metabolic functions. Many drug side effects are due to this compromising of
  liver function. It follows, then, that during a course of prescription
  medication it is useful to support and strengthen liver function. At the
  least a daily dose of milk thistle will offer some protection.

Sleeping Agents

Given that one of the most fundamental physiological disturbances in FMS is
sleep, it seems reasonable to attempt to rectify this problem. Unfortunately,
using drugs to induce sleep is often counterproductive. In many cases, the
deep, healing delta sleep is rarely reached or sustained, and people wake feeling just as tired as if they hadn't taken anything. Sometimes, indeed, they feel

worse because there is a significant hangover from the drug, causing morning grogginess and disturbed cognitive function. The greatest help from sleeping agents is probably psychological because you were actually knocked out all night and so you can think you have slept well. For the most part, though, the side effects outweigh the benefits and these drugs are best avoided by most people. If you do take sleeping agents, you should start at the lowest dose possible and only increase the dosage if needed. Be aware that tolerance builds up and increased doses will be needed over time to achieve the same level of benefit, which, of course, may result in increasing side effects too.

The most commonly prescribed drug for FMS is amitriptyline, sold under the brand name Elavil. This is a tricyclic antidepressant, a class of drugs that generally work by blocking the reuptake of specific neurotransmitters, thus prolonging their actions. Blockage of serotonin or noradrenaline reuptake has antidepressant effects while blockage of dopamine reuptake has stimulating effects. Additionally, it increases the effects of endogenous opiates, natural painkillers in the central nervous system. This drug and other antidepressants, are not necessarily being prescribed because the physician thinks the patient is clinically depressed, but because they induce sleep and relieve anxiety. Side effects are common and include weight gain, dry eyes and mouth, blurred vision, constipation, urinary retention, poor concentration, reduced perspiration, photosensitivity, confusion, and arrhythmias. Some people also experience restless leg syndrome which actually disrupts sleep further. These side effects are probably induced by incidental reuptake inhibition affecting histamine and the muscarinic acetylcholine parasympathetic fibers. A normal starting dose of amitriptyline is 10 mg but can rise to over 100 mg in some cases.

Venlafaxine HCl (Effexor), trazodone (Desyrel), doxepin (Sinequan), and nortriptyline HCl (Pamelor) are other tricyclic drugs used to treat FMS. Pamelor is often better tolerated than Elavil but has been associated with depression so care should be taken when using this drug in case it worsens any depression already present. Additionally, some people find paradoxical stimulation from Pamelor and instead use it in the morning for daytime alertness and energy.

Benzodiazepine tranquilizers are commonly prescribed for anxiety, especially alprazolam (Xanax). Diazepam has the added advantage of being a muscle relaxant. The pharmacology of this class of drugs has not yet been definitively established, although benzodiazepine receptors do occur in the brain and it is hypothesized that binding of the drug to the receptor increases the effect of gamma-amino butyric acid (GABA), an inhibitory neurotransmitter. Recognized side effects include skin rashes, nausea, headaches, vertigo, lightheadedness, loss of libido, drowsiness, and ataxia (gait abnormalities and difficulty walking). Additionally, habituation can occur even with low doses and the side effects of withdrawal can include aggravation of original symptoms including acute panic attacks, insomnia, muscle spasms, dizziness, and headaches. Interestingly, the herb valerian, traditionally used to induce deep and restful sleep, acts on the same receptor sites in the brain but has no side effects, except an occasional morning headache with very large doses, and is not habit forming. However, caution suggests that it is inadvisable to combine valerian and benzodiazepines due to possible potentiation of effects.

Other sleeping agents that may be used in FMS include zolpidem tartrate (Ambien) and diphenhydramine (Benadryl). Side effects of weight gain, constipation, arrhythmias, lethargy, and slowed thinking are common. Ambien may cause depression and is only recommended for very short-term, occasional use. Benadryl was developed and is still marketed as an antihistamine although it is widely used in compound pharmaceuticals as a sleep inducer. It specifically promotes delta phase sleep and is said to be safe even for children and not habit forming. About 20 percent of people respond to Benadryl with paradoxical stimulation. So far no research has been done on the immune response to long-term use of antihistamines and it is possible that problems may arise.

Recently two other drugs have shown promise in treating FMS—cimetidine (Tagamet) and ranitidine (Zantac). These are better known as antiulcer medications, but they also block the absorption of histamine, a stimulating neurotransmitter, and seem to promote delta phase sleep. They also increase the effectiveness of amitriptyline and allow for the use of lower doses.

The histamine response modification that is common to both Benadryl and cimetidine/ranitidine suggests more immune involvement in sleep disturbance and FMS than has previously been acknowledged. Although no specific allergen has been found common in FMS, histamine can be elevated in people with FMS. Additionally, there is inappropriate rupturing of mast cells in the skin of people with FMS, which goes a long way toward explaining the strange dermal symptoms many people experience.

Histamine is the key inflammatory substance released during an allergic incident. Is it possible that FMS is triggered or at least aggravated by allergic responses to food or environmental particles? This would support the experience of clinicians who report improved symptoms and decreased severity of FMS with cleansing and detoxification programs that alleviate stress on the immune system, and with avoidance of known allergens. Clearly more research needs to be done into the histamine release response in people with FMS and whether there are abnormal surges that correspond to symptom flare-up.

Regulators of Neurotransmitters

Selective serotonin reuptake inhibitors (SSRIs) have been tried with mixed results in FMS. They tend to reduce sleepiness and fatigue. Fluoxetine hydrochloride (Prozac) does not appear to be very effective, while sertraline (Zoloft) appears to reduce pain and fatigue. Paroxetine hydrochloride (Paxil) is both a serotonin and norepinephrine reuptake inhibitor and may cause insomnia. Prozac is most indicated for patients with severe concurrent depression who sleep excessively. Side effects may include paradoxical insomnia, dry mouth, headaches, nausea, diarrhea, loss of libido, restlessness, and weight loss. St. John's wort, long recognized as a gentle sedative, has a noted SSRI function, (hence its modern use for depression), and may be of benefit to people with FMS. Contrary to recent medical literature, herbalists have often combined St.

John's wort with SSRI drugs as part of a protocol to reduce dependence on the prescription drug, and no significant side effects have been reported. This should only be done under the supervision of a trained herbalist.

A meta-analysis of sixteen clinical trials reviewing the efficacy of antidepressant medication in treating FMS suggested that patients receiving medication were four times more likely to report improved alleviation of symptoms, especially reduced pain.

Recently a novel approach to treating symptoms of FMS has been the use of serotonin receptor antagonists. 5HT3 (serotonin) receptor antagonists are rapidly absorbed and readily penetrate the blood-brain barrier. They are metabolized by the cytochrome P450 enzyme series in the liver and excreted in the urine. They do not modify the behavior of animals nor alter physiological parameters in healthy human adults. They are generally well tolerated, headaches and gastrointestinal disturbance being the most common side effects. They are routinely used in the treatment of chemotherapy-induced or postoperative nausea and vomiting. They have been noted to reduce serous secretions and diarrhea caused by increased intestinal serotonin content, to exert a limited antiarrhythmic activity, and to reduce sensations of pain. Additionally, 5HT3 antagonists reduce symptoms of anxiety, improve age-associated memory impairment, and reduce alcohol cravings, Parkinsonian psychosis, and migraines. A large study of over four hundred FMS patients given 5 to 15 mg of oral tropisetron (a strongly selective competitive inhibitor of serotonin receptors) showed improved mood and anxiety states, reduction in pain and tender points, less dizziness, and less sleep disturbance. Five mg was found to be the most effective dose. Benefits were most pronounced after ten days of treatment, and twenty-eight days' use by a smaller group of patients fostered continued improvement and very good tolerance of the drug. Other research by some of the same authors suggests that 2 mg given intravenously may have a quicker and more pronounced effect. A study of ninety-six FMS patients evaluated the interrelationships of tropisetron and various neurotransmitters in the blood and revealed that patients with the lowest levels of plasma serotonin and/or the highest levels of dopamine responded best to the drug. This suggests a possible method of evaluating candidates for drug therapy.

Muscle Relaxants

Greatly increased muscle tension contributes to physical discomfort in FMS. Warm baths, massage, stretching exercises, and various herbal remedies are helpful here. The pharmaceutical approach includes the use of cyclobenza-prine (Flexeril), which is described as a muscle relaxant but is actually very similar to amitriptyline. Flexeril has anticholinergic (antiparasympatho-mimetic) activity and potentiates norepinephrine, thus being somewhat stimulating. It relieves muscle spasm through a central action, possibly at the brain stem level, with no involvement of the neuromuscular junction or the muscle tissue itself. It tends to reduce muscle pain and tenderness and increase mobility. Side effects include gastric disturbance such as indigestion, nausea and vomiting, dizziness and blurred vision, dry eyes, headache, con-fusion, drowsiness, fatigue, and a sense of detachment or unreality. It is contraindicated in people with arrhythmias or heart block and in those who wear contact lenses or suffer from dry eyes or glaucoma.

Klonopin (clonazepam) is a member of the benzodiazepine class of drug, here used as an antispasmodic and muscle relaxant but subject to the same long list of side effects as when this class of drug is used for depression. It is com-monly prescribed where nighttime bruxism (tooth grinding) is disturbing the sleep and is helpful when restless leg syndrome or other muscle jerking occurs at night. Carisoprodol (Soma) is a powerful drug, acting on the central nervous system to reduce the generation and transmission of motor impulses to the muscles. It works rapidly and is generally well tolerated. It helps patients detach from their pain and reduces the sensation of sensory overload. Lioresal (Baclofen) is sometimes prescribed for FMS, although it is most commonly used as a skeletal muscle relaxant for multiple sclerosis and other spinal cord lesions. Baclofen reduces muscle spasticity and pain and improves bowel and bladder function as well. The exact mode of action is not clear, but it is believed to block afferent pathways (transmission of nerve impulses to the spinal cord), possibly by serving as an inhibitory neurotransmitter or by hyperpolarizing receptor sites in the afferent pathway and thus inhibiting release of excitatory neurotransmitters such as glutamate and aspartic acid. Baclofen may cause a number of side effects, some of which may even mimic FMS. These include headache, dizziness, confusion, drowsiness, fatigue, insomnia, weakness, lethargy, increased urinary frequency, increased or reduced blood pressure, and seizures. In higher doses, such as are sometimes given for FMS, Baclofen may cause depression of the central nervous system. Due to a theoretical potentiation of Baclofen by valerian or kava, some authorities recommend not using these herbs concurrent with the drug. Conversely, this possible interaction holds promise for those persons wishing to wean themselves off prescription pharmaceuticals and replace them with natural remedies. If valerian and kava do work in the same pathways and have similar effects to Baclofen, then why not use them instead?

Chlorzoxazone (Parafon) is another centrally acting muscle relaxant occasionally used for FMS. It is thought to alter the perception of pain and, through influencing the central nervous system, to cause sedation and a reduction in muscle spasms. It is not recommended in pregnancy and when breast-feeding due to lack of research and clinical information. It is contraindicated in renal or hepatic disease, central nervous depression, and the elderly. There is a possibility of liver toxicity from this drug and it is not often recommended any more.

Pain Management

For the management of most muscular aching and stiffness, as well as the pain of arthritis, the nonsteroidal anti-inflammatory drugs (NSAIDs) are effective and readily available over the counter, but are not without side effects. They generally work by blocking the activity of either cyclo-oxygenase or lipoxygenase enzymes that manufacture prostaglandins from fatty acid substrates. Aspirin is known to cause gastric disturbance and to inhibit proper hydration of cartilage, hence contributing to joint stress and consequent inflammation. Acetaminophen is very damaging to the liver by impairing proper enzyme activity in the detoxification pathways. Ibuprofen is probably the best over-the-counter analgesic to use, with the bonus that it is also quite effective as an antispasmodic and muscle relaxant. However, no painkillers should be used long term. If improvement does not occur with appropriate treatment and painkillers are a necessity, then vary the type every couple of days and take precautions to protect the liver and kidneys from toxic damage. Avoid using narcotics and opiates because of their addictive nature, which will become a serious problem in a chronic disease such as FMS. Corticosteroids have not demonstrated benefits in FMS and should be avoided due to their significant detrimental side effects.

Tramadol hydrochloride (Ultram) is a nonnarcotic agent in a fairly new class of analgesics called the *centrally binding binary agents* (CABA). It is an opiate, but has a low abuse potential and is becoming more commonly pre-scribed. Patients report that it is necessary to take it continuously for best results; it is not very effective when taken on an "as needed" basis.

For management of tender-point and trigger-point pain there are two main therapeutic approaches, often applied in conjunction. "Spray and stretch" utilizes a local anesthetic and passive stretching of the affected part. For severe or unremitting pain, injection of 1 percent lidocaine into the point may be helpful.

Guaifenesin

An endocrinologist and professor of medicine at UCLA named Dr. R. Paul St. Amand has spent many years researching the effects of a common over-the-counter cough medication on FMS. His discoveries and conclusions are startling to some, and yet very familiar to anyone trained in principles of natural health. The new and still experimental drug therapy is simply re-creating through pharmaceutical means a process of cleansing and detoxification that natural healers have promoted for years with herbs and diet.

Guaifenesin is classified as an expectorant—it reduces the viscosity, stickiness, and surface tension of mucus and enables productive coughing to clear congestion from the lungs. In this it can be likened to the soothing, mucilaginous expectorants of herbal medicine. It is commonly sold in combination with other antitussive remedies in such over-the-counter products as Fenesin, Phenasin, Hytuss, Pneumomist, Robitussin, Benylin, Calmylin, Breonesin, and Resyl.

Dr. St. Amand, himself suffering from FMS, tried the drug and found that after an initial worsening of all symptoms, he later felt a significant improvement. Thus encouraged, he offered it to FMS patients and they had similar results. He found that with the use of guaifenesin they were all excreting abnormally elevated levels of phosphoric acid in their urine. He theorized that some hereditary defect of phosphate metabolism might be at the heart of FMS. He noted that it is a decrease in adenosine triphosphate (ATP) that actually causes the muscle stiffness of FMS, and that its availability is impaired by high mitochondrial levels of inorganic phosphates. Today we consume a very high percentage of inorganic phosphoric acid in our diet, mainly through food additives and canned sodas. Perhaps, he suggests, inorganic phosphoric acid binds up the phosphate required for cellular metabolism, resulting in reduced ATP production and cellular fatigue. Guaifenesin causes elimination of unwanted phosphoric acid from the body and thus a reactivation of energy production in the cell.

So far, this is still all theoretical and experimental. Dr. Robert Bennet in Oregon carried out clinical research on forty women with FMS that showed guaifenesin equal to placebo in reducing symptoms. The major drawback to this study was that the dose for all the women was 600 mg twice daily, which was probably not sufficient for at least some of them. Additionally, since that research was published in 1995, Dr. St. Amand has continued his clinical research and discovered even more about how the drug works and how it can be blocked inadvertently by patient behavior. First, he determined that the presence of reactive hypoglycemia will reduce the actions of guaifenesin. Dr. Devin Starlanyl and Mary Ellen Copeland report using guaifenesin in over one thousand FMS patients and finding as many as 85 percent have blood sugar imbalances. Working with high-protein and low-carbohydrate diets they have been able to aid some patients to better results from using guaifenesin. Additionally, Dr. St. Amand has discovered that the action of the drug is blocked by the presence of salicylates in the diet or in medications. Salicylates are very common naturally occurring substances, found in apples, peaches, apricots, cherries, aspirin, sunscreens, Pepto-Bismol, Listerine, Alka Seltzer, wart removers, ultrasound gels, and analgesic muscle rubs. Many herbs are also rich in salicylates, which have an anti-inflammatory action (see Chapter 6). These should be strictly avoided if you are planning to take guaifenesin. Guaifenesin is considered to be a risky drug for pregnant or nursing mothers. It is contraindicated in heart failure, in chronic obstructive pulmonary disease, and when taking ACE inhibitor medication.

Effective doses for FMS have ranged from 300 mg twice daily to as much as 2,400 mg daily. It is recommended to start with the lowest dose for about two weeks, then work up as required. Be aware that the side effects can be very unpleasant. As described in the literature, guaifenesin causes a classic "cleansing and healing crisis." Allopathic literature describes the symptoms of higher doses as abdominal pain, diarrhea, nausea, and vomiting. In the moderate to large doses required to benefit FMS, common cleansing effects include headaches, fatigue, aching, a flulike feeling, and lots of mucus secretion—eyes, nose, vaginally, rectally. Bad breath, burning urination, skin rashes, and body odor have also been described. These side effects may continue for several days and may recur episodically as treatment continues. It is important to get plenty of rest during this time and to protect and support the liver and kidneys. Guaifenesin may be continued for extended periods. It should be possible to slowly reduce the dose as symptoms subside. If a flare-up occurs, maintain at that dose until symptoms abate, then continue reducing. Some people may require a low-maintenance dose long term. If Dr. St.

Amand's theories of genetically induced phosphate dysregulation are true, then lifelong guaifenesin therapy will be required, much like insulin for diabetics and thyroid hormone for people with hypothyroidism.

Remember that this is still experimental. I have not had personal or clinical experience with guaifenesin yet but am intrigued by the concept. I wonder if using herbs, diet, supplements, and other natural depurative and tonic therapies would reduce the severity or frequency of the guaifenesin flare-ups. I asked herbal database wizard Dr. Jim Duke, formerly of the U. S. Department of Agriculture, if he knew of any herbs that would increase phosphoric acid elimination and he replied that he had no such listings. We can make the educated guess that herbs that increase uric acid elimination (parsley, celery, silver birch) might also aid FMS, but no hard evidence yet exists.

There is some suggestion that guaifenesin may help fertility by thinning the cervical mucus and making the passage of sperm easier. If you do not wish to become pregnant then be sure to take adequate precautions against conception while using the drug.

Guidelines for Taking Guaifenesin

- Seek out the help and support of a doctor who is experienced in prescribing this treatment. Read Dr. St. Amand's book for a list of doctors who have trained with him.
- Guaifenesin is available for self-medication in the form of over-the-counter cough remedies. The problem with these is that they come laden with sugar, artificial color, and other ingredients such as ephedrine or pseudoephedrine that have an adrenaline-like effect on the body and are contraindicated in FMS. Guaifenesin is also available over the counter in 300 mg tablets and these can be self-prescribed, although this is not recommended. When larger doses are required it may be necessary to have a prescription.

- Before commencing drug treatment you should complete a good cleansing and detoxification program using herbs and diet. Take alterative herbs to cleanse the liver and milk thistle to protect it.
- Avoid all canned drinks, sodas, and foods.
- Drink lots of filtered water and herbal teas to flush out the kidneys and to help liquefy mucus.
- Get plenty of rest. Set aside at least two weeks of "downtime" after first commencing treatment, and be prepared for weeks or months of intermittent cleansing flare-ups.
- Take warm baths and use heating packs over the kidneys to encourage excretion.
- As much as possible, reduce or eliminate other medications to simplify tracking of guaifenesin results.
- Address any symptoms of hypoglycemia.
- Avoid *all* sources of salicylates in food, medicines, or personal care items.

Some compounding pharmacists are mixing guaifenesin into a gel containing the nonsteroidal anti-inflammatory substance ibuprofen. The gel breaks down the nitrous oxide barrier on the skin and allows the guaifenesin to penetrate the skin and reach the subcutaneous nerve endings. There it interacts with the ibuprofen and potentiates its anti-inflammatory effects. The actual mechanism of action is as yet unclear.

PART II

Holistic Approaches to Fibromyalgia

Everything man needs to maintain good health can be found in nature— the true task of science is to find these things.

PARACELSUS

CHAPTER FIVE

USING FOOD AS MEDICINE: BUILDING A HEALTHY DIET

*Let your food be your medicine and
your medicine be your food.*
HIPPOCRATES

October 1993

*One of the most frustrating things about this damned disease is that it makes it
hard to do so many ordinary things. Opening taps or tight jar lids, grating and
chopping vegetables, stirring a batter. It can take me twice as long to cook now
because I have to keep switching hands, resting, and changing positions. I have
become an expert in quick and easy but still nutritious meals, not to mention
deli takeout dinners. Doing simple things like hanging laundry can be murder
because I can't keep my arms raised like that very long. Or ironing because the
heaviness makes my hand ache. In clinic it is a real problem when I am taking
notes because I get cramps in my hand and have to stop writing. In general,
exercise seems to help but repetitive movements aren't good. It is the little things
like this that really get me down sometimes. Other times I know from what
I see in the clinic that really I am very lucky. I can still function, albeit sometimes only with great effort of will. It could be much worse.*

The Paleolithic Diet

The basic nutritional needs of the body—the core of what it takes to stay alive—are protein and fat; even carbohydrate, at least in the form of grains, is optional. We also require a steady supply of vitamins, minerals, and trace elements, and plenty of clean water. The controversy arises over what the optimum amounts are and how to obtain them. Low-fat diets have completely failed to stop the rise of heart disease, and diabetes has risen dramatically since the American Diabetes Association began promoting the high-complex carbohydrate diet. America has the dubious distinction of being the first country in the world where over half of the population is officially overweight according to standard life insurance tables. We may have conquered many infectious epidemic diseases such as cholera and typhoid, but the morbidity and mortality from chronic degenerative diseases such as cardiovascular disease, rheumatoid arthritis, and cancer has risen inexorably over the past couple of hundred years. So what is going on here? Why aren't people responding well to the diets promulgated by the medical establishment?

The problem is actually quite simple. Our diet has evolved faster than the rate of adaptation that our bodies are capable of, and our physiology and biochemistry are becoming profoundly disturbed as a consequence. We are suddenly eating a totally new diet and the rate of evolution is inadequate to manage the change. This is the so-called "evolutionary discordance theory" that suggests that an organism will be adversely affected by sudden changes in the environment and that its subsequent survival will depend upon the ability to adapt rapidly and appropriately.

The human genome evolves very slowly, perhaps only a 0.5 percent spontaneous mutation rate for DNA in a million years. This translates into only a 0.005 percent change since the agricultural revolution 10,000 years ago, and yet our diets today are so different as to be unrecognizable. Some farsighted nutritionists today are advocating that we eat a *Paleolithic diet,* one more like that of our primitive ancestors. They suggest that we will be healthier, stronger, and have more stamina if we eat as we have evolved to eat over millennia. A close examination of the criteria of this diet reveals that it provides the physiologically and biochemically preferred balance of essential nutrients for optimal health.

If the genus *Homo* is imagined as being one day old, then we began eating grains in the last six minutes, drinking milk in the last three minutes, and eating soy less than one minute ago. Even just a few generations ago, the vast majority of people were rurally based and ate locally grown food in season. Preservation of foods was limited to salting, drying, and pickling. Transport of most foods was not practical because there was no way to keep food fresh and no transportation infrastructure. Foods were rich in enzymes because they were often eaten with fermentation commencing, a preputrefaction phase. Still today in developing countries such as India, as much as 80 percent of the population is primarily agricultural. This contrasts with America and the rest of the developed world where only 2 to 4 percent of the population now makes its living off the land. The vast majority of people in the developed world purchase food that has been preserved and stored in some fashion, often by the addition of artificial preservatives, and is rarely locally grown or eaten fresh in season. We buy canned, bottled, frozen, dried, processed, packaged stuff and call it food, when it would probably be almost unrecognizable to the farmer!

The closest primate relative of the human species is the chimpanzee. We are approximately 1.7 percent different at the genetic level and yet are clearly far apart in phenome expression—how this genetic programming is manifested. We broke away genetically from chimps five to seven million years ago and have evolved differently since then. This came about largely in dietary differences. A chimp eats approximately 94 percent plant foods, mostly ripe fruit, and all raw. The remaining 6 percent is made up of eggs, insects, grubs, small lizards, bats, and so on if the animal happens upon them, incorrectly characterizing the chimp as an opportunistic omnivore. Chimps use sticks to dig for termites as well as using them for tools, even teaching young chimps this skill. Some organized hunting of other smaller monkey species does occur, but it accounts for only a small percentage of their diet.

Long before the primates had appeared, small mammals—bats, rodents, and other animals—evolved, eating grass, insects, and each other, and these

evolved into larger carnivores. Two to three million years ago, as polar glacia-
tion expanded and the last full ice age commenced, dense forests in East
Africa opened up into a mosaic of savannas, or prairies. Chimps living on the
forest's edge, venturing into the grasses sometimes, would come upon the
abandoned carcasses left by other animals, and feast on the remains. Carniv-
orous animals always eat the organs, brain, and bone marrow first because
they contain dense "depot" (storage) fat and hence provide the highest caloric
value. However, early prairie carnivores may not always have had teeth strong
enough to crack a skull or a large thighbone. These they would leave behind
to be found by chimps, who quickly learned to drop rocks to crush the bones
to get at the tasty, nutrient-laden contents.

The particular fatty acids, notably docosahexanoic acid, and the cholesterol found in these foods—and not found in vegetable foods—allowed
rapid development of brain tissue. For brain activity to occur, fats with
twenty and twenty-two carbon chains are required. These occur naturally in
animal fats, but vegetable fats contain only eighteen carbons and must be
processed by the body before they can be used. Herbivores have developed
liver enzymes capable of doing this, while carnivores do not have the ability
at all. The human body has a low ability to carry out this desaturation and
elongation process and, although technically capable, does not preferentially
do it. Hence, a diet entirely free of animal fats is potentially quite harmful to
normal brain development and function. Cranial capacity nearly tripled in
size from 375 to 550 cc at the time of *Australopithecus* approximately 3.5 million years ago to 775 to 1225 cc by the time of *Homo habilis* 2.5 million years
ago. This rapid increase in brain size required a high dietary intake of the correct fats and fatty acids to build the tissue. Some paleoanthropologists suggest
that the introduction of more and more animal foods allowed for intellectual
development and that fats became a rate-limiting factor in brain growth.

The early hominids were very small and unable to hunt large animals. They
had no spears or speech, and most meat was scavenged. A chimp uses most of
its basal metabolic rate to fuel the search for and consumption/digestion of
food, and just 8 percent of its basal metabolic rate to fuel brain activity. This is

in contrast to modern man, who uses as much as 20 to 25 percent of his basal metabolic rate to fuel brain activity. To fuel this growth and development of the brain, it was necessary to eat more nutrient-dense food and to reduce the metabolic requirements of other body parts. This was achieved by learning to hunt meat and catch fish, and by eating eggs, all of which are fiber free and have no cellulose. By reducing cellulose (plant fiber) intake, our earliest ancestors were able to reduce cellulase enzyme normally present in herbivores to break down plant cell walls and access the nutrients within. Cellulase requires a long gut that provides plenty of time for it to act. Reducing plant fiber intake in the diet, and consequently enabling the gut to shorten considerably, saved energy expenditure in the digestion and assimilation of foods. This explanation of the physiology of human development is called the *expensive tissue hypothesis* and suggests that it was calorically more efficient to develop in the way we did, using progressively less and less physical exertion to digest our food. This correlates neatly with the "optimum foraging theory," which suggests that an animal will always choose the food that provides the most nutrient density to offset the energy expenditure in obtaining that food. In the context of modern, mechanical, mass-production agriculture, it is calorically more efficient for us to collect food by strolling around the shopping mall than to grow it ourselves.

Homo habilis first appeared about 2.4 million years ago and was the first primate descendant to use stone tools. The modern dimensions of *Homo erectus* were attained 1.7 million years ago. Anthropologists believe that this was the first hominid to control and use fire and the first to leave Africa and travel north and east toward what is now Asia. As they traveled north, these primitive peoples needed to eat more meat because the cold weather caused seasonal shortages of plant foods, and they also required greater caloric intake in the form of fats for insulation. Because of these pressures the early humans began to hunt, but the first use of spears didn't appear until a million years later.

Four hundred thousand years ago, in Germany, spears were used for the first time that we know of. This implies significant brain complexity, providing the ability to think, plan, and execute a hunt. Modern man *(Homo sapiens)* first appeared around 120,000 years ago. These people worked in teams, with considerable planning, to hunt even large animals such as woolly mammoths. They were the first humans known to gather and consume shellfish (mainly mollusks) and fish. Their protein (meat) intake was prodigious and their carbohydrates came exclusively from fruits and tubers. Vigorous physical activity resulted in low body fat and a high muscle-to-adipose-tissue ratio. These early people were tall, lean, and very strong. Evidence from archaeology and anthropology tells us that they had a high bone mass and density and very few fractures, as well as strong, healthy teeth. Population scarcity precluded most infectious or epidemic diseases and there were few parasites, but these people had short life spans due to the stresses of nomadism, climate, and warfare. Few women died in childbirth due to a notably high pelvic inlet depth index that facilitated delivery, but in general women died younger than men due to the stress of multiple pregnancies on top of the stress associated with the requirements for food gathering and moving camps. Infant mortality is estimated at 20 to 30 percent, which is high compared to modern times, but compares very favorably with wild animals at 60 to 80 percent.

The first cultivation of grain occurred in the Middle East around ten thousand years ago. This required sudden and rapid improvements in tools to allow for turning ground and harvesting, threshing, grinding, and cooking the grain. Dairy products, probably initially from goats, first appeared about five to seven thousand years ago. Within the space of just a few thousand years, the diet underwent drastic changes through reductions in the amount of meat, fruits, and vegetables consumed and in the introduction of novel foods in the form of cereals, legumes, and dairy products. As the dietary intake of grain and dairy increased, we began slowly to produce more of the enzymes that digest starch and milk constituents (protein and sugar).

However, this process could not begin to keep pace with the rapidly increasing predominance of grain and dairy in the diet. Starting with the first agriculture (the Neolithic period) and continuing today, fossil records show increasing incidence of osteoporosis and bone fractures, as well as declining dental health until modern dentistry developed. This has been attributed to two key issues: the presence of compounds in cereals called *phytates* that bind minerals and prevent absorption, and the high ratio of calcium to magnesium in milk that tends to displace magnesium in the body and contribute to bone weakness. Additionally, a marked reduction in meat consumption, as much as 80 percent less than these people's immediate forebears, may have contributed to protein deficiency and failure of anabolism. Within three thousand years of the first grain cultivation, average adult male height fell from 5 feet 9 inches in late Paleolithic times (up to 9000 B.C.) to as low as 5 feet 3 inches in late Neolithic times (5000 to 3000 B.C.) and has now slowly climbed back up to a modern average of 5 feet 8 inches. It is also interesting to note that cranial capacity, a measure of brain size, has decreased by 11 percent in the past 35,000 years, the bulk of it (8 percent) in the past 10,000 years.

In today's hunter-gatherer societies, the average amount of plant foods, calculating all fruits, vegetables, and grains together, rarely exceeds 35 percent. Up to 75 percent of the diet is hunted and scavenged meat and seafood. The further north the society exists, the higher the reliance on animal foods, the most extreme example being the Inuit of northern Canada who traditionally subsisted almost exclusively on whale and seal, including massive amounts of blubber, and who had no symptoms of heart disease until they began to adopt the white man's lifestyle and diet. Our ancestors ate much if not most of their food raw, including seafood, fish, and meat, within minutes or hours of killing or gathering. The freshness of the food preserved nutrients, especially many vitamins. Without cooking, vital enzymes in the food were retained, promoting the digestive process. In wild, unprocessed, and raw foods there are also significant quantities of nonnutrient phytochemicals, including aromatic compounds, polyphenols, anthocyanidins, isothiocyanates, organosulfur compounds, and flavonoids. The synergistic effect of all these assorted molecules, presented to the body in a whole plant form, as nature made it, provided our primitive ancestors with numerous direct and indirect health benefits.

Extrapolating from studies of primitive peoples today, we can assume an average plant-to-animal ratio in the primitive diet of 35:65. From this we can easily calculate that the ancient diet was significantly higher in many nutrients and nutrient cofactors than our modern, refined, processed, cooked diet provides. Of course this supports sales of nutritional supplements to the concerned consumer, but is this really the answer? Wouldn't we be better off changing our diets and providing our bodies with foods as nature made them?

The Building Blocks of Health

Protein

Our Paleolithic ancestors ate at least 35 percent of their daily energy requirement as protein, in the form of meat, fish, seafood, and nuts. Modern man, in contrast, eats around 12 percent of his daily energy requirement in the form of protein and much more from carbohydrates. Primates studied in the wild eat between 1.5 to 5.9 g of protein per kilogram of body weight per day; Stone Age people are estimated to have eaten 2.5 to 3.5 g/kg/day; and modern man eats around 0.6 to 1.6 g/kg/day.

Protein is a critical component of the immune system, tissue fluid dynamics, blood clotting, tissue repair, and tissue growth. Prolonged protein deficiency will result in immune impairment, muscle wasting, and decreased physical performance. The World Health Organization (WHO) provides a formula for calculating the minimum requirement of protein for sustained health. It suggests 32 g of protein per day for a 150-pound man. Another way to calculate individual protein needs is by caloric value. There are 4 calories in a gram of protein. The WHO formula suggests an average adult obtain a minimum of 128 calories per day in the form of protein, or about 5 percent of the total caloric intake (based on a 2,500 total calorie intake/day). The Food and Nutrition Board recommends that we obtain 0.213 g of protein per pound of body weight, or 31.95 g for a 150-pound man. For optimum health, nutritionists have typically doubled the WHO allowance and have recommended 50 to 75 g daily for an average adult. Compared to our ancestors, though, this is still very little. They are thought to have eaten 150 to 200 g of protein daily and, due to frequent total calorie restraints, this might have represented 30 to 50 percent of their daily intake of calories on a 1,000- to 1,500-calorie diet.

This is a huge discrepancy in volume, but the biggest difference, actually, may be in the quality. A cow is designed to walk on the range and eat grass and leafy herbs. A chicken is designed to run around on the ground and eat insects, worms, and plants. Today, meat is farmed in intensive agribusinesses where the animals are kept penned up, fed grains and other unnatural diets laced with hormones, and routinely given antibiotics. Not only may the resulting meat on your plate contain toxic residues, but the fatty acid profile is quite different from meat from an animal that is allowed to move about freely and eat its natural diet.

Today's meat is markedly high in saturated fats that are thought to be atherogenic and proinflammatory when not properly balanced by other fatty acids. Modern agribusiness meat production also promotes the formation of arachidonic acid (AA). The arachidonic acid found naturally in meats has an evolutionary advantage in that it tends to promote insulin sensitivity of cells, which would have helped the Paleolithic people to properly metabolize and store all the sugars they could obtain. But too much AA can disrupt the finely calibrated prostaglandin mechanism and can be proinflammatory. Wild or range-fed meats, as well as game and fish, in contrast, are rich in eicosapentanoic acid (EPA) and docosahexanoic acid (DHA), which inhibit the proinflammatory tendency of AA by altering enzyme pathways. Additionally, whereas wild meat may be only 15 percent fat by kcal of energy generated, modern commercial meat is selectively bred and induced by hormones to have up to 70 percent fat by kcal of energy. Thus modern meat eaters get less protein, fewer anti-inflammatory fats, and more proinflammatory fats than their ancestors evolved to handle.

As if this wasn't enough evidence of the physiological need to eat more high-quality protein, it has now been shown that eating animal protein may improve the ratios of blood lipids, causing decreased formation of very low density lipoprotein (VLDL) and low density lipoprotein (LDL) fractions; it also causes raised high density lipoproteins (HDL) fractions, and hence reduces the risk of atherosclerosis. LDL molecules are made in the liver and are used to transport cholesterol to peripheral tissues for storage. They are responsible for atherogenesis (plaque formation) when they become oxidized. This occurs most readily when the blood lipid profile changes sharply after eating, and is exacerbated by the addition of carbohydrates to a fatty meal.

Does vegetable protein confer the same health benefits as flesh foods? This is a controversial issue. As an avowed vegetarian for seventeen years, a proselytizing vegan for about eight years, and now a fish eater again, I feel I am qualified, at least by experience, to comment on this. The fact is that vegetable protein is not the same, but mostly only because it is not so nutrient dense. In other words, a vegetarian must eat more bulk to get a given amount of protein compared to a meat eater. For vegetarians with small appetites it is actually quite difficult to get enough protein to meet one's needs. Protein powders and bars are an option, but these are highly processed and not really a natural food at all.

Additionally, for vegetarians there is the problem of finding foods with the eight essential amino acids. There are twenty-two amino acids that make up the building blocks of protein. Endless permutations of these create all proteins, including enzymes, which are the biological catalysts of all reactions in the body. All amino acids have a nitrogenous base and many are interconvertible. Eight, however, cannot be synthesized by the body and must be found regularly in the diet. Most meats provide all of these, so there is no likelihood of shortage for the meat eater. In vegetables, legumes, and grains at least one, and sometimes several, are missing. Thus, it is necessary to combine vegetable foods to ensure a complete array of all the amino acids. This is easier than it sounds because the liver stores excess amino acids in an easily accessible reservoir. As long as one eats a variety of vegetable foods over a day or two, one will almost certainly get a sufficient variety of amino acids. Of particular importance to the health of the brain and nervous system and to the detoxification processes of the liver are the sulfur-containing amino acids methionine and its breakdown products cysteine and cystine, which are found in abundance in eggs and meat but are much less common in vegetables.

The problem for vegetarians, therefore, isn't so much one of availability as one of volume. Few people can eat sufficient bulk of vegetable protein to provide their daily nutritional needs. Providing all the protein needs of the Paleolithic diet with vegetables alone isn't just impractical; it also contravenes the whole concept of eating as our ancestors did. It is also worth pointing out that most legumes contain the so-called protease inhibitors, particularly trypsin inhibitors, that reduce the ability of the body to digest proteins. They need to be soaked and slow cooked or fermented to prevent these from disrupting protein digestion. Even then, they are still present in bean dishes and products and can contribute to protein indigestibility. Leiner states that:

> because of the necessity of achieving a balance between the amount
> of heat necessary to destroy the trypsin inhibitors and that which may
> result in damage to the nutritional or functional properties of the protein,
> most commercially available edible-grade soybean products retain
> 5 to 20 percent of the trypsin inhibitor activity originally present in the
> raw soybeans from which they were prepared.

Phytic acid, present in grains and beans, may bind up minerals in the gut and it, too, can be inhibited by soaking. Soaking and cooking of grains and beans markedly increases their digestibility, and sprouting them increases nutritional value. Traditional methods of preparing soybeans in Eastern countries involve fermentation or very slow cooking and skimming of rising scum. In this way the antinutrients can be minimized. Modern mass food production doesn't allow for these techniques and the antinutrients are inadequately removed. Tofu, soy milk, and soy cheeses and soy meats are not natural foods; they are not even health foods, for they are highly processed and exhibit poor digestibility. Alpha-amylase inhibitors may reduce carbohydrate digestion, contributing to fermentation, and gas and molecular mimicry may cause or contribute to auto-immune disease.

In summary, then, our ancient ancestors ate a high proportion of animal foods, obtaining a significant portion of their daily requirement of calories from protein. The meat they ate was wild and contained a high percentage of unsaturated fatty acids that are antiatherogenic. They ate no grains or dairy products. They ate large amounts of fresh fruits and vegetables. Their blood lipid profiles were remarkably healthy and they had strong bones and teeth.

What About Dairy Foods?

Dairy foods do contain a significant amount of protein that is readily bioavailable. Unfortunately, some of those proteins are likely contributors to autoimmune disease through molecular mimicry. This means that a protein in food is structurally similar to a protein in the body and, if the food protein sets off an allergic response, then the body can have a chronic immune reaction against its own tissues. For example, wheat allergy is implicated in rheumatoid arthritis and milk allergy is implicated in Type 1 diabetes. Additionally, only a small percentage of the world has developed the gene that codes for adult production of the lactase enzyme that digests milk sugar. About 5 percent of preagricultural peoples are believed to have continued to produce lactase enzyme as adults. This has risen to around 70 percent in fair-skinned, blue-eyed people whose ancestors domesticated cows early in the agricultural revolution (i.e., northern Europeans). The inability to produce this enzyme in Asian and African peoples today is still almost 100 percent. Without this enzyme, consumption of dairy products leads to fermentation of milk sugar and causes gas, bloating, belching, and diarrhea.

Furthermore, modern dairy foods from commercial herds of cattle are laced with antibiotic and hormone residues, just as the meat is, and this can adversely affect our health when we consume them. Pasteurization of milk to reduce disease transmission compounds the problems. Heating milk to pasteurize it destroys the lactic acid–forming bacteria that protect against pathological bacteria in the gut. Pasteurization also alters the amino acids lysine and tyrosine, which causes the protein in the milk to be poorly absorbed, and promotes rancidity of milk fats and loss of water-soluble vitamins. Loss of vitamin C from pasteurization can be as high as 50 percent. Pasteurization causes calcium, chlorine, magnesium, phosphorus, potassium, sodium, sulfur, and many trace minerals to be less readily absorbed, and increases the absorption rate of lactose (milk sugar), which disrupts pancreatic function and predisposes to diabetes. Homogenization, a process that forces fats in milk through tiny pores under pressure, results in fat particles so small that they stay in suspension and the cream doesn't settle out on the top of milk. This makes the fat more susceptible to rancidity and oxygenation, and may contribute to heart disease.

Many dieticians today contend that dairy consumption is required for healthy bone formation and prevention of osteoporosis in old age. Nothing could be further from the truth. A calcium:protein ratio (mg:g) greater or equal to 20 is considered necessary today for healthy bone maintenance. Based on a plant-to-animal ratio of 35:65 in the Paleolithic diet, the calcium:protein ratio would be only about 2:5. Even if we allowed a plant-to-animal ratio of 65:35, the calcium:protein ratio would still only be about 6:5. And yet fossil records clearly show strong, healthy bones. This apparent paradox can be explained in several ways:

- Paleolithic people did not consume added dietary salt (sodium chloride) beyond the trace amounts that occur naturally in many foods. Because the kidney is obliged to excrete calcium with sodium, high levels of dietary sodium are now recognized as being one of the major causes of osteoporosis.
- The calcium:magnesium ratio was about 1:1 in preagricultural diets, as compared to about 4:1 in the modern Western diet. This is largely due to the high consumption of dairy products that have a calcium:magnesium ratio of about 12:1. Because magnesium is known to be essential for bone strength, and because elevated calcium can cause magnesium deficiencies even when magnesium intake is adequate, it is possible that the exceptionally high level of calcium in milk could actually weaken bones and predispose to fractures.
- Bone mass is dependent upon the relative acidity/alkalinity of the blood and urine. Acid generated by the diet is excreted in the urine and

requires calcium to be attached to it to make it neutral. This has the effect of drawing calcium out of the body. Meat, fish, dairy, and cereals have a high potential renal acid load (PRAL), while fruits and vegetables have a low PRAL, meaning they are already alkaline and do not use up calcium in their excretion. In fact, fruits and vegetables act as alkaline buffers themselves and actually have a calcium-sparing effect even when animal protein consumption is high. In this way our primitive ancestors, who ate a lot of meat, maintained strong bones in part through their very high consumption of fruits and vegetables, and by not eating cereals or dairy.

- Vitamin D, which is manufactured by the influence of sunlight on cholesterol in the skin, is critical to the absorption of calcium from the diet. Our ancestors probably had much greater exposure to sunlight on their skin than we do today, and hence a higher level of vitamin D that promoted optimum calcium absorption.

- Hunter-gatherers were much more physically active than modern man, and this would have contributed significantly to bone strength.

Dairy foods are neither natural nor necessary to good health in human adults. They are responsible for many cases of chronic digestive disturbances, especially gas, indigestion, bloating, and diarrhea. In many cases, they are a contributing factor to allergies, including sneezing, sinus congestion, eczema, hives, and asthma. They may contribute to bone weakness and fractures and may be a causative factor in the development of Type 1 (insulin-dependent) diabetes through molecular mimicry and autoimmune damage to the pancreas.

If dairy foods are included in the diet, they should be from raw, unpasteurized milk, taken from animals raised organically. Cultured and fermented dairy foods provide beneficial probiotics and are traditionally eaten by many long-lived cultures around the world. Such items as yogurt, kefir, quark, clabber, sour cream, and blue cheese all feed the beneficial bowel flora and are notably easier to digest than nonfermented dairy foods such as regular cheese and milk. The natural fats found in milk products are not unhealthy provided they are not heated or otherwise damaged, and providing the source animal was naturally raised. Avoid pasteurized and homogenized milk.

See Table 5.1 for an overview of dairy and other sources of protein.

Carbohydrate

In the five to seven million years of human evolution, it has been beneficial to have a very effective mechanism for assimilating and storing the energy presented to us in the form of sugars, against times of future hunger. This has been likened to having a "thrifty gene," possibly one that codes for glycogen synthase and that enhances survival in marginal food situations. The body has evolved a complex and carefully calibrated method for storing food, but modern diets are straying far from the evolutionary norm, and the consequent inbalance has serious health implications.

Proponents of the Paleolithic diet contend that today we are eating far more grain than our bodies have evolved to handle and, to add insult to injury, we refine it and strip it of nutrients and fiber. We don't digest it well and it frequently ferments, causing belching, bloating, flatulence, diarrhea, loss of healthy bowel flora, and eventually overgrowth of yeast that feed on the poorly fermented foods in the large intestine. This is aggravated by the fact that grains and beans contain glycoproteins (protein/carbohydrate molecules) called lectins that can bind to intestinal epithelial cells and alter their permeability. This contributes to movement of inadequately digested food particles from the gut to the bloodstream, and also causes overgrowth of harmful gut bacteria. Eventually this can lead to overgrowth of various pathogenic bacteria, as well as *Candida albicans* yeast, leaky gut syndrome, multiple food allergies, vulnerability to parasites, and compromise of the entire immune and digestive functions.

Lectins from cereals and grains can cause the expression of the so-called "intercellular adhesion molecules" (ICAM) in lymphocytes. These bind bacteria to immune cells and move them from the gut to distant tissues where they can be deposited and may cause Type III (immune complex) allergic

Table 5.1 Sources of Dietary Protein:
Grams per 100 g (3.5 ounces) of Uncooked Food

Animal, Fish, & Dairy	Grams	Grains	Grams
Egg	3	Quinoa	18
Fowl	16–24	Amaranth	16
Red meat	17–21	Spelt	15
Organ meats	20	Wheat	14
Oysters	9	Oats	13
Clams	14	Buckwheat	12
Cod & bass	18	Millet	10
Anchovy & mackerel	19	Rye & corn	9
Sardines	24	Barley	8
Tuna	29	Rice	7
Whole milk & yogurt	3		
Cottage cheese	14		
Hard cheese	25–30		

Nuts, Seeds, & Beans	Grams		
Filberts	13		
Almonds	19		
Sesame seeds	19		
Sunflower seeds	24		
Tofu	8		
Sprouted bread	10		
Tempeh	20		
Aduki beans	22		
Lentils	25		
Soybeans	35		

Seaweeds are protein rich but hard to consume in sufficient quantities.
Vegetables and fruits range from 1 to 5g/100g.

responses, including such diverse conditions as glomerulonephritis, rheumatoid arthritis, and systemic lupus erythematosus (SLE). About 80 percent of food allergies involve some degree of Type III response. The same lectins also cause increased inflammatory cytokines such as tumor necrosis factor alpha (TNFa), interleukin-1, and interleukin-6.

The modern dietary recommendation (from the American Dietetic Association food pyramid) is to take 55 to 60 percent of the diet as cereals, grains, and starches. This is in direct contrast to the traditional diet of *Homo sapiens*.

Bad news, indeed. The Paleolithic diet offers a solution to this problem. We do need carbohydrate as a source of fuel for the cells, but our ancestors obtained theirs for millennia from fruits and tubers, unprocessed, with naturally occurring fiber, vitamins, minerals, and other metabolic cofactors. This is processed quite differently than cereal and grain. Carbohydrate is converted in the body into glucose and used as the primary fuel source. A full 65 percent of the circulating glucose in the blood will be used by the brain. The body is genetically programmed to take any spare carbohydrate that is not used immediately and convert it to glycogen and triglycerides (fat) for storage against future times of need. Glycogen is stored in either the muscles or the liver. Muscles may store about 400 g of glycogen and it is for the exclusive use of the muscles. Only glycogen made in the liver may be released later for use elsewhere in the body. The liver has a limited storage capacity, about 90 g, at most enough for a day, so there is a backup storage supply in the form of triglycerides in the adipose, or fat, tissue. The liver converts excess carbohydrates to fat, hooks them up to proteins, which it also makes, forming the so-called lipoproteins, and in this fashion delivers them to the circulation for distribution to the thighs or tummy, where the fat can be stored against times of need. The lower the density of the lipoprotein, the more fat it has and the more potential there is for depositing of fats into blood vessels (atheroma).

Digestion of starch commences in the mouth with the secretion of amylase enzyme and continues in the small intestine under the influence of amylase from the pancreas. Alpha-amylase inhibitors are found in many grains and these can reduce the efficacy of the digestive enzyme. In the gut, carbohydrate is absorbed as simple sugars—either glucose, fructose, or galactose. Glucose is made primarily from grains, pasta, bread, cereals, starches, and some vegetables; fructose (sucrose plus glucose) is found in fruits; and galactose (glucose plus lactose) comes from milk products. All these sugars pass from the gut through the hepatic portal circulation to the liver, where the glucose may be released directly into the systemic circulation for delivery to the cells. Fructose and galactose must first be reconfigured by the liver into glucose, which significantly slows the rise of blood sugar levels after a meal of fruit, while grains and cereals generally create a rapid rise. Dairy falls somewhere in between. The rapidity of the blood sugar increase that occurs after eating is called the glycemic index. (See Table 5.2.)

The pancreas, in synergy with the liver and adrenal glands, regulates how much sugar enters the bloodstream and how much glycogen gets used and made.

Summary of the Role of Carbohydrate

While carbohydrate is essential to life, it must be the right kind, in the right amount, and packaged along with other essential cofactors that promote proper cell metabolism of glucose. This can only occur in whole, unprocessed foods, with the emphasis on organic vegetables and fruits.

The process of converting glucose into cellular energy takes place in three stages: glycolysis, the Krebs cycle, and the electron transfer chain. At each step of the way, enzyme-mediated reactions are taking place, making one molecule out of another in an endless stream of interconversions, and each enzyme requires specific nutrient cofactors. Refined carbohydrates (sugars), where the vitamins and minerals have been discarded along with the fiber, fail to deliver these cofactors. These sugars are called "negative nutrients" because they require vitamins and minerals that they do not contain and so rob them from other physiological processes.

Luckily for us, grain is not the only source of carbohydrate. Our primitive ancestors ate a lot of carbohydrate, almost exclusively in the form of fruits and vegetables, especially tubers and roots. These unrefined carbohydrates

Table 5.2 The Glycemic Index. Foods with the lowest score are preferred.

Food	Grams	Food	Grams
Breads		*Legumes*	
White	100	Baked beans (canned)	60
Whole wheat	99	Butter beans	46
Whole rye	58	Kidney beans	48
		Soybeans	21
Cereals		Chickpeas	49
Buckwheat	74	Garden peas	65
Brown rice	96	Red lentils	43
White rice	104		
White pasta	72	*Vegetables*	
Brown pasta	61	Boiled potato	81
Corn	87	Baked potato	135
All-Bran	73	Sweet potato	74
Cornflakes	119		
Puffed rice (rice cakes)	132	*Dairy*	
Oatmeal	71–96	Ice cream	54
Shredded wheat	97	Skim milk	46
		Yogurt	52
Fruit			
Apple	53	*Sugars*	
Banana	79	Fructose	30
Cherries	32	Glucose	138
Grapefruit	36	Honey	126
Grapes	62	Maltose	152
Orange	66	Sucrose	86
Peach	40		
Pear	47		
Plum	34		
Raisins	93		

retain assorted nutrient cofactors and a high fiber content. In contrast, modern urban dwellers eat just 23 percent of their carbohydrate from natural, fresh fruits and vegetables. Anthropologists suggest that our ancestors ate about three times as many fruits and vegetables as we do today. Additionally, the high fiber content of whole fruits and vegetables delays the uptake of sugars from the gut, and this, combined with the fact that their sugar is fructose, which is delivered slowly to the blood, gives fruits and vegetables consistently beneficial scores on the glycemic index.

The significance of the glycemic index is that it shows how unstable or how far removed from homeostasis a food can make you. Foods with a high glycemic index cause the blood sugar to skyrocket. Despite their high percentage of vitamins and minerals, fresh juices cause significant elevation of the blood sugar because of the removal of fiber. Insulin release is proportionate to the blood sugar level so eating something really sweet like a candy bar will cause plenty of insulin to pour out of the pancreas. It acts quickly to reduce the blood sugar, too quickly in fact, and often after some time the symptoms of low blood sugar occur, including hunger, craving for sweets, feeling cold, headaches as the brain is deprived of fuel, tremors, and irritability. If you then eat something sweet again, the blood sugar rises steeply and the whole cycle starts over. The blood sugar is now on a roller coaster and the whole physiology becomes deranged (see Figure 5.1). This is a predisposing condition for Type 2 (adult-onset) diabetes and Syndrome X (pre-diabetic blood sugar elevation, abnormal weight gain, deranged blood lipids, and increased heart disease).

Fats

There are several strands or threads to the story on fats—both qualitative and quantitative—and there is a world of difference between the types of fats eaten 100,000 years ago and fats eaten today. Before we can discuss the meaning of the changing fat content of the modern diet, we need to define some terminology. Fats and fixed oils (those which are not volatile), along with

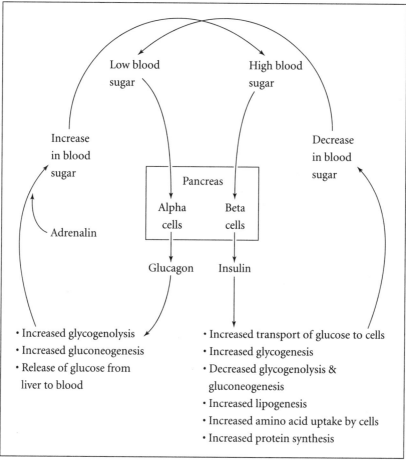

Figure 5.1 The Control of Insulin and Glucagon

fatty acids, waxes, and phospholipids constitute the general group called *lipids*. The fats and oils are composed of fatty acids attached to an alcohol. The commonest form is the triglyceride where three fatty acids link with a glycerol molecule. The fatty acids form the basis of the fats and oils. There are many different fatty acids, but they all have the same basic form: a chain of carbon atoms with attached hydrogen atoms plus a methyl (CH_3) or *omega* group on one end and a carboxyl (COOH) or *delta* group on the other end.

The number of carbon atoms in the chain is generally between four and twenty-four. The short- and medium-chain fatty acids (four to twelve carbon chains) are absorbed into the bloodstream from the gut and transported directly to the liver. They contribute antibacterial and antifungal activity to the gut and confer a quick energy source to the body. Long-chain fatty acids (fourteen to twenty-four carbon chains) must be emulsified in the gut by bile salts and are absorbed into the lymphatic system for delivery to the blood supply returning to the heart, and only reach the liver as part of normal systemic circulation. They tend to be used as storage fats. Thus butter and coconut oil, which are composed mainly of short- and medium-chain fats, do not contribute as much to weight gain as do olive oil and vegetable oils that are higher in long-chain fatty acids. The longest-chain fatty acids (twenty to twenty-four carbon chains) are used for structural purposes, forming the cell membranes, hormones, and prostaglandins.

If every carbon atom in the chain carries two hydrogen atoms, then the fatty acid is said to be *saturated*. This is the form generally found in animal fats and tends to be solid at room temperature. Avocado, coconut, and palm oil are saturated vegetable oils used in foods. If the carbon chain is missing any hydrogen atoms and has formed one or more double bonds, then it is said to be *unsaturated*. This is the form generally found in plant oils and tends to be liquid at room temperature. An unsaturated fatty acid may have only one hydrogen missing, in which case it is called *monounsaturated* (such as in olive oil), or it may have several hydrogens missing, in which case it is called *polyunsaturated*. The carbon atoms in a fatty acid are numbered from the methyl (or omega) end to the carboxyl (or delta) end. Unsaturated fatty acids may be referred to as omega-3 or omega-6 fatty acids, which refers to the place on the carbon-hydrogen chain where hydrogen is missing.

Our primitive ancestors ate perhaps 6 percent of their daily energy (calories) in the form of saturated fats and another 15 to 20 percent of their daily energy in the form of unsaturated fats, for a daily total of 20 to 25 percent of their daily energy from fats. They are estimated to have eaten 450 to 500 mg of cholesterol daily. The wild meat, fish, and game they ate were rich in the anti-inflammatory fatty acids and had a relatively low proportion of the acids that tend to raise serum cholesterol. This, together with high protein and flavonoid intake and very low carbohydrate intake, protected them against cardiovascular diseases.

Dieticians today generally recommend that 30 to 35 percent of the daily energy be derived from fats and not more than 10 percent from saturated fats. Many people seem to have a very hard time keeping to this regimen, even though it is not so austere as the primitive diet. The fact is that we like fats in our food. Fat adds a richness, a creaminess, a smoothness to foods that we find very appealing, and fats "carry" other flavors. Even in this we can trace the influence of the Paleolithic in ourselves. For primitive people, fat was a very desirable food because it packed a lot of calories and allowed growth of brain tissue, and hence furthered the biological imperative.

Fats serve many essential roles in the body. Fat is an insulator of nerve fibers, permitting much more rapid transmission of nervous impulses; an insulating layer and energy storage site under the skin in the form of subcutaneous fat; a storage site for noxious substances and metabolic wastes; a thermoregulatory mechanism that ensures minimal core temperatures; a substrate for the formation of the sex hormones (estrogen, progesterone, and testosterone), aldosterone, and vitamin D; and, perhaps most important of all, the substrate for the formation of eicosanoids.

Eicosanoids and the Essential Fatty Acids (EFAs)
EFAs cannot be made by the body from other fats, and must be consumed regularly (see Figure 5.2). They include linoleic and linolenic fatty acids and are found only in plant foods. They fulfill a critical metabolic and structural role. They:

- Are a major component of all cell membranes.
- Regulate the ratio of high-density to low-density phospholipids (HDL/LDL) in the blood
- Form the prostaglandins, (eicosanoids) which are a type of hormone with a very short life span that regulate metabolic processes on a minute-by-minute level

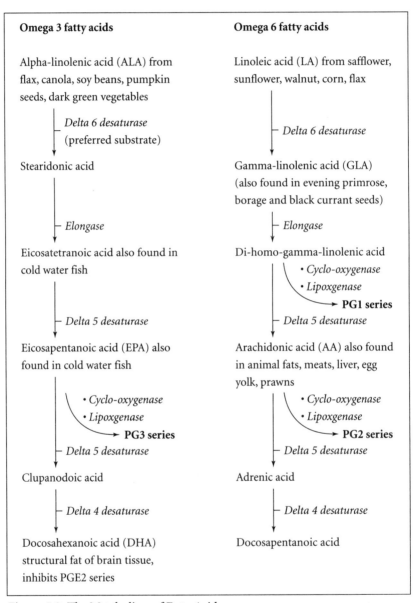

Figure 5.2 The Metabolism of Fatty Acids

Eicosanoids or prostaglandins are a form of microhormone, surviving only seconds or minutes after release from a cell, and acting locally in the tissue where they are manufactured. They are the micromanagers of the body, constantly adjusting the details of physiology and calibrating homeostasis. They generally exhibit opposing functions, acting like a check or a brake on each other in a delicate dance of negative feedback. Eicosanoids are the original, most primitive control mechanism in the body, and are estimated to have first appeared more than 500 million years ago. Even today, some of the eicosanoids we make are identical to those made by primitive creatures such as the sea sponge. The first eicosanoids, discovered in 1936, were isolated from the prostate gland and were given the name *prostaglandins.* These are now known to occur in many other tissues as well, but the name has stuck.

To manufacture the eicosanoids we require two essential fatty acids. These are alpha-linolenic acid (ALA), an omega-3 fatty acid found in flax, pumpkin seed, soybeans, and dark green vegetables; and linoleic acid (LA), an omega-6 fatty acid found in safflower, sunflower, corn, walnut, and flax oils. Each of these is reconfigured by the cells under the influence of several enzymes. The first of these enzymes, delta 6 desaturase, is considered a "gatekeeper" enzyme in that it controls and is pivotal to the whole cascade. Unfortunately, many of the lifestyle and dietary habits of modern man inhibit or diminish the function of this enzyme.

The prostaglandin PG1 series activates cyclic AMP formation, which enhances cellular energy production and transmission of hormone messages, inhibits platelet formation, causes vasodilation, inhibits excessive inflammatory responses, and activates T lymphocyte function. The prostaglandin PG3 series become incorporated into cell membranes all over the body and make them more fluid, permitting enhanced membrane function including transmission of nerve impulses and hormone messages. The prostaglandin PG2 series has generally opposite effects, being proinflammatory and causing platelet aggregation, vasospasm, and reduced lymphatic flow. The PG2 series includes the leukotrines and the thromboxanes, which are made from arachidonic acid under the influence of the enzymes cyclo-oxygenase and lipoxygenase.

Factors That Adversely Influence Delta 6 Desaturase Function

- Deficiency of B_6, magnesium, and zinc in the diet
- Presence of excessive saturated fats in the diet
- Presence of transfatty acids
- Atopic tendency (asthma, hayfever, eczema in the family)
- Diabetes
- Consumption of alcohol
- Ionizing radiation
- Large intake of glucose
- Aging
- Chronic exposure to adrenaline and cortisol (chronic stress, caffeine, television, anxiety, etc.)
- Low protein intake
- Tobacco
- Environmental pollution and toxins
- Many recreational and prescription drugs

Because of the vulnerability and unreliability of delta 6 desaturase, many nutritionists recommend supplementing the diet with fatty acids from further down the cascade. These include evening primrose, borage, and black currant seed oils. Note that eating fish provides us with eicosapentanoic acid, (EPA) which converts directly into the PG3 series and also bypasses the need for delta 6 desaturase. Delta 5 desaturase is dependent upon vitamin C, niacin, and zinc in the diet for optimal function. Biotin (a B vitamin) is also required for the elongation and desaturation of fatty acids and this, as well as zinc and other minerals, is known to be sequestered by phytates in whole grains.

Thus eating a diet high in whole grains can cause disturbances of fatty acid metabolism and prostaglandin formation. Anyone living under chronic stress and sympathetic dominance, such as the person with FMS, may not have adequate delta 6 desaturase activity and may not be manufacturing adequate amounts of anti-inflammatory prostaglandins. An excessive amount of linoleic acid in the diet, which is especially likely with a high consumption of vegetable oils, can inhibit the body's ability to adequately synthesize docosahexanoic acid (DHA), which is crucial for proper brain development and function.

Transfatty Acids

Transfatty acids are a particular problem in the modern diet. These are formed when fat is subjected to heat and other artificial influences. Incorporated into cell membranes, they disrupt cell membrane function and disturb cellular metabolism. Learning from our ancestors once again, we observe that they ate their fats unprocessed, in a whole, natural form. Today's consumer demands clear, odorless oils that must be subjected to heat, filtration, bleaching, and deodorizing before sale. Even when we start with a perfectly harmless oil such as sunflower, this processing is damaging in the extreme. It produces an end result that blocks delta 6 desaturase, promotes oxidative stress in the body, raises serum cholesterol levels, reduces HDL levels in the blood, and is carcinogenic. Commercial salad dressings may contain 15 percent transfatty acids, tub margarine up to 25 percent, and stick margarine up to 35 percent transfatty acids. Beware the words *hydrogenated* or *partially hydrogenated* on food labels. These terms signal the presence of transfats. Any oil that is not specifically labeled "cold pressed" or that has been subject to heat in any way will contain transfatty acids.

Saturated Fats and Cholesterol

It is a deeply ingrained myth that eating animal fats will raise cholesterol and that this is a bad thing. First consider the hunter-gatherer with a cholesterol intake of as much as 450 mg daily and yet having very low plasma cholesterol levels as demonstrated by modern studies of current hunter-gatherer societies, with virtually no incidence of heart disease. Despite a high cholesterol intake these people have average blood cholesterol levels of 90 to 135 mg/dl compared to modern man with an average around 200 to 250 mg/dl. A marked difference is seen, also, in the relative intake of saturated and polyunsaturated fats. The hunter-gatherer typically eats a polyunsaturated-fat-to-saturated-fat ratio of around 1:2, while modern man eats a ratio of 0:4. This decrease in intake of polyunsaturated fats has a clear negative impact on cardiovascular health and many other physiological processes.

Polyunsaturated fats are the dietary source of the omega-3 and omega-6 essential fatty acids. The precise ratio of omega-3 to omega-6 fats is critical to good health. In traditional diets the ratio was anywhere from equal amounts to four times as much omega-6 as omega-3. The modern diet is distorted into providing anywhere from ten to twenty times the omega-6 intake as omega-3. Thus we see modern hunter-gatherers with an omega-6:omega-3 ratio of around 2.8:1, while Americans have 17:1.

Elevated omega-6 is known to promote insulin resistance of the cell membrane. The elevated omega-6 has come about partly because we generally eat less fish and seafood, and because the quality of fats in meat has changed dramatically. Because omega-3 and omega-6 fatty acids compete for the same desaturase and elongase enzymes, an excess of one may cause progressive deficiency of the other.

Specifically, delta 5 desaturase prefers to work on the substrate of omega-3 fatty acids and, providing there is sufficient omega-3 present, will tend to cause the formation of the beneficial PG3 series rather than the problematic PG2 series. Our elevated modern intake of omega-6 oils tends, on the other hand, to promote the formation of the health-damaging PG2 series.

Our ancestors obtained omega-6 fats from nuts and seeds. However, the modern Western diet derives almost all polyunsaturated fats from vegetable oils. In the sixty-year period from 1910 to 1970 the proportion of animal fat in the diet fell from 83 percent to 62 percent, with vegetable oil consumption rising about 400 percent. Butter consumption fell from 18 pounds per year to just 4 pounds. Yet heart disease, supposedly caused by saturated fats, increased from almost nothing to causing 40 percent of all deaths in America today.

The moral of this story is that we should eat only range-fed meats and wild-caught fish—no farmed animals. We should not shy away from animal fats but should ensure that we get plenty of the correct ones in the correct proportions. Eating fatty fish such as salmon, herring, mackerel, and sardines; range-fed beef and lamb; and free-range poultry and their eggs will be beneficial. Fresh (not old or rancid) nuts and seeds should be eaten liberally. All margarine and processed fats should be avoided. These habits are in keeping with our evolutionary history and may promote health and prevent disease in many ways.

Enzymes

Enzymes are protein compounds that occur in all living things and are essential for all biological reactions, speeding up metabolic processes and enabling life as we know it to occur. There are over five thousand known enzymes, broadly divided into three types: metabolic enzymes, digestive enzymes, and food enzymes. There are many digestive enzymes and they are made mostly in the pancreas. They include amylase, which breaks down starch; lipases, which break down fats; and proteases, which break down proteins. For optimal functioning both the digestive and the metabolic enzymes require adequate supplies of many nutrients. Enzymes are complex protein molecules that require various coenzymes and cofactors to do their work. Many of these secondary substances are found in the diet.

Food enzymes are present in raw foods but, being protein in nature, are destroyed by cooking. Enzymes present in raw foods initiate the process of digestion in the upper stomach. Foods are held in this area for some time before being released into the lower stomach and thence into the small intestine, where endogenous enzymes are delivered from the pancreas to further activate digestion of foods. Thus, eating a diet rich in fresh, raw foods and high in naturally occurring enzymes will reduce the amount of enzymes required from the body for proper digestion. Most people feel much healthier and more vibrant when they introduce a large amount of raw foods into the diet.

Research into traditional diets reveals that almost all peoples, the world over, traditionally incorporate fermented, soured, or yeasted foods into their diets regularly. Fermented vegetables such as sauerkraut, pickled cucumbers, and beets, or Korean kimchee provide beneficial *Lactobacillus* bacteria, as do yogurt, kefir, clabber, koumiss, and cultured buttermilk or butter. Fermented soy provides tempeh, miso, natto, and tamari. Raw fish and meat, which was extensively eaten by primitive people, was eventually replaced with hanging and marinating meats, both of which enable innate enzyme reactions to occur and predigestion to commence. Slow cooking of meats also helps to retain enzymes. Sprouting of wheat and other grains liberates large amounts of enzymes that are unavailable in the unsprouted grain. Nuts, seeds, and legumes are also rich in enzymes after sprouting, and this has the added benefit of deactivating the phytic acid present in these foods, which otherwise tends to bind with minerals and make them less easy to absorb. Fruits and vegetables are generally low in enzymes, with the notable exceptions of papayas, mangos, kiwis, pineapples, olive oil, raw honey, figs, avocados, bananas, and dates, all of which are beneficial in the diet.

The use of digestive enzymes as a nutritional supplement may be indicated. A very weak, depleted and deficient person may have low "digestive fire" or reduced ability to manufacture enzymes. Here the enzymes in the form of a supplement may be helpful to improve digestive function and enhance absorption of nutrients. Some digestive enzymes, notably papain, betaine, and bromelain are also remarkably effective as an anti-inflammatory for arthritic joints when taken between meals.

There is some slight concern that prolonged use of supplemental enzymes will cause the body to manufacture even less itself. For long-term treatment it may be preferable to use the bitter herbs, which promote the body's own production of digestive enzymes. For the person with FMS a balance must be struck between promoting digestive function and not cooling the person down too much with bitters. See Table 5.3.

Table 5.3 Nutrient Cofactors Required for Enzyme Systems

Nutrient	Enzyme system
Cobalt	Transferases
Copper	Ferro-oxidases, tyrosinase, cytochrome oxidase dismutase
Iron	Oxidoreductase, cytochrome oxidase
Manganese	Kinases, peptidases, pyruvate carboxylase, dydrolases
Molybdenum	Oxidases
Selenium	Glutothione peroxidase, transferases
Zinc	Peptidases, dehydrogenase, transferases, oxidoreductases, isomerases

Choosing and Using Nutritional Supplements

If the diet is optimally balanced and there are plenty of fresh foods, then the need for supplementation diminishes. But, sad to say, even many organic fruits and vegetables are picked green, and artificially ripened or are old and past their prime. Growing your own is certainly the best but impractical for most of us today. People with FMS are likely to have impaired digestive function and reduced absorption due to years of excess adrenal stimulation. It may be especially important for them to use nutritional supplements. For enhanced absorptive capacity, bitter herbs should be taken fifteen minutes prior to taking the supplements.

If possible, take each product in divided doses through the day to maintain a steadier state in the blood. Capsules and tablets may not dissolve easily in the gut, especially where there is weak digestive function. Liquid nutritional supplements are preferred, or you can open capsules or crush tablets before taking them. Do not do this if the product is labeled "enteric coated," because the contents will then be broken down by stomach acid. See Table 5.4 for recommended daily nutrient values.

Table 5.4 Recommended Daily Nutrient Intake

Vitamin or Cofactor	Adult Dose	Comments
Vitamin A (retinol)	5,000 IU	Not more than 2,500 IU during pregnancy.
Beta-carotene	5,000 to 25,000 IU	
Vitamin D	100 to 400 IU	Dark-skinned people and those who spend a lot of time indoors or live in northern latitudes require higher doses.
Vitamin E (d-alpha tocopherol)	400 to 1,200 IU	A high dose may raise the blood pressure.
Vitamin C (ascorbic acid)	500 to 5,000 mg	Take to bowel tolerance.
Bioflavonoids	500 to 2,000 mg	
Vitamin B_1 (thiamine)	50 to 100 mg	Take the B vitamins in the form of a B complex.
Vitamin B_2 (riboflavin)	50 to 100 mg	
Vitamin B_3 (niacin)	50 to 100 mg	Niacin causes flushing but is best for reducing cholesterol. Niacinamide does not cause flushing but is best for treating arthritis and diabetes.
Vitamin B_5 (pantothenic acid)	50 to 100 mg	
Vitamin B_6 (pyridoxine)	50 to 500 mg	
Vitamin B_{12} (cyanocobalamin)	100–400 mcg	
Folic acid	400 mcg	
Biotin	100 to 300 mcg	
Inositol	50 to 100 mg	
Choline	50 to 100 mg	

Table 5.4 Recommended Daily Nutrient Intake, *continued*

Mineral or Cofactor	Adult Dose	Comments
All minerals are best absorbed in the chelated form.		
Boron	1 to 6 mg	
Calcium	500 to 1,500 mg	Higher doses for women at risk of osteoporosis. Use the citrate form.
Chromium	150 to 400 mcg	
Copper	1 to 3 mg	
Iodine	50 to 200 mcg	
Iron	15 to 30 mg	Only use if there is demonstrable iron deficiency.
Magnesium	500 to 1,500 mg	Use the malate form for FMS; take at least as much as calcium or more.
Manganese	5 to 10 mg	
Molybdenum	10 to 30 mcg	
Potassium	100 to 400 mg	
Selenium	100 to 200 mcg	
Silicon	20 mg	
Sulfur (MSM)	2,000 to 5,000 mg	
Vanadium	10 to 100 mcg	
Zinc	14 to 45 mg	

Additional Supplements	Adult Dose	Comments
Carnitine	1,500 mg	
Phosphatidyl serine		Dose not yet established.
Phosphatidyl choline	1,000 mg	
N-acetyl glucosamine	1,500 mg daily	
N-acetyl cysteine	1,500 mg daily	
Cetyl myristoleate	500 to 2,000 mg	
Essential fatty acids	2 to 4 g daily	

Continued overleaf

Table 5.4 Recommended Daily Nutrient Intake, *continued*

Additional Supplements	Adult Dose	Comments
Amino Acids		
Methionine	up to 1 g	
L-aspargine	up to 500 mg	
GABA	up to 750 mg	
L-glutumate	up to 500 mg	
L-glutamine	up to 2 g	
Glycine	up to 500 mg	
Phenylalanine	up to 500 mg	
Taurine	50 mg daily	For long-term use
	up to 1 g	For acute conditions
Tryptophan	1 g	For sleep
	up to 5 g	For depression
Tyrosine	up to 100 mg per kilo of body weight daily	
Coenzyme Q10	100–300 mg	
Malic acid	1,500 mg	
S-adenosyl methionine	1,500 mg	
NAD	1 to 10 mg	
DHEA	5 to 10 mg	

Vitamins

B Vitamins

Thiamine (B_1) is a key component of the enzyme thiamin pyrophosphate, which is required for cellular energy production and nerve cell metabolism. Thiamine (B_1) deficiency is known to contribute to impaired mental function and, in extreme cases, psychosis. Up to 30 percent of admissions to mental wards are found to be deficient in this vitamin. Up to 100 mg daily is recommended as a general dosage and up to 5 g daily in people with severely disrupted mental functioning. It is found in soybeans, sunflower seeds, brewer's yeast, and nuts. Do not consume with alcohol, tannins, or sulfites.

Riboflavin (B_2) improves the cellular production of energy by acting as a key component of two enzyme systems. It also aids in the regeneration of glutathione, the major intracellular antioxidant. Doses of up to 100 mg are generally used, preferably in divided doses of 20 mg each for maximum absorption. Almonds, mushrooms, whole grains, soybeans, and leafy green vegetables are good sources.

Niacin (B_3) is essential in the production of energy. Severe deficiency will cause pellagra, characterized by dermatitis, diarrhea, and dementia. When ingested in doses over 50 mg, niacin causes transient flushing. The use of inositol hexaniacinate will prevent this. In therapeutic applications, niacin is mostly used to treat elevated cholesterol, or in the nonflushing form, to treat arthritis and early-onset Type 1 diabetes. It also regulates the production of adrenal hormones. It is helpful to combine this B vitamin with others because they all work synergistically to regulate energy production in nervous tissue and elsewhere. A standard dose as an adjunct to other B vitamins would be 100 mg daily of niacinamide. Organ meats, eggs, fish, and peanuts are the richest food sources. Legumes, whole grains, milk, and avocados also contain beneficial amounts.

Pantothenic acid (B_5) is critical to the metabolism of fats and carbohydrate and to the manufacture of adrenal hormones. It is sometimes called the "antistress vitamin." Doses up to 250 mg daily have been used to treat adrenal exhaustion or insufficiency, chronic stress and anxiety, and allergies. Organ meats, fish, milk, and poultry are the best food sources, followed by whole grains, yeast, legumes, and some fruits and vegetables.

Pyridoxine (B_6) is involved in the manufacture of serotonin, dopamine, melatonin, epinephrine, norepinephrine, and other neurotransmitters, as well as being critical to the production of energy in nervous tissue. Pyridoxine requires riboflavin and magnesium as cofactors for its conversion into pyridoxal-5-phosphate, the active form. This conversion occurs in the liver, so people with advanced liver disease may not be able to carry out this function and should consider injectable forms of the vitamin. A normal adult dose is 100 mg daily. Whole grains, legumes, seeds, nuts, bananas, and yeast are good dietary sources.

Folic acid is used in DNA division and is critical to cellular reproduction. Maternal deficiency during pregnancy will lead to neural tube defects, and deficiency in adults may lead to depression, irritability, early onset of senility, and memory loss. Folic acid acts as a methyl donor and increases production of serotonin, which has a marked antidepressant effect and is known to be deficient in people with FMS. In the absence of folic acid, homocysteine cannot be converted to methionine and this will predispose to development of atherosclerosis and osteoporosis. Measuring plasma homocysteine levels is the most effective way to assess folic acid levels. Folinic acid is the most bioavailable form and supplements up to 400 mcg daily are recommended, in conjunction with B_{12} because folic acid deficiency may mask B_{12} deficiency. High doses should be avoided in epilepsy. The best dietary source is leafy dark green vegetables.

Cobalamin (B_{12}) works in conjunction with folic acid in the replication of DNA and cellular reproduction and is required for the manufacture of myelin, which insulates nerve fibers. Numbness, depression, multiple sclerosis–like lesions, and memory loss are common effects of B_{12} deficiency. A daily dose of 100 mcg is recommended as a baseline supplement and up to 1 mg daily for clinical application. Animal foods are the only reliable source, including milk, eggs, cheese, and meats. A trace amount occurs in seaweeds and miso (fermented soybean paste).

Inositol is a minor B vitamin that functions with choline as a lipotropic to export fat from the liver. It is also required for the proper function of several neurotransmitters in the brain, including serotonin and acetylcholine. It has demonstrated significant benefits in treating depression and panic disorders. It is found in citrus fruits, whole grains, nuts, and seeds. Doses up to 10 g daily have been used for clinical application.

Vitamins E and C

Vitamin E has an anti-inflammatory action due to its effect on prostaglandin and leukotrine formation and it acts synergistically with other antioxidants as a free radical fighter. It inhibits the enzymatic breakdown of cartilage and stimulates cartilage synthesis. The dose should be 400 to 600 IU/day in the form of d-alpha-tocopherol.

Vitamin C, or ascorbic acid, is needed in the diet by only a few species on this planet: humans, monkeys, and guinea pigs. For us it is absolutely essential to life. It acts as a powerful antioxidant to soak up free radicals, promotes immune function, serves as a catalyst to many metabolic processes, strengthens connective tissue, maintains the integrity of skin, bones, and teeth, increases the absorption of iron and calcium, enhances resistance to carcinogens, assists the production of neurotransmitters in the brain, reduces cholesterol levels in the blood, and inhibits the formation of atheromatous plaques in the blood vessels.

Vitamin C is a very sensitive substance that is readily broken down by heat, light, and oxygen. In a growing plant the vitamin C is stable, but if the plant is bruised or picked, then an enzyme promotes the breakdown of the vitamin C by oxygen. For this reason, and because of our polluted environment and stressful lives, it is often hard to obtain the necessary amount of vitamin C from diet alone. People who are seriously deficient in vitamin C may develop scurvy, but this is very rare in our culture. However, subclinical deficiencies certainly exist and may cause tiredness and lethargy; swollen gums and loose teeth that rot easily; swollen wrists and ankles; shortness of breath; tendency to colds, flu, and other infections; poor wound healing; and easy bruising.

The required dose is different for everyone; it changes (up or down) as events occur in life. Because vitamin C is water soluble, the body cannot absorb more than it needs. Any excess will simply leave the body through the intestines and the kidney where it will act as a diuretic and a laxative. This provides an easy way for you to judge your own requirement.

Take 1 g of vitamin C daily for a week. Powder, capsules, or tablets are fine as long as it is always natural-source vitamin C with bioflavonoids. After a week start adding 500 mg per day, preferably in divided doses (two or three times daily). At a certain point you will notice a looseness in the stools. Don't go as far as diarrhea, just until you feel a shift in the bowel habits beginning to happen. At this point, cut back the dose of vitamin C by 500 mg and the bowel habits should normalize. This constitutes *your* optimum dose at this present time. Remember that your requirement will change over time, so keep adjusting the dose up and down, always keeping just within bowel tolerance. Even if your normal dose is around 3 or 4 g per day, if you are coming down with a bad cold or have some other acute condition, then your requirement may go as high as 10 g or more per day. If you are pregnant do not take more than 5 g per day.

Good dietary sources of vitamin C include acerola cherry juice, black currants, parsley, broccoli, citrus fruits, watercress, kale, beet tops, sweet peppers, spinach, cantaloupes, papayas, pineapples, mangos, chard, tomatoes, brussels sprouts, asparagus, and onions.

Minerals

Calcium is essential for normal transmission of nerve impulses and normal muscle contraction. It is involved with the maintenance of pH in the body and enhances immune function by strengthening cell membranes. Absorption of calcium is inhibited by caffeine, sugar, phytic acid, and alcohol. Absorption is promoted by the presence of vitamin C. Excretion of calcium is increased with the consumption of sodas, the use of tobacco, and an acid-forming diet. Supplementation with calcium citrate is recommended at doses of 500 to 1,000 mg/day. Note that this should be taken in the citrate form for maximum absorption, and with an equal amount of magnesium for optimum utilization.

Selenium is a powerful free radical scavenger and antioxidant that appears to work synergistically with vitamin E and is a cofactor for glutathione peroxidase. It also inhibits the production of leukotrines. Serum levels of selenium are usually low in people with rheumatoid arthritis and this suggests that it is useful to supplement with 200 mcg/day.

Methylsulfonylmethane (MSM) is a nonmetallic, crystalline source of sulfur. Sulfur is the eighth most abundant mineral in the body and essential for proper immune function and connective tissue integrity. It is a structural protein in joints, ligaments, tendons, hair, nails, blood vessel walls, and skin. Sulfur contributes to the flexibility of cell walls and improved fluid dynamics. It is also required as a critical enzyme activator for detoxification processes in the liver, where it has been likened to the "match" that sparks the fire of life. Sulfur occurs as a component of several other nutrients, including thiamine, pantothenic acid, biotin, lipoic acid, methionine, taurine, and cysteine. It is present in appreciable amounts in some foods, notably onions, garlic, the cruciferous vegetables (cabbage, broccoli, kale, turnips, etc.), eggs, fish, and meat. MSM is metabolized in the presence of vitamin C to sulfur. A normal daily dose is 2 to 5 g.

Magnesium is critical to energy production in the brain and indications of magnesium deficiency may include irritability, forgetfulness, mental confusion, anxiety, and problems with nerve conduction leading to muscle cramps. It is best given in a chelated form, bound to intermediates of the Krebs cycle such as citrate, malate, fumarate, aspartate, or succinate. For people with FMS the malate form appears to be the best. The starting dose is 6 mg per kg of body weight per day. Good food sources include soybeans and other legumes, seeds, nuts, whole grains, and leafy vegetables.

Potassium, *sodium*, and *chloride* function synergistically in the body, regulating water content and hence blood pressure, as well as being intricately involved in the transmission of nerve impulses. The average American has a potassium:sodium ratio of less than 1:2, and the ideal is considered to be greater than 5:1. The higher the consumption of fruits and vegetables, the higher the ratio will be. Potassium deficiency manifests as muscle weakness, fatigue, mental confusion, dizziness, irritability, heart disturbance, and problems with nerve conduction and muscle contraction. A supplementation of up to 2 g daily may be helpful.

Zinc is a cofactor in many enzyme functions. Most enzymes involved in DNA replication and repair require zinc, and a chronic low-grade deficiency may be one of the underlying causes of Alzheimer's. The dosage range is 10 to 50 mg daily, preferably in the picolinate form for maximum absorption. Good dietary sources are oysters and other shellfish, fish, red meat, whole grains, legumes, nuts, and seeds. Zinc is easily bound to phytic acid in plants, which limits absorption. Soaking the grain, nut, or seed in water will reduce this effect.

Manganese is involved in carbohydrate and fat metabolism and occurs in many enzyme systems including superoxide dismutase (SOD), a major cellular antioxidant. It is critical to proper glucose utilization within the nervous tissue, as well as to adenylate cyclase activity and neurotransmitter control. Doses of up to 30 mg daily are recommended. In very high doses it may cause psychiatric disturbance, including hallucinations and violent behavior. Food sources include nuts, whole grains, dried fruits, and leafy vegetables.

Amino Acids

In nature, amino acids are delivered to the body in the form of complex protein structures (polypeptides) that must be broken down in the gut into dipeptides, then free amino acids for absorption. Taking isolated amino acids may not seem wise because there is potential to disturb the natural proportions of stored amino acids held in the liver, and yet, individually, they do clearly show some significant health benefits. If you are careful to eat plenty of high-quality protein foods on a daily basis, then you may not need to use isolated amino acids except for certain specific therapeutic circumstances. If you do take them, you should also take a complex protein supplement such as a protein powder every day.

Methionine is a sulfur-containing amino acid that is incorporated into cartilage and can thus act to improve the strength and integrity of the joint in arthritis. It is best taken in combination with choline at a dose of 1 g of each per day. This will also help to enhance liver function and the tissue-cleansing process.

L-asparagine is useful as a regulator of brain function, acting to either stimulate or sedate, as required.

Gamma-aminobutyric acid (GABA) is an inhibitory neurotransmitter in the central nervous system. When taken as a supplement, in doses up to 750 mg in conjunction with niacinamide and inositol, it acts as a powerful yet gentle antianxiety agent. It may be helpful in weaning patients off tranquilizers.

L-glutamic acid (L-glutamate) is a major fuel for the brain and has a stimulating effect on brain function. It is helpful in treating depression, memory loss, and impaired cognitive function.

L-glutamine is converted to glutamic acid in the brain and has shown promise in the treatment of schizophrenia, epilepsy, senility, and mental retardation.

L-glycine has an inhibitory action in the central nervous system and may be helpful in treating epilepsy, anxiety, hysteria, and bipolar depression.

L-phenylalanine aids in the manufacture of norepinephrine and is helpful in treating depression, impaired memory, and cognitive dysfunction. It is a mood elevator and reduces awareness of pain.

L-taurine acts as a building block for many other amino acids and is critical to normal functioning of the central nervous system. Epilepsy, anxiety, hyperactivity, and learning disabilities are related to deficiency of this amino acid.

L-tryptophan is used by the brain in the production of melatonin and serotonin and is beneficial in the treatment of sleep disorders, hyperactivity, stress, and depression. It is most commonly available in the form of 5-hydroxy-tryptophan (5HTP).

L-tyrosine is a mood elevator and is helpful in treating depression, anxiety, and mental fatigue.

Additional Supplements

Carnitine is responsible for the transport of long-chain fatty acids into the mitochondria to make energy. Carnitine is also involved in the interconversion of amino acids. L-acetyl-carnitine (acetic acid plus L-carnitine) is made in the brain and this is the form in which it is usually taken as a supplement. L-acetyl-carnitine is structurally related to acetylcholine and also acts as a powerful antioxidant in the brain. Age-related memory defect is also improved with l-acetyl-carnitine supplementation. Doses of 500 mg three times daily are recommended. The best dietary source is red meats.

S-adenosylmethionine (SAMe) comprises methionine and adenosine-triphosphate (ATP) and is dependent upon adequate availability of methionine, B_{12}, and folic acid. It is the most effective methyl donor and so far is known to be involved in over forty biochemical reactions in the body. It is required for the manufacture of all sulfur-containing compounds, including glutathione. SAMe is required for the manufacture of many neurotransmitters, phosphotidyl serine, and phosphotidyl choline. It causes increased levels of serotonin and dopamine and improved binding of neurotransmitters to receptor sites. It is a very effective antidepressant and is especially indicated for postpartum depression and during drug withdrawal. Doses of up to 400 mg four times daily should be used, taking several weeks to build up to this dose to avoid nausea or gastrointestinal disturbance.

Phosphatidyl serine is a naturally occurring phospholipid that is especially concentrated in the brain and nervous tissue. Human trials going back over twenty years have demonstrated a significant effect on cognitive capacity (the ability to think clearly and rationally); on concentration; and on the ability to recall faces, words, and numbers. It is believed that phosphatidyl serine improves the functioning of neuronal membranes and regulates production of a variety of neurotransmitters, including acetylcholine, serotonin, dopamine, and norepinephrine. This supplement is absorbed rapidly and crosses the blood-brain barrier within minutes after ingestion. It is recommended to be taken during the day, as nighttime use may retard sleep onset.

Phosphatidylcholine, also known as lecithin, is involved in liver and brain function and has recently been designated an essential nutrient. Choline itself is part of the family of B vitamins and occurs as free choline in some vegetables, especially cauliflower and lettuce, as well as in liver, soy, and whole grains. As a supplement, it is usually consumed as phosphatidylcholine, combined with two fatty acids and a phosphate group. In the liver, choline acts as a methyl donor, which is necessary to remove fat from the liver. A choline-deficient diet will lead to fatty degeneration of the liver and other liver malfunctions. Additionally, choline is a component of acetylcholine, a major neurotransmitter. Supplementation with phosphatidylcholine has shown promise in reducing memory loss from Alzheimer's disease, in treating bipolar depression, and may be helpful in protecting the myelin sheath in various demyelinating diseases. Note that many commercial preparations have from 10 to 30 percent phosphatidylcholine, and the "inert" ingredients often cause gastric upset. Some newer preparations are available with up to 90 percent phosphatidylcholine and these are preferable. For treating Alzheimer's and bipolar depression, doses of up to 30 g daily are recommended. Dietary sources include whole grains, legumes, soybeans (an excellent source), and egg yolk.

Supplementing the diet with fish oils that provide *eicosapentanoic acid* (EPA) enhances the formation of anti-inflammatory prostaglandins and inhibits the formation of the inflammatory leukotrines. Clinical trials have shown that 1.8 g per day is an effective dose. *Gamma-linolenic acid* (GLA) is the active constituent of the pressed oils of evening primrose, borage, and black currant seed. By enhancing the production of anti-inflammatory prostaglandins, GLA minimizes arthritic pain. A dose of 2 to 3 g per day is usually effective. Do not continue use beyond six months because it may promote arachidonic acid and leukotrine production if allowed to dominate the prostaglandin pathways.

Betaine HCl, bromelain, and *proteolytic enzymes* may be especially useful in people with rheumatoid arthritis where there are associated food allergies and impaired digestive function. By augmenting the body's own digestive juices, the allergenic component of arthritis may be minimized. The enzymes also serve to reduce soft-tissue swelling and pain. Papaya, pineapple, kiwi, and mango are good sources.

Coenzyme Q10 is used in the electron transfer chain in the mitochondria as part of the final common pathway for the formation of energy in the cell.

It is also called *ubiquinone* because it is ubiquitous, being found in every living cell. Deficiencies will lead to impaired fuel utilization and may cause tissue fatigue. CoQ10 has long been known to regulate energy supply in the heart. Recent research has also indicated a significant benefit for generalized muscle fatigue. It is useful in FMS, chronic fatigue syndrome, multiple sclerosis, and other causes of physical fatigue and lack of energy. Doses of 100 to 300 mg are normal. CoQ10 requires fat for proper absorption in the gut, and should be taken with food.

Malic acid plays an essential role in the metabolism of glucose and the production of energy through the Krebs cycle. It tends to spare oxygen and provide greater stamina and endurance in muscle cells. It is found in abundance in apples and may contribute to the traditional use of apple cider vinegar as a treatment for rheumatism. Research from the Texas Health Science Center in San Antonio demonstrated significant benefit from the use of magnesium malate in FMS. Malic acid also helps to remove aluminum, which may contribute to significant cellular disruption, from the tissues. Doses up to 1,500 mg/day are normal. It is often taken in the form of magnesium malate and this is particularly helpful in FMS.

Cetyl myristoleate (CMO) is a long-chain fatty alcohol (cetyl alcohol) bound to a long-chain fatty acid (myristoleic acid). Both these substances are natural surfactants, being employed to reduce friction. These surfactants occur in the body in joints, the lungs, the pleura, and the pericardium. In the 1970s a particular species of laboratory mouse, the Swiss albino, was observed to be constitutionally devoid of arthritis problems, to the extent that it was routinely excluded from clinical trials for arthritis medications. Research at the National Institutes of Health (NIH) resulted in the isolation of CMO from mice, and it was found to be an "immunity factor" preventing development of arthritis. Crude CMO is poorly absorbed and is best taken by injection, which causes vary rapid reduction in symptoms of inflammation. Recent human trials have used doses ranging from 150 mg to 2.5 g and a dose-dependent result has been observed. The exact mode of action has not yet been determined, although an influence upon T-cell function and a regulation of prostaglandin activity is indicated. Inhibition of leukotrine function has been observed.

Nicotinamide adenine dinucleotide (NAD) is a coenzyme precursor for the manufacture of adenosine triphosphate (ATP), or cellular energy. It is found in every cell and is found in the highest concentrations in heart and brain tissue. It is thought to enhance the production of neurotransmitters. It is also one of the most powerful antioxidants available as a dietary supplement and assists in the regeneration of other antioxidants. Deficiency of NAD will reduce cellular energy production and cause fatigue. Clinical trials have indicated a benefit in cases of chronic fatigue syndrome, Parkinson's disease, Alzheimer's disease, multiple sclerosis, amyotrophic lateral sclerosis (ALS), depression, learning impairment, and memory loss.

Dr. Georg Birkmayer of Vienna, who did most of the original research on NAD as a clinical agent, recommends a graduated dose scale according to symptoms. Thus for general maintenance in a younger person, he recommends 2.5 mg twice weekly, rising to 5 mg daily in older people. For depression he recommends up to 7.5 mg daily and for cognitive dysfunction as much as 10 mg daily. Those tissues with the highest workload and highest energy requirement have the greatest amounts of NADH; for example, the heart of an animal and the flight muscles of a bird. It is found in appreciable amounts in meat and fish.

N-acetylcysteine (NAC) is a small peptide that provides glutathione for metabolic functions. Glutathione is a tripeptide consisting of cysteine, glutamic acid, and glycine. It is a primary antioxidant and critical to the detoxification pathways. Chronic viral infections, chronic stress, and poor dietary habits all contribute to glutathione deficiency and impaired detoxification of the body. NAC is used to supplement glutathione in doses of 1,500 mg daily. Good food sources include whey, yogurt, eggs, wheat, and meats.

Melatonin is a hormone produced in the pineal gland from tryptophan. Taken as a supplement it can significantly aid in regulating the sleep cycle and promoting restorative sleep. For rapid absorption and delivery it is often taken as a sublingual tablet, thirty minutes before bed. The adult body normally makes about 0.5 mg in twenty-four hours, mostly at night. Taking high doses (2 to 6 mg) may be necessary when commencing treatment, but this dose may cause nightmares and should be adjusted down. A dose of 0.5 to 1 mg is suitable for long-term use. Many people find that after several weeks of taking melatonin, they can cycle it—one or two days on and several days off. Because melatonin is a hormone, it is best to have the body level tested prior to commencing treatment and to take the lowest dose possible for the shortest time necessary to bring the body level back into optimum range.

Chlorophyll and *green foods* such as spirulina, chlorella, alfalfa, and blue-green algae can aid in the removal of toxins, especially heavy metals, and promote cellular energy production. Chlorophyll is easily converted into hemoglobin for enhanced oxygen delivery. No standard doses have been established and there are many proprietary products now available. Sprouts and wheat grass are excellent sources of chlorophyll, as are all leafy dark green vegetables.

Dehydroepiandrosterone (DHEA) is a steroid hormone manufactured in the adrenal glands that acts as a precursor for the manufacture of several other hormones, including cortisol and the sex hormones. Secretion of DHEA follows a diurnal rhythm, being highest during deep sleep. Sleep disturbance, especially of phase 4 (delta) sleep, will cause disruption to DHEA secretion and this may cause secondary disturbance of other hormone systems, including the menstrual cycle, sperm production, and stress management. Circulating DHEA sulfate may be measured in the blood and salivary DHEA may also be measured. It is important to note that fasting may cause a transient elevation of DHEA.

Measuring DHEA is a useful way of assessing degrees of adrenal exhaustion. In the early phase of adrenal depletion there will be elevated cortisol and normal DHEA. As adrenal depletion progresses, DHEA diminishes and finally cortisol is reduced as well. Testing should be done prior to supplementation with this hormone to determine the required dose. Normal starting doses are 5 to 10 mg daily, and up to 50 or 75 mg may be useful in an adrenal crisis or an acute flare-up of an autoimmune disease.

Biochemical Individuality

What has been described so far in this chapter provides the broad brush strokes for using diet and nutritional therapy to restore and maintain optimum health and well-being. We have discussed the importance of eating animal protein and animal fats, good-quality omega-3 fatty acids, and fruits and vegetables, and of limiting the consumption of grains, processed and refined carbohydrates, processed fats, and dairy products. We have examined the major nutritional supplements—vitamins, minerals, and others—that contribute to optimum health. Now we need to fine-tune this mass of information to account for biochemical individuality and personal physiological needs. No two people are biochemically and physiologically alike; hence, no single diet plan can work for all individuals. While the general principles described above do hold true, for optimum wellness we need to personalize a dietary program just as we personalize an herbal formulation. What we are seeking has been called a "patient-specific program," in contrast to "disease-specific programs," which are the norm in modern Western medicine.

Within the body there are five core homeostatic balance mechanisms that work to maintain the "steady state" that best predisposes to good health. They provide an oscillatory dynamic equilibrium resulting from the alternate operation of opposing forces. Imbalance in one or more of these homeostatic mechanisms can have profound effects on the body. All pathology represents a dysfunction of one or more of these fundamental control mechanisms. This may come about through inherited genetic faults or predispositions, or may be acquired through faulty nutrition, stress, or disease vectors such as bacteria, viruses, and other pathogenic microbes. The five fundamental balance mechanisms are as follows:

1. Water/electrolyte balance (relative hydration level)
2. Anaerobic/dysaerobic balance (degree of oxidative stress)
3. Glucogenic/ketogenic balance(use of glucose or fats as primary fuel)

4. Acid/alkaline balance (tissue and serum pH)
5. Sympathetic/parasympathetic balance (relative stress load)

In the office of your health care provider these balance mechanisms can be tested using a very simple, integrated series of forty-six physical and biochemical tests, which take about fifteen minutes to administer and less than ten minutes to analyze. No special equipment is required and the results can be correlated against any other analytical testing methods, if required. This system is called the Nutri-Spec system and further information can be obtained by contacting the address given in Appendix Two at the end of this book.

Other testing methods may be employed to ascertain the specific biochemical individuality of the patient. In my clinical practice I make extensive use of VEGA testing. This is a computerized electrode that measures electrical resistance in the skin over meridian points when the patient is exposed to various substances. This allows assessment of food and substance sensitivities and allergies; organ strengths and weaknesses; vitamin, mineral, hormone, or enzyme imbalances; heavy metal toxicity; parasites; *Candida*; and much more. Like all testing methods there is some inherent subjectivity, but very little. It operates on the same principle as muscle testing but allows much less room for operator bias.

Other measurements, such as pH, resistivity, and redox potential of blood, urine, and saliva; hepatic clearance function and renal clearance function; and secretory immunoglobulin A and hormone panels, can also indicate much information about one's biochemical individuality.

The Low-Oxalate Diet

As mentioned in Chapter 2, following a low-oxalate diet may be of some benefit for people with interstitial cystitis and vulvodynia, conditions commonly associated with fibromyalgia. Urine is normally saturated with calcium oxalate, uric acid, and phosphates. These substances remain in solution due to finely calibrated pH control; availability of nutrients such as citrate, which keeps calcium in solution; and the secretion of various protective substances. If these protective mechanisms are overwhelmed, crystallization occurs and minerals precipitate out of solution. Small amounts will cause tissue irritation and larger amounts may cause a kidney stone. If the etiologic theories of Dr. R. Paul St. Amand are correct in the case of fibromyalgia, a genetic defect results in renal inability to adequately excrete phosphates. This disturbs the solutions and predisposes to the precipitation of oxalates, which cause irritation of the delicate epithelial lining of the ureters, bladder, and urethra. Dr. C. C. Solomons has determined that a low-oxalate diet is beneficial in interstitial cystitis, and this is now being successfully applied to people with fibromyalgia. In severe cases it is wise to follow a comprehensive dietary program designed for alleviating kidney stones (see Table 5.5).

Table 5.5 High- and Medium-Oxalate Foods to Be Avoided or Moderated

High-Oxalate Foods (Avoid)	Medium-Oxalate Foods (Moderate)
Black tea	Beet greens
Coffee	Cranberries
Cocoa	Nuts
Chocolate	Sorrel
Spinach	Chard
Rhubarb	Grapefruit
Parsley	Kale
	Peanuts
	Sweet peppers

Dietary Guidelines for Enhanced Renal Clearance

- Drink lots of water.
- Increase the intake of leafy dark green vegetables (except those listed in Table 5.3, pages 128 to 130) and dietary fiber.
- Eat foods with a high magnesium: calcium ratio, such as avocados, bananas, lima beans, potatoes, and most whole grains.
- Reduce dairy products and other sources of dietary calcium.
- Avoid all refined sugars, which increase the urinary calcium concentration.
- Supplement with pyridoxine (B_6), 100 to 250 mg daily, and magnesium citrate, 200 mg twice daily.

Diet for Hypoglycemia

Hypoglycemia is a condition of low blood sugar (glucose), which can lead to many frightening physical and mental symptoms (see Figure 5.3). It is usually caused by long-term overeating of refined carbohydrates (sugar, white bread and white-flour products, white rice, etc.). When refined carbohydrates and sugar are eaten, they are rapidly digested and absorbed and cause a rapid rise in blood sugar. This enhances the production and secretion of insulin from the pancreas, which acts to lower the blood sugar again.

The drop in blood sugar is often extreme and the cells of the body and especially of the brain temporarily fail to get sufficient nourishment. The onset of symptoms is often sudden, and usually occurs before breakfast, a few hours after eating, after exercise, or after emotional stress.

The treatment of hypoglycemia involves eating a well-balanced diet with plenty of *unrefined* carbohydrates that have a low glycemic index. These are broken down slowly by the body to yield glucose without dramatically raising the blood sugar. If the hypoglycemic person does not follow this type of diet, he or she runs the risk of eventual pancreatic exhaustion when no more insulin can be produced, leading to diabetes or hyperglycemia (too much blood sugar). It is also very important to eat plenty of protein, at least 75 g daily, to delay the absorption of sugar.

Recommended Foods

- All vegetables and fruits, unless mentioned below as being restricted
- Unsalted nuts and nut butters
- Sesame paste (tahini)
- Beans and peas
- Lean, organic meat; poultry and fish

Emotional Symptoms	Bodily Symptoms
Impatience	Fatigue or exhaustion
Phobias	Backache
Irritability	Bloating
Loss of purpose or sense of meaning in life	Diarrhea
	Abdominal pain
Bad temper	Cold sweats
Suicidal feelings	Muscle and joint pain
Crying	Palpitations
Depression	Insomnia
Anxiety	Hunger
Nervous Symptoms	**Intellectual Symptoms**
Headaches	Confusion
Blurred vision	Loss of concentration
Dizziness	Forgetfulness
Twitching of muscles	Spaciness or foggy feeling
Trembling	
Sensitivity to light	
Numbness	
Fainting	

Figure 5.3 Symptoms of Hypoglycemia

Limited Intake
- Full-fat cheese
- Grapes
- Whole grains and their products (whole grain pasta, brown rice, etc.)
- Dried fruits
- Bananas
- All fruit juices

Avoid Completely
- All refined and processed foods
- All sugar and honey
- Cakes, chocolate, all sweets, pastries, and puddings
- Cereals with sugar
- Ice cream
- Jam and marmalade
- Ketchup, relish, sauces, pickles, and mustard
- Tea and coffee
- Alcohol
- Soft drinks and chocolate drinks
- White bread, pasta, or rice
- Medication with caffeine, cough syrups, and laxatives

General Advice
Eat a small meal every two to three hours and avoid snacking in between. When hungry, try eating a high-protein snack; it will often give you more lasting satisfaction and energy than carbohydrates.

Putting It All Together

Let us now examine the special use of therapeutic diet for the person with fibromyalgia. The diagnosis of FMS is indicative of multiple organ dysfunctions stemming from environmental, social, and individual stresses causing chronic adrenal excess, and eventually resulting in metabolic depletion. This may be compounded by genetic defects and phosphate accumulation leading to cellular and mitochondrial disturbance and failure of energy production. The diet is critically important in aiding this situation. We cannot necessarily change our job, our environment, or some of the stresses of living, but we do have ultimate control over our diet. This is one place we can take charge and make real, positive, life-affirming choices that will promote optimal health. Eating well can remove a significant level of stress from the body and provide maximum nutritional support for metabolic functions.

Those with FMS have a deficiency of "vital force" and judicious use of diet will build a solid foundation for true healing to occur. FMS patients are typically cold, tense, and given to anxiety, jitteriness, poor sleep, cramping of muscles, and feelings of stiffness. They need to be warmed up, loosened up, and encouraged to be more relaxed. The use of warming, spicy, aromatic foods, rich and heavy foods, and plenty of root vegetables, nuts, fat, and protein will all aid the symptoms of FMS. Avoid sour or bitter flavors, except therapeutically to encourage the digestive function where needed.

According to traditional Chinese medicine, the preferred foods for this type of "deficient yin" state include yams, dates, molasses, barley malt, blackberries, raspberries, mulberries, bananas, watermelons (despite their cooling nature), grapes, sardines, duck, cabbage, kale, broccoli, brussels sprouts, turnip greens, wheat germ, millet, and barley. Plants that grow underground—root vegetables such as carrots, turnips, rutabagas, beetroot, parsnip, and so on—are considered warming, as are red, orange, and yellow-colored foods, and cooked foods in general. Adzuki beans, black beans, and lentils are especially good. Oats, spelt, and quinoa are the only warming grains. Rice, corn, buckwheat, and rye have neutral energy; they may be eaten in moderation and preferably sprouted. All other grains (including wheat) are cooling and should be avoided. Foods that are watery or mature quickly, such as lettuce, spinach, cucumbers, and radishes, are cooling and should be avoided. Many aromatic spices are warming and stimulating and can be added freely to food. These include ginger, turmeric, cinnamon bark, cloves, basil, rosemary, angelica root, fennel, dill, anise, caraway, cumin, coriander,

chili, garlic, and black pepper. Butter is a warming food; other dairy products
are cooling.

In addition to the above general principles, the person with FMS needs to
address the specific issues of oxalate avoidance and hypoglycemia, if applicable, and avoid all allergenic foods. Following the Paleolithic diet is very helpful
for most people. One should eat plenty of high-quality protein and good fatty
acids, loads of fruits and vegetables, very little starch, and no dairy products.
To prevent additional allergies, it is best not to eat the same food day after day.

The biggest problems are likely to be that you are simply too tired or weak
to cook and that your family may not want to eat what you are having. There
are, of course, no easy answers to these problems. However, it is imperative
that you eat properly if you want to achieve and maintain wellness. Actually,
the basic principles of the healthy diet given below are equally applicable to
all members of the family, no matter what their state of health. These general
principles can be universally applied.

Most of the general principles of the low-oxalate and hypoglycemic diets
are the same as those of the basic guide to healthy eating that follow. To make
the transition easier, write a week's worth of menus and shopping lists at one
time. Buy a write-on/wipe-off board to hang in the kitchen and write down
everything to do or buy when it pops into your head. Once a week you can
sort it out, write your menus and shopping lists, and wipe the board clean to
start again. This will simplify your life and help to ensure that good food will
be abundant and delicious on your new program.

Basic Principles of a Healthy Diet

A healthy diet includes eating lots of fruits and vegetables, eggs, fish (especially oily ones such as salmon, sardines, and mackerel), nuts and seeds, moderate amounts of meat and game, and beans and legumes. Ideally, one should
eat no grains at all. The best carbohydrate comes from fruits and starchy vegetables. If you must eat grains, try oats, barley, rice, spelt, quinoa, millet,

buckwheat, and amaranth. Avoid wheat; it is hard to digest adequately due to the presence of alpha-amylase inhibitors and it has a high acid residue. The Paleolithic diet does not recommend eating dairy products, but if they are consumed, butter and fermented products (yogurt and kefir) are preferred. If you eat cheese, go for the blue ones that have live bacterial cultures that can be beneficial for the bowel flora. It is always best to eat organically raised food whenever possible. Be sure to drink plenty of filtered or bottled water each day (one 8-ounce glass for every 20 pounds of body weight), and avoid all stimulating drinks such as coffee, tea, and cola.

For the person with FMS it is important to eat foods that are alkalizing to the body and reduce the deposition of acid waste materials in the tissues and joints. Acid waste, especially uric acid, is formed when animal protein is digested in the body. There is a finite amount the kidneys can excrete and excess may be deposited into muscles, contributing to tender and trigger points, and into joints, contributing to arthritis. A high consumption of fruits and vegetables reduces the acid level of the body fluids and seems to protect against this to some extent, and drinking lots of water also helps. This intake must be calibrated to suit the level of vital force depletion as well. If the person is notably cold and deficient, raw fruits and vegetables should generally be avoided. Light steaming, poaching, and broiling are suitable cooking methods. Deep frying and barbecuing should be avoided.

Fruits

There is no upper limit on fruit consumption unless it causes excessive cooling. Fruits are best eaten between meals or at least half an hour before other foods, and fresh fruit, in season, is preferred over stored, bottled, or frozen fruit.

The following fruits are recommended:

apples	oranges	bananas	pears
peaches	cherries	grapes	strawberries
kiwis	plums	gooseberries	raspberries
grapefruits	nectarines	fresh figs	

Dried fruits include apricots, raisins, and dates. These are very high in sugar, which makes them a good food for quick energy unless one suffers from hypoglycemia. In any case, don't eat too many, as an excess of sugar is not good for anyone.

Vegetables

Vegetables should comprise 50 percent of each meal or of the total daily intake of food. Almost all vegetables can be eaten raw, or at the most lightly steamed. Some root vegetables that are usually eaten cooked (turnip, parsnip, beets) are quite delicious raw when finely grated. The trick to enjoying salads on a regular basis is to be imaginative. Try as many unusual combinations as you can think up—most of them will be delicious!

The following vegetables are recommended:

beans	beet tops	beets	bok choy
broccoli	cabbage	carrots	cauliflower
celery	collards	cucumbers	eggplant
fennel	leeks	lettuce	onions
parsley	peas	peppers	radishes
spinach	squash	tomatoes	zucchini

Legumes

Legumes, or dried beans, can comprise up to 15 percent of each meal or of the total daily intake of food. They are an excellent source of protein, carbohydrate, and dietary fiber. They also contain variable amounts of vitamins and minerals. The best way to eat them is sprouted. Soak a handful overnight, then rinse them and put them in a jar with a gauze covering. Rinse and drain them twice a day and eat them when you see shoots beginning to appear. If you wish to cook unsprouted beans, all types, except lentils, need to be pre-soaked. This is done in cold water overnight and reduces phytic acid activity. After soaking, the beans should be thoroughly rinsed. Do not add salt to the cooking water, as this makes them tough. Rinse again after cooking, as this makes them more digestible and less likely to cause gas and flatulence and removes some of the protease inhibitors.

Beans can be added to salads or incorporated into many hot dishes. They can also be pureed with seasoning to make delicious dips and spreads. Avoid tofu, soy milk, and other processed soy products. The processing of soy destroys much of the nutritional value. Try tempeh or whole soybeans instead.

The following legumes are recommended:

adzuki beans	mung beans	green beans	lima beans
lentils	kidney beans	navy beans	black-eyed peas
garbanzos	pinto beans	split peas	

Fish/Wild or Range-Fed Organic Meats/Naturally Raised Fowl

Eat these protein-dense foods several times a week. This may be particularly useful where there is weakness, debility, poor immune function, or chronic disease. Be sure to buy only organic or you will get a dose of antibiotic, hormone, and pesticide residue.

Seeds and Nuts

Seeds and nuts can comprise up to 5 percent of each meal or total daily intake of food. High in protein and fats they also provide a variety of vitamins and minerals. They also make a delicious snack if toasted and drizzled with tamari or soy sauce. Seeds and nuts are also available as pastes and butters

The following seeds and nuts are recommended:

sunflower seeds	sesame seeds	pumpkin seeds	almonds
filberts	pecans	walnuts	Brazil nuts
cashews			

Technically peanuts are a type of legume. They are high in a fat implicated in certain heart problems and therefore shouldn't be eaten in large quantities. Also, many people are highly allergic to them.

Oils

Oils should always be used in moderation, and frying should be kept to a minimum. Always use cold-pressed oils. The best oil to use for salad dressings is flaxseed, followed by safflower, olive, or sunflower. For cooking, olive, safflower, or sunflower are good. Avoid margarines, even those that claim to be high in polyunsaturates. Blended, high-omega 3 and 6 oils are available also.

Better Butter

Take 1 pound of organic butter and soften to room temperature. Beat in 8 to 16 ounces of cold-pressed olive oil. This will set in the fridge to the texture of margarine and provides all the good fatty acids of olive oil with the richness of butter, but has only half the saturated fat of pure butter.

Additional Items

Honey and molasses in moderation, apple cider vinegar, tamari or soy sauce, herbs and spices, yeast flakes (give a cheesy flavor), carob powder, garlic powder, miso (fermented soybean paste), and many other natural condiments such as sea vegetables and salsas are acceptable. Avoid anything with added salt, sugar, colorings, artifical flavors, or preservatives.

Beverages

Drink plenty of water, about 8 ounces for every 20 pounds of body weight. Green tea is okay if you want a caffeinated beverage, but avoid coffee and too much black tea. Herbal teas are good. Avoid all sodas, and bottled and canned drinks. Especially avoid aspartame (artificial sweetener) in diet drinks. This is metabolized by the body into methanol or wood alcohol, which can cause some serious adverse reactions. Phosphoric acid in canned drinks inhibits calcium and magnesium absorption and contributes to bone fragility. Avoid large amounts of fruit juices because they lack beneficial fruit fiber and are high in sugar.

CHAPTER SIX

HERBAL APPROACHES TO HEALING FIBROMYALGIA

He causeth the grass to grow for the cattle
and herbs for the service of man.
PSALMS 104:14

July 1992

It is a year since the accident and I still feel lousy. You would think that as an

herbalist I should be able to deal with this and get over it. Makes me doubt

sometimes that I know at all what I am doing. How can I help others when

I can't seem to help myself? I am taking a powerful mix of Siberian ginseng,

blue vervain, licorice, stinging nettle, and kelp. Also various supplements,

including spirulina, calcium, magnesium, and bee pollen. I should be feeling

better, but I'm not. I had three weeks off recently and that helped a lot—

if only I didn't have to earn a living! I am also trying some acupuncture and

Chinese herbs. The herbs are disgusting. I have to brew up a big decoction

and they smell and taste foul. God knows what all is in there, but I am willing

to try anything. I am wondering about homeopathy. Maybe there is some

miasm or emanation in my psyche that is causing this sort of constitutional

malaise. In the meantime I am working hard and trying to keep going.

Sometimes I struggle not to get depressed from living in chronic pain and feeling helpless. I cannot allow myself to feel hopeless. I cannot afford to give in to this affliction. I must continue to function and make a living.

The History and Philosophy of Western Herbal Medicine

From the time when man first roamed the earth, and continuing in every country and in every culture down through the ages, people have been seeking to understand and control disease processes. In all parts of the world, as mankind and his belief systems evolved, so did the systems within which man viewed his physical state. Sometimes illness was seen as divine retribution and the sick person was seen as a sinner being cleansed. Sometimes illness was seen as a visitation by evil spirits that required exorcism by a shaman. Around the world, though, there was a common thread in that there was always a belief in something larger than the self—a greater power, a higher being. Whatever their individual differences, virtually all traditional systems of healing were and still are alike in that they center around the idea of a *vital force* or *life force* that gives energy and vitality to the body. While their traditional healing systems may have radically different philosophical frameworks, all cultures believe that human life is somehow more than just the physical body. Whether we call this life force the soul, chi, prana, or spirit, all reflect the principle that *the whole is both greater than and different from the sum of its parts.*

In traditional healing systems around the world there was usually a reverence accorded to this life force and the body was regarded as the temple of the spirit. Thus medicine tended to be very respectful of the body and avoided intervention unless absolutely necessary. In many cases a direct appeal was made to the life force to allow healing to occur, possibly taking the form of a ceremony or sacrifice. When therapeutic intervention did take place it tended to be simple and gentle initially, and only if this failed would more drastic measures be taken.

As the centuries passed and Christianity gained an ever-stronger grip on the spiritual life of people in the West, the Christian church took on more and more of the task of healing the psyche and soul, leaving the physical body to the medical doctor. The effect of this was a separation of the body from the spirit and the resultant loss of the spiritual basis of healing. Concurrently, the esoteric science of alchemy was just beginning to gain a foothold in Europe and with it came a tendency to view the world more analytically than emotionally. Alchemists experimented with many inorganic substances, both in chemical reactions and as medicines. Interesting chemical combinations were created in laboratories and then prescribed in experimental doses. This was empirical learning in its most extreme form—trial and error as cure or kill! However, just enough cures were successful to encourage the alchemists in their endeavors. This, in fact, was the beginning of what we know today as allopathic medicine.

One of the most influential people in this process was Sir Isaac Newton. This great thinker is best known for deducing the principle of gravity, but he was also the originator of a whole school of scientific thought based on the principle of *reductionism*. Whereas the traditional belief systems acknowledged the "wholeness" of all things and their interrelatedness, the reductionists considered the world to consist of no more than multiple chemical building blocks, and the body to be no more than a mechanistic series of parts. Their aim was to look closer and closer into the body at smaller and smaller parts until they could understand every aspect of its functioning.

Through this divisive process the human body and the planet that we inhabit came to be seen from a purely mechanistic perspective. As a logical corollary of this, disease was regarded as something that came from outside the body rather than the result of internal imbalances or disharmonies. In a machine if a part is defective in some way, it is simply replaced. In its most extreme medical application, this mechanistic viewpoint is seen in the phenomenon of organ transplants. However, on a more day-to-day level, the mechanistic belief is seen in many surgical procedures and even in modern "silver bullet" drug therapy. Thus, for example, varicose veins are stripped out without consideration given to the lack of exercise that may have brought them about in the first place, or teenage acne is treated with long-term antibiotics without consideration of the young person's diet.

Without a doubt modern medicine is lifesaving in certain acute or critical situations, but in daily life, this mechanistic, reductionist perspective totally fails to take into account the life force inherent in a human being. The body's own innate healing powers are ignored or even suppressed (through antipyretics, anti-inflammatories, immunosuppressives). The modern doctor has such a complex understanding of disease processes that he is desperately trying to control all of them instead of attempting to access the body's own healing potential. There is no room in his understanding for a bodily process that cannot be seen or measured. He simply cannot conceive of such a thing as a life force.

For almost four hundred years in the developed world, science has promulgated and promoted the mechanistic model and this has permeated every facet of our society. However, the most recent generation of scientists, especially physicists, are beginning to challenge this belief system.

James Lovelock's Gaia Hypothesis suggests that the earth can be considered as an organism, an intricate network or web of life in which all things are interconnected and interdependent. If you take a holographic image and cut off a small piece of it, you will find that the whole picture is still visible in the part. Thus in any piece of a hologram there is contained the whole picture, but in the context of the larger image only a small part will be revealed. This is comparable to the phenomenon of each body cell that contains all the same genetic information as every other cell, but in which only a portion is revealed.

From the understanding that all things are connected we can see that each one of us is a part of a greater whole. We can also see that, whether we are talking about plants, animals, humans, rivers, forests, or oceans, one part of the system cannot be affected without affecting all the other parts. The health and well-being of every living creature on the planet is ultimately dependent on the health and well-being of all other living creatures and the health of the planet on which we live.

While acknowledging the usefulness of modern medicine in certain acute situations, it cannot be denied that as an overall system of health care it has some serious drawbacks. Certainly there are some wonderful, lifesaving drugs, but they tend to be best at dealing with truly life-threatening diseases and provide little pharmaceutical help for chronic degenerative diseases such as arthritis, heart disease, and most cancers. From the belief that the body consists merely of a series of parts has come the assumption that a drug can be designed to act on and affect single parts of the machine without impinging on other parts. In fact, of course, there is no such thing as a drug with a single, specific action with *no* effect elsewhere. When you consider the close intimacy of all parts of the body with their common circulatory, hormonal, and nervous systems, then it should come as no surprise that, for example, a drug affecting the kidneys will affect the lungs as well.

In the past hundred years or so a fairly typical pharmaceutical procedure has been for a traditional herbal remedy to be examined in a laboratory and its active constituents identified, isolated, extracted, and, if possible, synthesized. Through this procedure it becomes possible to make pure drugs suitable for double-blind placebo-controlled crossover trials. After such "provings" a drug can be patented, licensed, and sold. From the holistic perspective this is a direct contravention of the natural laws of life. By treating a plant in this way, no credence is given to the life force of the plant. The artificially synthesized drug, while it may be chemically identical to an actual plant constituent, not only has no life force of its own, but it will deplete the life force of the organism to which it is administered.

It must be remembered that plants and humans have evolved side by side for millennia. We all came from the same primeval mud and we all contain the same basic chemical building blocks. The DNA genetic material of an oak tree is fundamentally no different from that of the Queen of England; the only differences lie in the amounts of DNA and in the sequences of gene codons. When we ingest a plant, its chemical constituents are completely familiar to our bodies, which know how to process them and incorporate them into our physiological processes. Thus herbal remedies tend to be supportive, nutritive, and tonic, gently moving the body toward its own healing processes.

This is in contrast to the allopathic drugs that, by virtue of their inherent foreignness to the body, tend to actively interfere with body processes and to force the cells into certain courses of action, regardless of the appropriateness of such actions. Such foreign substances must also be processed and detoxified by the liver and this can stress the organ. The metabolism and excretion of herbal remedies utilizes existing biochemical pathways that have evolved specifically to deal with these very molecules. Allopathic drugs may also use these pathways, but in so doing, frequently inhibit the correct biochemical reactions from occurring there. This is partly why herbal remedies have so few toxic reactions when compared to allopathic drugs.

Another factor that deserves consideration is the natural system of checks and balances in a plant remedy. A perfect example is seen in the case of *Ephedra sinica* (Ma Huang). This plant was safely and effectively used in China for countless generations as a remedy for asthma. Twentieth-century laboratory examination revealed the presence of the alkaloid ephedrine that was shown in clinical trials to dilate the bronchi. However, the isolated alkaloid also significantly raised the blood pressure, an effect that was only very rarely noticed when utilizing the whole plant remedy. The reason for this was that in the whole plant there are at least six other related alkaloids, some of which act to reduce the blood pressure. So, not infrequently, a whole plant remedy is actually safer than the isolated constituents ingested out of context.

What Is Holistic Medicine?

The following definition of holism and holistic medicine is drawn from the manifesto of the British Columbia Holistic Healing Association, written in 1991 by myself and Chris Shirley, a professional reflexologist in Vancouver. It provides a concise and comprehensive summary of the principles of holistic medicine.

The terms *holistic* and *holism* refer to a way of being that is loving and respectful of the essence of life in all of its forms. In healing, this love and respect supports and empowers a person to engage in and actively direct his

---

The Seven Principles of Holism and Holistic Healing

1. Human beings live within a holographic context that describes their integral relationship with other living organisms and ecosystems, the earth, and the universe.
2. A human being is a dynamic living energy system rather than simply a mechanistic arrangement of parts.
3. Holistic healing regards any disease in body, mind, spirit, or environment as a reflection of disturbance in the whole system.
4. Holistic healing recognizes the essential strengths and resources of each person and seeks to empower people and liberate these resources to facilitate wellness.
5. Holistic healing seeks to expand clients' conscious awareness of their dynamic relationship with all levels of their disease, and hence may be considered educational.
6. Holistic healing recognizes that ultimately all choice and responsibility rests with the client and encourages a healthy independence in relationship with healers and healing modalities.
7. Holistic healing recognizes that expansion of consciousness and knowledge is the essence of human evolvement and seeks to serve that process.

---

or her own healing process. Holistic health is a conscious, vibrant experience of well-being, characterized by optimal integration of body, mind, spirit, and environment.

Herbal Medicine in the Holistic Context

Herbal medicine alone cannot cure fibromyalgia. FMS is a complex syndrome with multiple overlapping causes and consequently many ways of treating and managing it. Individualized approaches are required to address the unique personal experience of each patient. Holistic practitioners know this and recommend using herbs as part of an overall approach including diet, lifestyle, physical therapy, counseling, and remedial therapy as necessary. Herbal medicine is generally safe and suitable for long-term use, an important point when treating chronic conditions like FMS. The herbs are used to enhance the body's own innate healing capability. They generally do not force the body to cooperate nor do they suppress natural, desirable bodily responses. Many of the herbs have a tonic effect, enhancing overall metabolic efficacy and promoting optimum functioning of the whole body.

For the person with fibromyalgia, herbal medicine can offer some significant benefits. Perhaps herbs are most notably beneficial in the area of tonics and adaptogens. They nourish the body, providing energy without draining or exhausting it, support and promote healing, and improve resistance to stress and strain, wear and tear. Herbs may also be used to treat many of the symptoms of FMS. Pain, muscle spasm, impaired sleep, fatigue, palpitations, chills, poor memory and concentration—all can be aided through the judicious use of carefully selected herbal formulas.

Although herbal medicines can be used for acute conditions, they really shine when treating chronic, debilitating disease. A well-designed formula can create symptomatic improvement within a few days to a few weeks and lasting change can be effected after several months of use.

Building an Herbal Formula

Pathological Correction and Physiological Support

In holistic medicine the practitioner starts with the premise that the normally functioning body is free from disease, capable of resisting disease, and capable of healing from disease. Based on this belief, the major focus of holistic medicine is on supporting and enhancing this inherent ability of the body to heal itself. Physiological support, it is thought, will bring about a deeper and more profound healing than pathological correction that interferes directly with the healing process.

An example of this fundamentally different approach to treating disease is seen in the treatment of colds and flu. The allopathic physician will recommend aspirin to bring down the fever, a decongestant to dry up the mucous membranes, and an antitussive to reduce coughing. The holistic practitioner, in contrast, will recommend a warm bath and a diaphoretic (sweat-promoting) tea to bring up the fever and induce a sweat, which will allow natural cooling. This temperature spike will enhance white blood cell activity against the invading microbe, and will reduce the microbe's virulence. Additionally, the holistic practitioner will use inhaled essential oils to deliver antibiotic properties directly to the mucous membranes and open the airways, as well as plantain and goldenrod infusion to thin the mucus and make it easier to clear out. Mucus production is an important form of primary defense in the body and should be encouraged, not suppressed. Coughing is also part of the primary defense system and, again, will be promoted by the herbalist with gentle soothing expectorants.

If frequent colds and flu are a pattern, the allopathic physician may prescribe antibiotics, which suppress the immune response, and flu vaccinations. The holistic practitioner, on the other hand, will address aspects of diet and lifestyle to improve immunity, as well as recommending herbs and supplements to boost immune response. Enhancing the natural defense mechanisms of the body may obviate the need for stronger, symptomatic medicines. Pathological correction makes sense as a response to an acute and severe symptom, but should be quickly followed with physiological support to ensure rapid recovery and increased resistance to future disease states.

In clinical practice one of the most useful techniques is to pinpoint the actual sequence of disease, that which master herbalist Kerry Bone has called the "causal chain" of disease. He suggests that every disease consists of three phases: predisposing, excitatory, and sustaining. For example, predisposing causes of disease might include diet, attitude, environment, genetics, and constitution. Excitatory causes might include viruses, bacteria, yeasts, physical trauma, emotional trauma, and sudden or severe stress. Sustaining causes could include sleep disturbance from pain, chronic inflammation, or the side effects of drugs. Bone suggests that if the practitioner can determine, for any given disease state, which part of the causal chain can be attributed to predisposing, excitatory, or sustaining causes, he can refine and focus the individualized formula for that patient. For the person with FMS, for example, the simplified causal chain might be explained thus:

High stress → increased intake of caffeine → stimulation of the adrenal glands → insomnia → lowered production of melatonin → weakening of the immune system and impaired release of growth hormone → problems with muscle repair → microtrauma to the muscle → spasms, pain, and formation of tender points → further impaired sleep → beginning of a vicious cycle

In this example, the predisposing causes are stress, caffeine intake, and disturbed sleep; the excitatory causes are impaired melatonin and growth hormone; and the sustaining causes are compromised muscle repair, pain, tender-point development, and disturbed sleep. By considering the specific needs for physiological support we could use herbs to treat the predisposing causes, such as modulating the adrenal reaction to chronic stress and balancing the stress hormones. Treating the excitatory and sustaining causes could utilize pathological correction in the form of herbs to deepen sleep, enhance circulation, relax muscles, and enhance tissue repair. It is usually more effective to give a larger quantity of a single herb than small amounts of many different herbs. Five or six herbs in significant quantities (which vary with each herb) is usually the most effective number; it allows for all the herbal actions needed and yet doesn't confuse the body with too many chemical combinations simultaneously.

The traditional and time-honored approach suggests that a formula should have within it:

- 2 or 3 parts specifically active against the particular components of the condition.
- 1 part soothing and relaxing to the affected area or to the nerves in general.
- 1 part nourishing and strengthening or tonic to the affected area or to the body in general.
- 1 part eliminative/alterative/depurative.

Traditional Chinese medicine bases the structure of the formula on the principle of government. Thus there is an "emperor" that determines the overall approach, various "ministers" that support and carry out the wishes of the Emperor, "assistants" that create the agenda for government and set the political climate and tone, and "servants" that carry out the actual work. In the context of the herbal formula this means that the herbs are layered, that each is considered in relation to the other parts of the formula as well as for its own merit. The Chinese art of compounding, or making herbal formulas, is impressive and China's energetic principles may be applied to Western herbs as well. Similarly, Western herbal medicine draws threads from Ayurveda and many other indigenous herbal traditions. There is no right or wrong when making a customized formula; there is only the question of whether it is effective for the individual. By careful analysis of the condition, careful assessment of the herbs, and regular monitoring of progress, you will know if you are on the right track.

Herbal Therapies for Fibromyalgia

The specific approach to FMS should be tailored to the needs of the individual, but the overall action will include energizing and tonic, relaxing, warming, adaptogenic, immune regulating, connective tissue strengthening, and cleansing.

Some of these objectives may be achieved by internal use and some by topical applications. Some herbs fit in more than one category and can double up in purpose; some herbs may be used in food and some as essential oils in a massage or bath. See Appendix One for details on individual herbs and for directions on how to make the herbal remedies. Table 6.1 gives typical formulas for treatment.

Clinical Approaches to Treating Fibromyalgia

Alteratives for the joints
Diuretic/uricosuric alteratives
Triterpenoid saponins anti-inflammatories
Sulfur anti-inflammatories
Resin anti-inflammatories
Salicylate anti-inflammatories
Steroidal saponin anti-inflammatories
Essential fatty acid anti-inflammatories
Volatile oil anti-inflammatories
Rubefacients
Cerebral circulatory stimulants
Warming tonic circulatory stimulants
Central circulatory stimulants
Peripheral circulatory stimulants
Adaptogens
Connective tissue tonics
Sedative nervines
Nervines that have a muscle-relaxing effect
Gentle, relaxing nervines
Tonic nervines
Sialogogues

Table 6.1: Typical Formulas for Treating Fibromyalgia

For muscle stiffness and pain

Piper methysticum	15	Zanthozylum spp.	15
Cimicifuga racemosa	15	Apium graveolens	15
Harpagophytum pro.	15	Boswellia carterii	5
Glycyrrhiza glabra	15	Phytolacca spp.	5
			100 ml

For lack of energy

Eleutherococcus senticosus	20	Urtica dioica	20
Glycyyrhiza glabra	15	Fucus vesiculosis	15
Verbena officinalis	15	Schizandra chinensis	10
Zingiber officinalis	5		
			100 ml

For pain and lack of sleep

Valeriana officinalis	25	Lactuca virosa	10
Piscidia erythrina	20	Scutalleria lateriflora	20
Chamomilla recutita	15		
			90 ml

For joint pain and inflammation

Fucus vesiculosis	15	Betula alba	15
Salix alba	15	Dioscorea villosa	15
Viburnum opulus	10	Withania somniferum	10
Boswellia carterii	10	Zanthoxylim spp.	10
			100 ml

For depression and digestive disturbance

Chamomilla recutita	15	Leonurus cardiaca	20
Melissa officinalis	20	Verbena officinalis	20
Gentiana lutea	5	Hypericum perforatum	20
			100 ml

For brain-fog impaired memory

Ginkgo biloba	20	Vinca major	10
Centella asiatica	15	Verbena officinalis	10
Rosmarinus officinalis	10	Avena sativa	10
Mentha piperita	10	Baccopa monierra	10
Acorus calamus	5		
			100 ml

Note: Where there is poor sleep at night and fatigue during the day it is best to design two different formulas: one for morning and one for nighttime use.

Demulcent herbs for the digestive system
Astringent tonics for the digestive system
Anti-*Candida* agents
Gentle sedative analgesics
Muscle-relaxing analgesics
Stronger analgesic herbs with a central nervous system effect
Topical muscle relaxants
Warming muscle relaxants
Antispasmodic herbs for the urinary tract
Demulcents for the urinary tract
Antispasmodic herbs for the digestive system

Adaptogens and Tonics

Adaptogens increase the resistance of the body to stress, whether it be physical, emotional, biological, or chemical. They enhance the restoration of homeostasis and reduce the debilitating effect of chronic disease. Often they increase available energy and vital force without taxing the system. Frequently they exhibit balancing or regulating actions. For example, ashwagandha (*Withania somniferum*) can be used to improve energy through the day and to encourage sleep at night.

These herbs are of paramount importance in FMS. With more energy, one will feel better all over. Some herbs have a long and rich history as adaptogens, such as licorice, Siberian ginseng, and ashwagandha; others, such as alfalfa, kelp, oats, nettle, and gotu kola, are nourishing herbs. Some adaptogens are believed to work through the presence of triterpenes, which may interact with hormonal receptor sites much as the steroidal saponins do. In many cases, though, we are still not clear what the active constituents are, but we see empirical evidence of their efficacy through hundreds of years of successful use. Adaptogens are especially popular in Asian medicine, where they are often referred to as the "harmony" herb in a formula. Korean ginseng has been shown to act directly in the hypothalamus, the region of the brain that governs the production and release of many hormones from the pituitary gland. Others may work more directly in the adrenal glands, and still others by as yet unknown mechanisms.

Adaptogenic Herbs

Borago officinalis (Borage)

Eleutherococcus senticosus (Siberian ginseng)

Ganoderma lucidum (Reishi)

Glycyrrhiza glabra (Licorice)

Oplopanax horridum (Devil's club)

Panax ginseng (Korean ginseng)

Panax quinquefolium (American ginseng)

Pfaffia paniculata (Suma)

Rhodiola rosea (Arctic rose)

Schizandra chinensis (Wu Wei Zi)

Verbena officinalis (Blue vervain)

Withania somniferum (Ashwagandha)

Alteratives

In times past there was a popular health concept called "bad blood," which implied that some foreign, toxic material had entered the system and that cleansing was called for. In the wider, more modern view, depuratives—or cleansing herbs—are called "alteratives." They act to alter the metabolic processes in various ways so that assimilation and elimination, anabolism, and catabolism are regulated and balanced. Alteratives may act on any of the organs of elimination: the liver and biliary system, lymph vessels and glands, bowel, lungs, skin, or renal and urinary system.

The alteratives, along with lymphatic and circulatory stimulants, are especially effective in promoting tissue detoxification. By providing increased blood flow to an area and improved lymphatic drainage, and by stimulating liver detoxification reactions, this class of herbs can be an effective part of a cleansing program. Diuretic herbs may be helpful in removing acid wastes from the body.

Generally speaking, an alterative herb acts as a stimulant to the processes of cellular metabolism, aiding in the uptake of useful, nutritive substances and the elimination of waste products, toxins, and unwanted materials. This helps the body to maintain optimum biochemical balance and to heal from disease. Thus alteratives are the quintessential herbs of physiological support. Although there are many different alteratives with specific effects upon various parts of the body, they typically appear to act via the liver and kidneys, which are the major organs of cleansing and elimination. Some alteratives stimulate lymphatic function, further aiding the removal of toxins from the tissues. Alteratives are frequently bitter in taste and this is often the key to their activity. The bitterness triggers a reflex nerve response that stimulates all digestive functions: salivation; production of hydrochloric acid, mucus, digestive enzymes, and bile; liver functions; and peristalsis. It is important to taste this bitterness in order to elicit the beneficial effects. Do not gulp down this medicine or disguise the flavor with sweeteners.

Most people in the modern world, with or without FMS, accumulate a load of toxins in their systems, the residue of agricultural and industrial pollution in the food chain, the water, and the air. We almost all carry such loads; it is the price we pay for the privilege of living in the postindustrial age. In all cases, including FMS, it is helpful to remove some of these stored morbid wastes because they adversely affect liver function, speed up oxidative damage in the tissues, disrupt hormone function, and run down the immune system. Gentle detoxification programs can help here. Do not undertake rigorous fasts or other extreme cleansing methods while you are debilitated and weakened.

The secret is to build and cleanse, build and cleanse. In fact, fasting longer than one to three days is rarely necessary or advisable for people with FMS because they will become chilled, depleted, and more run down. What they need is not so much a short, intense detoxification program, but rather a new way of eating and drinking that enhances tissue cleansing and builds energy, a new diet plan for ongoing health and well-being. A mild to moderate cleansing program followed by sensible eating thereafter can help to reduce acids and metabolic wastes accumulating in the tissues and contributing to trigger points and muscle stiffness or arthritis. A healthy diet can be optimized by the use of bitter herbs to stimulate digestive functions and promote improved assimilation of nutrients. Some of these, such as blue vervain and rosemary, serve other useful functions as well. Some, such as dandelion greens or burdock root, can be added to food.

Alterative Herbs for Musculoskeletal Disorders
Bitter Hepatic Stimulants
Arctium lappa (Burdock)
Berberis vulgaris (Barberry)
Rumex crispus (Yellow dock)
Taraxacum officinalis folia (Dandelion leaf)

Lymphatic Stimulants
Fucus vesiculosis (Kelp)
Galium aparine (Cleavers)
Urtica dioica (Nettle)
Calendula officinalis (Marigold)

Alteratives Herbs for the Joints
(reduce acid deposits, regulate metabolism)
Equisetum arvense (Horsetail)
Guaiacum officinalis (Lignum vitae)
Harpagophytum procumbens (Devil's claw)

Diuretics

A great many herbs are considered diuretic, although only a few are truly strong enough to produce increased urine output in a normal, healthy kidney. Where there is metabolic overload and accumulation of acid wastes, several diuretic herbs are especially effective in encouraging the elimination of uric acid via the kidneys. This is of great benefit in treating musculoskeletal disorders because accumulation of acid wastes is a major contributor to muscle stiffness and the development of tender points. I have not found that any particular herbs can aid the body in eliminating phosphates, so herbs cannot be used as an adjunct to or replacement for the guaifenesin treatment discussed in Chapter 4.

Diuretic Herbs That Encourage Uric Acid Removal
   Apium graveolens (Celery)
   Betula alba (Birch)
   Filipendula ulmaris (Meadowsweet)
   Petroselinum crispum (Parsley)

Anti-inflammatories

In FMS there is often low-grade, localized, subclinical inflammation in the muscles, frequently along with arthritic changes in the joints. The use of herbal anti-inflammatories can be very helpful here. Interestingly, some of the best anti-inflammatories have other very important health benefits: licorice and turmeric are also an adaptogen and a liver agent, respectively; willow is also an analgesic; and meadowsweet can help if the stomach is irritated from nonsteroidal anti-inflammatories such as aspirin and acetaminophen.

Inflammation is the body's normal response to injury or irritation and simply suppressing it will often do more harm than good, as the natural healing response is inhibited and resolution does not occur. Herbal anti-inflammatories do not inhibit the bodily reactions, but actually nourish and support the body in its attempt to deal with the problem. Perhaps we should call them "pro-inflammatories" because they may actually stimulate the immune response, which is a required step before complete healing can occur.

How herbal anti-inflammatories actually work is only partially understood. There are six basic groupings based on known chemical constituents, although the isolated extracts only rarely seem to have anti-inflammatory properties. Apparently, for many therapeutic benefits to occur the whole plant is needed.

Salicin

Salicylates are all converted in the body into salicylic acid, which interacts with the enzymes that mediate inflammation.

The richest source of salicylates is in the willows (*Salix spp.*) and poplars (*Populus spp.*). Additionally, the *Viburnums* have significant amounts. There are five hundred species of willow and thirty-five of poplar and probably all have some medicinal value, but the ones typically found in commerce are white and black willow, and balsam poplar. These contain salicylates, the active form of which is salicylic acid, a potent mediator of the inflammatory response. Inflammation is regulated by a series of chemicals called *prostaglandins*. These can be thought of as microhormones, having a life span of less than a minute and acting locally in the tissues in which they are produced. Prostaglandins are made from essential fatty acids in a cascade reaction requiring many enzymes. (See Chapter 5 for more details on prostaglandin formation and effects.) Salicylates (and ibuprofen) inhibit the metabolic processes that result in inflammation.

Willow and other salicylate-rich plants have been used traditionally and with good results for arthritis inflammations.

For the person with FMS the problem encountered when using high amounts of salicylates is that the thermogenic effect tends to promote the use of protein as a fuel and this catabolic effect can acidify the system. Willow is traditionally not recommended for gout because of this. People with FMS are often very sensitive to increased acid load. It is therefore recommended that these very effective, non-habit-forming herbal anti-inflammatories be used only for a few days at a time, as needed.

It is important to note that people using the drug guaifenesin must completely abstain from using any herbs with salicylates for the duration of their treatment.

Salicylates are somewhat analgesic through an action on the pain perception centers in the brain. Methyl salicylate, the active ingredient of wintergreen (*Gaultheria procumbens*), is used topically as a powerful analgesic and anti-inflammatory.

Herbs Notably Rich in Salicylates and Traditionally Used as Anti-inflammatories

Filipendula ulmaris (Meadowsweet)
Gaultheria procumbens (Wintergreen)
Populus spp. (Poplar)
Salix spp. (Willow)
Viburnum prunifolium (Black haw)

Saponins

Saponins are glycosides with a steroid or triterpenoid skeleton. The steroidal form are structurally related to cholesterol, vitamin D, the sex hormones, and cortisol. The steroidal saponins from wild yams, soybeans, and sisal are used commercially to make the drug cortisone.

Both steroidal and triterpenoid forms of saponin appear to interact with hormones in the body and many have anti-inflammatory effects. The exact mode of action of the saponins is not yet clear, and ingestion of plants rich in saponins does not lead directly to increased circulating levels of cortisol, progesterone, or any other sterol-based substance. The steroidal saponin from the plant is very small compared to the body's own (endogenous) sterol molecules, so it has been suggested that the tiny plant molecule enters the receptor site for the hormone on the target tissue and acts as a partial agonist to "prime" the receptor site so it will respond more rapidly when the endogenous molecule enters it. In this way the plant molecule could promote the effect of the hormone without affecting the actual hormone levels.

In the case of the anti-inflammatory herbs it is likely that the steroidal saponins are interacting with receptors for cortisol and potentiating the effect of the endogenous hormone. Additionally, it is known that licorice inhibits an enzyme that normally catalyzes the conversion of active cortisol to inactive cortisone. This will have a sparing effect on the adrenals and in this way may help to down-regulate the hypothalamic-pituitary-adrenal axis.

Herbs Notably Rich in Triterpenoid Saponins
Traditionally Used as Anti-inflammatories
> *Bupleurum falcatum* (Chinese thoroughwax)
> *Glycyrrhiza glabra* (Licorice)

Herbs Notably Rich in Steroidal Saponins
Traditionally Used as Anti-inflammatories
> *Dioscorea villosa* (Wild yam)
> *Smilax spp.* (Sarsaparilla)
> *Trigonella foenum-graecum* (Fenugreek)
> *Yucca spp.* (Yucca)

Essential Oils

The essential, or volatile, oil of a plant may be very complex, containing several hundred different substances. Many essential oils are notably anti-inflammatory. They are usually applied topically in the form of liniments, lotions, baths, compresses, and massage oils. The monoterpene volatile oils have a counterirritant effect when applied over an inflammation. They cause local vasodilation and skin reddening. This approach has traditionally been used to bring increased circulation to an injured area, providing increased availability of oxygen and leucocytes, thereby stimulating the healing response. Both menthol and camphor are monoterpene volatile oils with a notable cooling effect that relieves pain. The sesquiterpene volatile oils are especially effective in reducing histamine-induced inflammation and as such are noted for their antiallergenic qualities. Certain essential oils from chamomile and *Guaiacum officinalis* are examples of sesquiterpene volatile oils that are anti-inflammatory to joints and muscles.

Herbs Rich in Volatile Oils
Traditionally Used as Anti-inflammatories
    Achillea millefolium (Yarrow)
    Betula alba/lenta (Silver/sweet birch)
    Chamomilla recutita (Chamomile)
    Cinnamonum camphora (Camphor cinnamon)
    Curcuma longa (Turmeric)
    Guaiacum officinalis (Lignum vitae)
    Juniperus communis (Juniper)
    Melaleuca leucadendron (Cajuput)
    Myristica fragrans (Nutmeg)
    Rosmarinus officinalis (Rosemary)
    Tanacetum parthenium (Feverfew)
    Zingiber officinalis (Ginger)

Another group of volatile compounds with noted anti-inflammatory action are those containing sulfur, found in garlic and onions, and the various mustard oil glycosides, which yield strongly rubefacient breakdown products.

Herbs Rich in Sulfur-Containing Volatile Compounds
Traditionally Used as Anti-inflammatories
    Allium sativa (Garlic)
    Allium cepa (Onion)
    Armoracea rusticana (Horseradish)
    Brassica niger/alba (Black/white mustard)

Essential Fatty Acids

Prostaglandins are responsible for mediating the inflammatory response in the tissues. They are made from essential fatty acids in a cascade reaction requiring many enzymes. Adequate provision of the essential fatty acids is required and they need to be in the correct ratio (omega-3:omega-6). Including flax, walnut, and safflower oils in the diet will be beneficial, as discussed in Chapter 5.

The availability of the enzymes responsible for catalyzing the cascade of conversions serves as a rate-limiting factor in the formation of prostaglandins. Many factors may adversely affect the first enzyme in the cascade, delta 6 desaturase. These include chronic stress, use of steroid drugs, hypercholesterolemia, ionizing radiation, very low dietary protein, increasing age, presence of saturated fats and transfatty acids in the diet, alcohol consumption, and blood sugar imbalances. If the body is deficient in this enzyme, then the fatty acids taken in the diet will not be adequately converted and prostaglandin imbalances and deficiencies may occur. Many of the prostaglandins are regulators of the inflammatory response and without them chronic inflammatory states can develop.

Fish oils and certain plant oils are exceptionally rich in fatty acids that can enter the cascade below delta 6 desaturase and thus allow the formation of more anti-inflammatory prostaglandins. They form an important part of the therapeutic protocol for such diverse conditions as eczema, multiple sclerosis, asthma, premenstrual syndrome, ulcerative colitis, and arthritis. In treating FMS, essential fatty acids may relieve some of the symptoms of subclinical muscular inflammation as well as definite arthritic changes in the joints.

Herbs Rich in Essential Fatty Acids
Traditionally Used as Anti-inflammatories

Borago officinalis (Borage seed)
Oenothera biennis (Evening primrose seed)
Ribes niger (Black currant seed)

Resins

Resins are complex compounds containing acids, esters, tannins, and alcohols. They are often found in association with oils or gums, or both. Many resins are diterpenes and are frequently left behind after distillation of volatile essential oils. In herbal medicine resins may be applied topically to obtain a counterirritant effect or may be taken internally to obtain a systemic anti-inflammatory effect. *Capsicum minimum* (cayenne) contains an oleoresin rich in a substance called *capsaicin,* which is strongly rubefacient and also reduces sensitivity of pain receptors, probably by down-regulating the production of Substance P.

Herbs Rich in Resins Traditionally Used as Anti-inflammatories

Boswellia carteri (Frankincense)
Capsicum minimum (Cayenne)
Guaiacum officinalis (Lignum vitae)
Liquidamber orientalis (Storax)
Myroxylon balsamum (Tolu balsam)
Myroxylon pereirae (Peru balsam)
Populus balsamifera (Poplar buds)
Styrax benzoin (Benzoin)
Zingiber officinalis (Ginger)

Mucilage

Mucilage is a complex polysaccharide that is said to have a demulcent, or soothing, effect on the mucous membranes of the digestive, respiratory, and urinary tracts when taken internally. When applied externally in the form of a soak, wash, or compress, the effect is said to be emollient. Mucilage in water becomes slippery, almost slimy, and this may be used to coat exposed nerve endings in an injured wound. In this sense it may be considered anti-inflammatory, specific for the gastrointestinal and genitourinary systems and for the skin.

Herbs Rich in Mucilage
Traditionally Used for Soothing the Digestive Tract
  Althea officinalis (Marshmallow)
  Plantago major/lanceolata (Plantain)
  Ulmus rubra (Slippery elm)

Herbs Rich in Mucilage
Traditionally Used for Soothing the Genitourinary Tract
  Agropyron repens (Couch grass)
  Althea officinalis (Marshmallow)
  Plantago major/lanceolata (Plantain)
  Zea mais (Corn silk)

Circulatory Stimulants

People with FMS generally feel chilly and are sensitive to the cold. They derive particular benefits from ginger, which is both a peripheral and a central circulatory stimulant, acting to equalize the circulation, preventing both excess and deficiency. Rosemary encourages peripheral and cerebral blood flow and is also slightly bitter, which has a carminative and tonic effect on the digestive system. For a tendency to chilliness, warming foods should be taken—baked root vegetables and squash, soups and stews. Adding black pepper, chili sauce, and other aromatic spices to food is helpful. Warm clothing, aerobic exercise, and hot applications can be helpful with locally impaired circulation.

The central circulatory stimulants (such as black pepper, ginger, cayenne) have a warming influence upon the digestive system and increase circulation to the heart and lung area and the pelvic basin. They are considered to be especially beneficial when using alteratives and undertaking a detoxification program, and by promoting circulation to the adrenal glands, they may be considered a tonic and stimulant. They are also often included in formulas as an adjuvant to enhance uptake of other herbal agents.

The peripheral circulatory stimulants tend to encourage blood flow to the limbs and head. Herbs that encourage cerebral circulation may be used to counter the effects of "brain fog," poor memory, and lack of mental clarity. In the case of FMS, by improving blood flow to the muscles where there is stagnation and accumulation of acid waste materials, the circulatory stimulants tend to warm and relax the muscles and ease pain. Additionally, white blood cells are provided to fight infection and reduce inflammation by cleaning up inflammatory debris. Hemoglobin can then deliver oxygen to reduce free radical damage and aid tissue healing. Inflammation itself promotes blood flow to the area (hence the redness, heat, and swelling that are the cardinal signs of inflammation). In the case of chronic musculoskeletal inflammations, it may be useful to enhance this process with peripheral circulatory stimulants, as well as with topical applications of rubefacient herbs.

Cerebral Circulatory Stimulants

Centella asiatica (Gotu kola)
Ginkgo biloba (Ginkgo)
Rosmarinus officinalis (Rosemary)
Vinca major/minor (Periwinkle)

Peripheral Circulatory Stimulants

Achillea millefolium (Yarrow)
Capsicum minimum (Cayenne)
Rosmarinus officinalis (Rosemary)
Zanthoxylum clavaherculis/americanum (Prickly ash)
Zingiber officinalis (Ginger)

Central Circulatory Stimulants

Achillea millefolium (Yarrow)
Capsicum minimum (Cayenne)
Zingiber officinalis (Ginger)

Warming Tonic Circulatory Stimulants
Marsdenia condurango (Condor plant)
Myrica cerifera (Bayberry)

Rubefacients

Rubefacients are not unlike circulatory stimulants, but they are applied topically. They greatly enhance blood flow into the affected area, which is particularly beneficial in the treatment of joint disease because internal joint surfaces are actually avascular and thus less effectively treated by internal methods. Stiff or sore muscles, as well, can benefit greatly from the additional oxygen and warmth. Rubefacients are used as counterirritants to increase local circulation and promote inflammation and resolution. Essential oils, and especially the volatile sulfur-containing herbs, are often employed for their rubefacient effect.

Herbs Rich in Sulfur-Containing Volatile Compounds Traditionally Used as Rubefacients
Allium sativa (Garlic)
Allium cepa (Onion)
Armoracea rusticana (Horseradish)
Brassica niger/alba (Black/white mustard)

Sialogogues

Herbs that increase salivation can be helpful in cases of dry mouth and Sjogren's syndrome. They include *Echinacea spp.* (echinacea) and *Zanthoxylum spp.* (prickly ash).

Collagen Tonics/Connective Tissue Regenerators

Connective tissue is made of collagen and elastic fibers, each of which contains multiple fine filaments bound together by molecular cross-links. It is the substance that holds all the body tissues together. It is found very widely throughout the body, including fascia, muscles, ligaments, and tendons. Vitamin C and a variety of different flavonoid substances are required for its formation and repair. Some herbs are traditionally reputed to strengthen and nourish the connective tissues of the joints, tendons, ligaments, and muscles. The pharmacological effect is generally accepted as being due to the presence of many flavonoids, which are strongly antioxidant. However, *Equisetum arvense* (horsetail), which is widely considered to be an effective connective tissue rebuilder, is not notably rich in bioflavonoids.

Many practitioners consider FMS to be a connective tissue/fascia disorder and this would indicate the desirability of using herbs to strengthen and nourish these tissues. Many people with FMS also have concurrent arthritic changes. These may come about because of excessive acid waste in the body, from misuse of the joints, or due to hereditary or lifestyle reasons. Where cartilage is damaged, bone can rub on bone and this will provide an ongoing source of irritation and inflammation. Besides the use of anti-inflammatories, certain herbs such as horsetail can be used to strengthen and nourish the cartilage and reduce friction in the joint.

Herbs Traditionally Used as Connective Tissue Regenerators
Centella asiatica (Gotu kola)
Crataegus oxycanthoides (Hawthorn)
Equisetum arvense (Horsetail)
Plantago major/lanceolata (Plantain)
Polygonum multiflorum (Fo ti)
Vaccinium myrtillus (Blueberry)

Muscle Relaxants

In FMS the muscles are significantly affected by impaired circulation, accumulation of acid wastes, chronic tension or contraction of the fibers, and eventual tender-point development. If the muscle can be induced to relax, then blood flow is improved at every level, from artery to capillary. Lymphatic drainage will also increase, helping in the removal of excess fluids and wastes from the tissues. Relaxation will also ease stiffness and pain and can reduce the sensitivity of tender points. Muscle spasms cause the colicky discomfort of irritable bowel syndrome and the urinary urgency and bladder pain of interstitial cystitis, both conditions commonly associated with FMS.

Herbs Used Topically for Muscle Relaxation
    Lobelia inflata (Lobelia)
    Viburnum opulus (Cramp bark)
    Any rubefacient herbs

Herbs That Work As Muscle Relaxants by Increasing Circulation
    Rosmarinus officinalis (Rosemary)
    Zanthoxylum spp. (Prickly ash)
    Zingiber officinalis (Ginger)

Nervines That Have a Central Muscle-Relaxing Effect
    Cannabis sativua (Marijuana)
    Cimicifuga racemosa (Black cohosh)
    Paeonia lactiflora (White peony)
    Piper methysticum (Kava kava)

The carminative herbs are also antispasmodic in the digestive tract. These include aniseed, caraway, cumin, fennel, dill, and cardamom.

Sedatives, Relaxants, and Tonic Nervines

Stress is a major component of FMS. People who don't handle stress well are often more prone to this type of condition. Adrenal burnout is one way to describe it. They put themselves under pressure to perform, then more pressure when they can't live up to that expectation. The stress of being disabled by FMS becomes just one more thing to worry about. Herbs can be very helpful here. They can be used to take the edge off anxiety and improve sleep patterns. They are completely nonaddictive and, except in the case of valerian, won't leave you hungover in the morning even if you take a whole lot. Some of the adaptogens fit in this category as well. It is best not to use hops because although this herb is an effective bitter and sedative, hops may actually contribute to depression. Note that, except for hops, all bitters are slightly antidepressant and uplifting.

Oats should be taken freely, preferably in the form of steel-cut oats (also known as oat groats or coarse oatmeal) soaked overnight in water, simmered ten minutes, and eaten as porridge. Chamomile tea can be found in almost every home and restaurant nowadays and is a pleasant, gentle sedative. It is also, surprisingly, classified as a bitter despite the deceptively sweet taste. The overall effect of the plant is a gentle digestive stimulation.

Gentle, Relaxing Nervines
Chamomilla recutita (Chamomile)
Melissa officinalis (Lemon balm)
Nepeta cataria (Catnip)
Scutalleria lateriflora (Skullcap)
Zizyphus jujube (Jujube date)

Sedative Nervines
Eschscholzia california (California poppy)
Lactuca virosa (Wild lettuce)
Passiflora incarnata (Passionflower)
Piscidia erythrea (Jamaican dogwood)
Valeriana officinalis (Valerian)

Tonic Nervines
Avena sativa (Oats)
Bacopa monniera (Brahmi)

Borago officinalis (Borage)
Centella asiatica (Gotu kola)
Hypericum perforatum (St. John's wort)
Polygonum multiflorum (Fo ti)
Vinca major/minor (Periwinkle)
Verbena officinalis/hastata (Blue vervain)

Analgesics

Analgesics are occasionally necessary for acute or chronic pain. Usually the really effective herbal painkillers are also sedative, which is probably nature's deliberate design to get you to slow down and rest until you are well.

The strongest analgesics work by depressing functions of the central nervous system and, as such, are potentially toxic. Some that were commonly used in the past but are now unavailable for over-the-counter purchase include *Gelsemium sempervirens* (yellow jasmine), *Papaver somniferum* (opium poppy), and *Atropa belladonna* (deadly nightshade). They may be available from a qualified herbalist or naturopath who is trained in their use. For self-medication we rely on gentler herbs. Some of these still work by a depressing effect on the central nervous system, while others may be muscle relaxants, circulatory stimulants, or sedatives or hypnotics.

In the management of chronic pain it is often helpful to relax the patient so that the responses to pain can be minimized. Herbal sedatives and hypnotics are nature's tranquilizers. Unlike their pharmaceutical cousins, though, they are nonaddictive and noncumulative, although overzealous dosing can certainly produce disagreeable effects such as headaches, impaired mental clarity, and confusion. These effects will wear off over several hours as the herb is cleared from the system, but it is recommended that dosing be moderate, especially if given long term.

Many gentle nervine herbs can be effective in treating mild or short-lived pain. These stop short of being true analgesics but do make the pain more bearable and ease the stress associated with pain. They may be particularly helpful in aiding the rest and sleep that is essential to the healing process.

Gentle Sedative Herbs Traditionally Used as Mild Analgesics
   Chamomilla recutita (Chamomile)
   Humulus lupulus (Hops)
   Hypericum perforatum (St. John's wort)
   Lavandula officinalis (Lavender)
   Melissa officinalis (Lemon balm)
   Passiflora incarnata (Passionflower)
   Scutalleria lateriflora (Skullcap)

Muscle-Relaxing Herbs Traditionally Used as Analgesics
   Cannabis sativua (Marijuana)
   Lobelia inflata (Lobelia)
   Piper methysticum (Kava kava)

Stronger Analgesic Herbs with an Effect on the Central Nervous System
   Corydalis ambigua (Yan ho suo)
   Eschscholzia California (California poppy)
   Lactuca virosa (Wild lettuce)
   Piscidia erythrina (Jamaican dogwood)
   Valeriana officinalis (Valerian)

Very Strong Analgesics for Practitioner Use Only
   Atropa belladonna (Deadly nightshade) for digestive spasms and pain
   Hyoscyamus niger (Henbane) for urinary spasms and pain
   Gelsemium sempervirens (Yellow jasmine) for neuralgias and acute pain
   Aconitum napellus (Aconite) for neuralgia and acute pain

Topical Applications

There are many topical treatments that may be of assistance in the treatment of fibromyalgia. These may be applied in the form of fomentations, poultices, or plasters; or as a bath, lotion, or ointment.

Kelp and Capsicum Plasters

These plasters are rubefacient, counterirritant, and nourishing and healing for the joints. They are made by evaporating the alcohol out of cayenne tincture over a water bath, adding powdered kelp and melted beeswax, and then soaking strips of cotton bandage in the resulting liquid. The strips are laid out to dry on newspaper and stored carefully because they are brittle. Before use they are warmed over a radiator or in a very low oven so they may be gently wrapped around the affected joint. They should be covered over with plastic wrap and a heating pad should be applied. Check frequently for excessive reddening of the skin and be sure to remove before any blistering occurs.

Warming Embrocation

Mix together 250 ml each of the infused oils of juniper and comfrey. Add 5 ml each of the following essential oils: juniper, wintergreen, marjoram, and black pepper. Apply over the affected joints as required. For added potency one of the infused oils may be made in castor oil, which penetrates deeply into the underlying tissues. (See Appendix One for an explanation of infusing oils.)

Cramp Ease Liniment

Take the formula for "Warming Embrocation," double the volume of essential oils, and add 250 ml each of the tinctures of lobelia and cramp bark. This can be used for any cramping or spasms of smooth or skeletal muscle, including menstrual cramps, exercise-induced cramps, tension headaches, muscle stiffness, and strains or sprains.

Russian Ointment (thanks to Medical Herbalist Janet Hicks for this recipe)
Melt together 150 ml of sunflower oil and 65 g of grated beeswax. Add 110 g
of lanolin and allow to cool slightly. Add 5 g of camphor powder dissolved
in 75 ml of turpentine oil. Now add 30 ml of methyl salicylate, 10 ml of capsicum tincture forte (made by evaporating alcohol off over a water bath),
35 ml of acetic acid 25 percent, and 5 g borax powder. Stir well, pour into
jars, and allow to set. Apply to joints as needed.

Hayseed Poultice

Hayseed (available from farm supply stores) retains heat very well and so
warms the underlying tissue when applied with moist heat to the skin. It also
contains volatile oils and coumarins, which themselves are rubefacient and
anti-inflammatory. The poultice should be prepared by placing hayseed in a
linen bag or wrapping it in a piece of muslin. This is then soaked for ten minutes in a pan of freshly boiled water. Squeeze out the excess water and place
the poultice over the affected area. Cover with plastic wrap and a heating pad
and leave in place for up to one hour.

Epsom Salts Baths

Epsom salts, or magnesium sulfate, is an old traditional remedy for circulatory insufficiency, lymphatic or liver congestion, arthritis, and all toxemia
conditions. By soaking the whole body or the affected part in a hot solution
of Epsom salts you can encourage blood supply to the area, supplying healing
nutrients and oxygen, and also draw out accumulated toxins, which predispose to irritation and inflammation.

Whole Body Treatment Draw a hot bath and add 2 to 4 cups of Epsom salts.
Get into the bath and keep adding hot water until it is as hot as you can bear.
Stay in the water for fifteen minutes, adding more hot water whenever the
bath cools a little. If you have arthritic joints, scrub the affected joints under
the water until they are red and tingling, using a soft brush. When you are
ready to get out of the bath, don't dry yourself. Just wrap up in an old sheet

and go straight to bed. Protect the mattress with a rubber sheet or lie on an old towel, and then pile on blankets and use a hot water bottle. The goal is for you to sweat all night, excreting many toxins through the skin. The sheet you are wrapped in may become quite stained.

Repeat this process once a week until the sheet is no longer stained in the morning, indicating that you are now excreting normally through the skin and have greatly reduced your toxin load.

Localized Treatment Use about ½ cup of Epsom salts to 4 cups of water. Place the salts in a basin and pour on hot water. Immerse the hands, feet, or elbows in the basin and soak for fifteen minutes. Do not dry afterward; allow the part to air dry or wrap in a cotton bandage to preserve the heat. For more awkward parts of the body (knee or shoulder), use a flannel cloth wrung out in the solution and laid directly over the skin, as hot as you can bear. Keep wringing out the flannel and make sure it stays hot.

CHAPTER SEVEN

ADJUNCTIVE THERAPIES
AND SELF-CARE

The part can never be well
unless the whole is well.
SOCRATES

October 1995

I have started taking Pilates classes and I love it! Kind of like mechanical
yoga—familiar yoga moves but done with a piece of machinery that has straps
and weights and springs and gives you resistance to move against. I am
going three times a week for an hour and it has toned my muscles and is giving
me greater strength and endurance. I am also walking forty-five minutes
to work or cycling twenty minutes there and back, two to three times a week.
Often I get leg cramps and have to stop a little while, but I persevere
because I know I feel so much better afterward. Exercise seems to clear my
head and give me energy and better sleep. But I have to pace myself
carefully. I am easily exhausted and inclined not to notice my fatigue
until suddenly it is overwhelming and I am about to drop. Still learning to
listen to my body.

191

For many of us the idea of taking responsibility for our own health is a novelty. In today's Western culture, we put responsibility for our health in the hands of doctors and other health care professionals, expecting them to fix all our problems or at least help us to cope with and manage our health crises. There is no emphasis on prevention, good nutrition, or self-care. This is in sharp contrast to the common practice in ancient China of paying the doctor only while the patient was well and ceasing payment if sickness occurred. How different our health care system would look if it was run like that!

Self-care and various mind-body therapies play a major role in healing FMS. Ensuring appropriate exercise and good sleep are probably the most useful things you can do to help yourself. Utilizing bodywork to relax and recondition the muscles and correct structural misalignments will allow unimpeded flow of blood, lymph, energy, and Qi, and reduce sympathetic stress. Accessing the power of the mind to heal the body is empowering and effective.

Many different therapeutic approaches have been used in treating FMS. Generally they modify symptoms or our responses and reactions to them, and some have proven quite effective. Some that research has validated include cardiovascular fitness training, EMG biofeedback, hypnotherapy, regional sympathetic blockade, and cognitive behavioral therapy. Obviously the field is vast and many options exist. I have chosen to write about those with which I have had personal experience, but don't let that limit your choices. Use this book as a springboard to better health through whatever approach works for you.

Sleep Management

The average adult requires approximately eight hours of sleep nightly, although this can vary widely from five or six to ten. Generally, people with FMS require more sleep than most and are often not refreshed even after a long sleep because they do not sleep deeply and soundly. They also often have reversal of normal sleep cycles, whereby they get a "second wind" in the evening and can stay up late, but then cannot get up in the morning. This is actually indicative of chronic and severe adrenal stress because the phenomenon of "second wind" is actually brought about by serotonin release when the adrenals are incapable of responding to energy demands. As described in Chapters 2 and 3, many factors can contribute to sleep disturbance and the impaired sleep will then contribute to many of the symptoms of FMS. (See Figures 7.1 and 7.2.)

Americans average nine days of paid vacation annually and routinely work fifty hours a week. This is in contrast to most other countries where

Psychiatric Disturbance
  Depression
  Anxiety
  Alcohol abuse
  Drug abuse

Medical Causes
  Sleep apnea
  Chronic or acute pain
  Arthritis
  Congestive heart disease
  Asthma
  Chronic obstructive pulmonary
    disease
  Gastrointestinal reflux
  Peptic ulcer
  Hyperthyroidism
  Hypoglycemia
  Nocturnal myoclonus
  Parkinson's disease
  Interstitial or infective cystitis
  Bruxism
  FMS
  Restless leg syndrome

Other Causes
  Excessive napping during the day
  Lack of exercise during the day
  Vigorous exercise near bedtime
  Spousal snoring or movements
  Heavy or spicy food near bedtime
  Fluids near bedtime
  Stimulation (parties, TV)
    near bedtime
  Children or other dependents
    needing attention
  Pets in the bedroom
  Noise or light pollution
  Uncomfortable bed
  Too hot or too cold

Figure 7.1 Possible Causes of Sleep Disturbance

- Antidepressants—especially monoamine oxidase inhibitors and tricyclic antidepressants
- Antihypertensives—beta blockers, clonidine, methyldopa, and reserpine
- Sympathomimetic amines—amphetamines, appetite suppressants, caffeine, beta adrenergic agonists, cocaine, decongestants, and antihistamines
- Barbiturates and hypnotics
- Marijuana and other street drugs
- Nicotine
- Alcohol
- Corticosteroids
- Levodopa
- Oral contraceptives
- Phenytoin
- Quinidine
- Theophylline
- Thyroid medications

Figure 7.2 Drugs That May Disturb Sleep

four or even six weeks of vacation is normal and the workweek is thirty-five to forty hours. In a typical American household, the husband and wife are now working five hundred more hours per year than they did in 1980. Men between the ages of thirty-five and fifty-seven who take annual vacations are 21 percent less likely to die young than age-matched control nonvacationers, and 32 percent less likely to die of coronary disease. Many of us are working too hard and making ourselves sick by it.

In many parts of the world—all around the Mediterranean, throughout Africa, Asia, and South America—an afternoon siesta is the norm. In northern Europe and allied cultures such as Canada and the United States, the notion of taking an afternoon nap is seen as luxurious, self-indulgent, slothful, even a little bit sinful. It goes against the ingrained work ethic and is rarely admitted to except as some sign of weakness and failing. This says a lot about our culture and our society. On a purely physiological level, the only problem with napping is that if you sleep too long you will enter deeper sleep from which it is harder to waken and which can leave you feeling groggy.

When you feel tired the body is sending a message that you need rest. This message is being sent for a reason. For the person with FMS, a short nap is a necessity, not a luxury. As described in Chapter 3, during the deepest phase of sleep growth hormone is released under the influence of melatonin, which causes the liver to release insulin-like growth factor for repair of muscle tissue. Even though you won't reach delta phase sleep in a short afternoon nap, and even though melatonin and hence growth hormone won't be released without darkness, napping in the day can shorten the lag time from entering sleep at night to commencing delta sleep. In other words, napping in the day can give you deeper and more restful sleep at night. If you are sleepy and you have an opportunity to nap during the day, by all means lie down for a half hour or so. Set a limit of twenty to thirty minutes so that you don't go into the deeper phases and wake up feeling groggy. Use an eye shade or a silk eye pillow filled with lavender and flax seeds; it will help you relax more deeply.

Tips to Improve Sleep

- Schedule an hour at the end of the evening for bedtime preparation. This will allow you time to unwind, relax, and get yourself in the mood for sleep.
- Set a regular bedtime and stick to it as much as possible. Up to thirty minutes' variance is okay, but try not to be later than this. The body usually responds well to routine. This doesn't preclude the occasional party, but know that you will probably pay for it the next day and need a few days to reestablish the routine again.
- Ensure that your bed is really comfortable. Sleep in the biggest bed you

can so that you never feel crowded. Get a good mattress and box spring. The mattress should be firm and you can top it with a egg-crate foam pad or a sheepskin cover if you have sensitive places that feel pressed in the night. Use cotton flannel sheets for immediate warmth when you get in bed. Use a hot water bottle if you are chilly (not an electric blanket because of electromagnetic frequencies). Use a warm, light quilt, not heavy blankets. If you want a blanket as well, use one with a waffle weave, which is warm and light. Make sure you have the best pillow you can buy. Try the contoured ones that are available from chiropractors or medical stores. Use a long, firm pillow between your knees when you lie on your side and under your knees when you lie on your back. This supports and protects the sacroiliac joints.

- Keep the bedroom cool with some fresh air, but no drafts. Consider using a humidifier if you live in a dry climate. Use aromatherapy to scent the room—lavender, orange blossom, rosewood.
- Prepare to sleep by turning out all the lights and using candles for the last hour before you go to bed. This will slowly adjust the brain chemistry to night mode. Be sure to sleep in absolute darkness. Use heavy curtains or wear an eye mask. Do not use digital bedside clocks and avoid night lights. If you must have a night light to see the way to the bathroom, position it low on the ground and do not look at it when you get up in the night.
- Have a warm bath scented with lavender before bed, light a candle, listen to soft music—make it a ritual.
- Avoid watching TV for a couple of hours before bed and don't read thrillers or scary books in the evenings.
- Nighttime hypoglycemia can waken people, so have a light snack before bed. Turkey, milk, soybeans, lentils, and tuna are all good food sources of tryptophan, which can hasten and deepen sleep.
- Take relaxing and sedative herbs.
- A magnesium and calcium supplement in the dosage range of 250 to 750 mg at night can relax muscles and ease leg cramps or restless leg syndrome.

- Avoid drinking alcohol to induce sleep. Avoid all caffeinated products—coffee, tea, cocoa, chocolate, kola nut, many sodas, guarana. Note that many over-the-counter medications such as painkillers and cold care products contain caffeine; read the labels.
- If possible, don't keep a clock in the bedroom. If you must see the time in the morning, or be woken by the alarm, then keep it in a place where you cannot see it from the bed. Resist the urge to check the time when you waken in the night and can't go back to sleep. This just creates stress and tension.
- Use the time waiting to fall asleep for a meditation practice, guided visualization, to imagine pleasant and happy things, or for any other thoughts that are positive and creative. Try not to use the time to rehash the day or plan tomorrow; avoid worrying and fretting.
- Use a relaxation technique from yoga. Lying on your back, hands loosely by your sides, feel your body getting very heavy and soft. Start with your feet and work slowly up the body, imagining each part relaxing, loosening, lengthening, softening, and becoming very heavy. Let your face and head relax, too, then watch the mind slip away.
- If there is a lot of noise, wear earplugs or listen to soft, instrumental music or sounds of nature.
- Don't exercise within three hours of bedtime. It is stimulating, invigorating, and will keep you awake.
- If you grind your teeth, get fitted for a night guard or splint. Be sure to have it made for the lower jaw. Splints on the upper jaw lock the bony plates of the skull into one position and inhibit the natural rhythmic contraction and expansion of the skull that moves cerebrospinal fluid around the brain and spinal cord.
- Reserve the bedroom for sleeping, meditation, and lovemaking. Don't use it to watch TV, read, work, make phone calls, and so on. Try to reserve it as a special space that is tranquil and calm.
- When you first waken in the morning, try to stay awake. Don't hit the snooze button on the alarm clock. Drifting in and out of sleep in the

morning will disrupt the wakening cue and make you groggy. Get up, go outside, and look up into the morning sky for a minute, with no windows, eye glasses, or contact lenses to filter the light. This will switch off the melatonin production and start the daytime boost of serotonin.

Light Therapy and the Serotonin/Melatonin Balance

One of the crucial elements in FMS is daytime serotonin deficiency. Serotonin is a neurotransmitter that concentrates in certain neurons of the brain stem. Made from the amino acid tryptophan and generally excitatory, serotonin regulates sensory perception, including pain control, mood, and temperature regulation. It induces sleep through its onward conversion into melatonin. In advanced cases of serotonin deficiency, severe depression and disturbance of all stages of sleep are known to occur.

Supplementation with serotonin is not helpful because it doesn't cross the blood-brain barrier. However, tryptophan may be taken to boost production of serotonin. A double-blind study with supplements of 5-hydroxy-tryptophan in FMS showed very positive results. Additional supplementation with vitamin B_6, magnesium, and niacin will aid in this conversion.

Tryptophan is absorbed into the hepatic portal circulation from the gut by active transport mechanisms that it shares with several other amino acids. Thus, eating a protein-rich meal may not result in elevated tryptophan, as the other amino acids will be absorbed preferentially. However, tryptophan supplementation coupled with a high-carbohydrate meal will result in improved serum tryptophan levels and consequent elevation of serotonin. A normal daily supplement of tryptophan would be in the range of 250 to 500 mg. For chronic or severe pain, depression, or insomnia, however, a dose of up to 3,000 mg may be required. Excessive serotonin can act as a stimulant, so really high dosing with tryptophan may be counterproductive and cause you to feel more wired and less able to relax or sleep.

Decreases in estrogen can also cause disruption of tryptophan metabolism and reduced serotonin production. Certain forms of premenstrual syndrome, characterized by depression, as well as postpartum depression and hypothyroid depression are associated with a relative excess of progesterone, relative deficiency of estrogen, and consequent deficiency of serotonin.

Two of the key elements to regulating serotonin production are appropriate intensity and duration of light. Over the eons of evolution, before the advent of electricity, we adapted our activities and sleep to the seasons. We were exposed to the sun daily and our physiology adjusted according to the intensity and duration of natural light received. We generally slept less in the summer and more in the winter. We tended to be outside a lot more than we are today and hence had greater exposure to the sun overall. In the modern world, where sunlight is filtered by windows and sunglasses, where we spend much of our time indoors, and where we are exposed to electric light more than sunlight, our natural rhythms are disrupted. We stay up later at night and sleep an average of one to two hours less per night than did our ancestors; that adds up to seven to fourteen hours less per week.

No wonder we feel tired! This lack of natural sunlight and overexposure to artificial lights that do not carry all the spectrum of light rays results in less melatonin being produced at night; it also leads to less serotonin being produced in the day in response to lack of sunlight, and a consequent relative excess of melatonin in the daytime which contributes to daytime fatigue.

The classic example of this is seen in the condition known as seasonal affective disorder (SAD). This is a type of depression affecting approximately 1 percent of the population in northern climates, with three times more women affected than men. People with SAD are depressed, weepy and moody, lethargic and sleepy, crave carbohydrates and sugars, and experience loss of libido. All these symptoms occur between November and March and are relieved by regular exposure to sunlight. The further away from the equator the person lives, the worse will be the symptoms and the longer they will last each year.

People with FMS often suffer from some degree of SAD and commonly report that their symptoms are worse in the winter or on cloudy days. Daily exposure to sunlight, without any filter or shade, is the best way to stimulate daytime serotonin production and to set the melatonin-induced sleep-wake cycles. If this is impossible due to inclement weather or physical disability, artificial lights can be used. To trigger serotonin release with full-spectrum lights that contain all known light wavelengths, exposure to 2,500 lux is required—equivalent to 2,500 candles. To achieve the same result with lights that are not full spectrum, 100,000 lux is needed. To put this in context, a cloudy winter day has a light intensity equivalent to about 4,000 lux. The easiest way to use light therapy, aside from being outdoors as much as possible, is to mount a series of three or four full-spectrum light tubes on a board and place the board in the room where you spend the most time. Several times a day you should look into the light for a few moments, without glasses or contact lenses. Carry the board from room to room as needed. You can also replace regular lightbulbs with full-spectrum ones so that you get a low level of exposure all the time.

Mind-Body Medicine

The following material on various mind-body therapies for FMS are written by experts in each field. These are all therapists whom I consulted on my healing journey, but many other forms of alternative healing may also help.

Psychospiritual Healing
Joanne Fallow, Vancouver, British Columbia

Joanne has over thirty years' experience in clinical psychology and indigenous healing ceremonies. She is also a practitioner and teacher in a mystical school akin to Tibetan Buddhism. She teaches, lectures, and has a clinical consultation and healing practice in directing energy to heal the body.

Although the source of FMS is not known, it is apparent that stress is a significant characteristic. This stress can be emotional, mental, or physical. Once the condition of FMS is established, the harmonious functioning of the body is interrupted, producing further stress. Finally there is the additional mental/emotional stress of having a disabling and painful condition that is little understood.

The human organism has a finite capacity for dealing with stress. In day-to-day living we cycle through ever-changing levels of stress. For example, we get the flu and our physical body is stressed, trouble on the job and the mental/emotional bodies are overloaded; but, with a good night's sleep or a holiday in the sun, we regenerate. We are constantly cycling and rebalancing multiple layers of stress within a channel defined by the capacity of our organism to rebalance. When extended multiple high levels of stress combine to prevent the body from carrying out its normal course of rest and recovery, capacity is eventually exceeded. From my personal experience, as well as observation of clients, I have observed that the effect of extended stress is linear up to a point, after which there is a paradigm shift. Before that shift, the way back to health and restedness is also linear—through rest, supplements, etc.; feed the body, feed the soul, and rest. However, once a paradigm shift has occurred the return is no longer linear. A good night's sleep no longer produces a sense of restedness. A holiday in the sun is no longer restorative.

Whatever the source of stress—be it physical, emotional, or mental—stress registers in the physical body as a threat. The physical body responds by preparing the body to do battle or flee the danger—the fight/flight response. The stress response may be acute (initiated by a specific current event), or chronic (a habitual and unconscious response to historic stress). Modern-day stresses are more likely to be produced on the mental or emotional level and a physical response is not appropriate or useful. Rather than being released, the energy provided by one's body remains contained, producing tension in the body. Further, even when the actual threat has passed, the body continues to produce the stress response, maintaining a state of preparedness that eventually leads to exhaustion. Once recognized, the domino nature of the stress response can be used to advantage to initiate a relaxation state. If one in the series of physiological stress responses can be consciously altered, then the domino effect can be reversed, producing a calm, restful state.

Of the physiological processes characterizing the stress response, the most easily accessed is the respiratory system. We cannot easily intervene to slow the heart or inhibit adrenal action, but we can control breath at will. Breath, therefore, is the key for initiating a state of relaxation. Bringing conscious intention to the breath, making it long and slow and full, the body begins to relax, needing less oxygen, thereby allowing the breath to slow further, and so on. This process of slowing the breath requires full attention. Initially there is often a period of interrupted attention as the mind wanders. If it is gently brought back to the breath eventually the relaxation cycle deepens and the mind lets go of its busyness and also comes to rest. In this way breath can be used as a bridge to shift awareness from the conceptual mind to the body. Further, as the focus of the analytical mind settles into awareness of the breath, it serves to bring us into the present moment. Simply by bringing ongoing awareness to our breath and through gentle intention, making the breath fuller and slower, we are able to initiate a state of relaxation, become present in the moment, and focus awareness in the body. The resulting reduction in stress is beneficial on all levels: physical, emotional, and mental.

Our emotional history is carried in our bodies, and when we journey in for the purpose of healing it is likely that unresolved emotional issues will make themselves known. If present, they are the first layer of work that must be done in order to facilitate the flow of energy. In the Tibetan view of health, it is said that the root of all illness is blocked energy. In my practice I have often found that the character of the blocked energy is unresolved emotional history. This has been particularly so with the clients I have worked with who have chronic fatigue and FMS. When this is the case, it is difficult, if not impossible, for the individual to practice mind-body techniques without addressing the emotional blocks. Such individuals are advised to work with a therapist who does a nonanalytical, body-centered form of therapy as a first stage of healing.

Guided imagery, properly and repeatedly used in the body, can also be very effective. But even without the imagery, healing can be accelerated simply by focusing awareness in the body. Literally where you place your awareness in your body there is a buildup of Qi (life force energy). Simply relax the body, bring awareness to the body, and move it to the injury or symptom site.

Guided Visualization

You may want to record this piece onto a cassette that can be played as you deeply relax.

1. Lying in a warm, comfortable room, allow your breath to settle into a long, slow, full, even, and relaxed pattern; then continue to breathe in this way as you move through the following steps.
2. Focus your awareness in your solar plexus and imagine a square yellow topaz radiating a brilliant yellow light of warm, peaceful security.
3. With three long, slow, full breaths feel the brilliant yellow light of warm, peaceful security expand to fill your body.
4. With three long, slow, full breaths feel the brilliant yellow light of warm, peaceful security expand to surround you, enclosing you inside an egg of energy.
5. With three long, slow, full breaths feel yourself as a body of yellow light floating inside an egg of light, surrounded by and infused with the brilliant yellow light of warm, peaceful security.
6. With three long, slow, full breaths feel that the egg of light becomes set and that it remains with you.
7. With three long, slow, full breaths focus your awareness on the square yellow topaz in your solar plexus radiating a brilliant yellow light of warm, peaceful security.

Repeat this process until you feel fully relaxed.

Therapeutic Bodywork

Chiropractic
Else Larsen, D.C., Vancouver, British Columbia

Else graduated from the Canadian Memorial Chiropractic College in Toronto in 1983 and has been in clinical practice in Vancouver since 1984. She is a certified instructor in sacro-occipital techniques and also holds a diploma in chiropractic orthopedics. Else has served on the board of the British Columbia College of Chiropractors since 1991 and currently serves as vice president and chair of the Standards of Practice Committee.

The science of chiropractic is a branch of the healing arts that is concerned with the restoration and maintenance of health through adjustments of the joints of the body, and is involved primarily with the relationship of the spinal column to the nervous system. The central concern of the profession has been the effect of improper function of the spinal vertebrae (due to subluxation) on the function and expression of the nervous system and, to a lesser extent, on the vascular system—vital elements that are intimately linked to the spine.

Chiropractic is not only interested in specific ailments. It has pioneered the holistic approach to health care now widely espoused in North America, through chiropractic education and practice in the areas of nutrition, lifestyle, exercise habits, sleeping habits, lifting techniques, and more. To the chiropractor, wellness is the state of health where the body is free of interruption or interference to any part of the nervous system, enabling the person to have full expression and enjoyment of life. Chiropractic philosophy uses the term *innate intelligence* to describe the guiding force that exists in all living matter. The chiropractor enables the innate intelligence by removing interferences of the nervous system. Chiropractic does not use drugs or surgery. Since its origins, the profession has always offered more conservative approaches, relying upon the body's natural ability to fight disease and achieve stable health. The guiding belief is that individuals have the ability to heal within themselves.

Doctors of chiropractic are primary health care providers, meaning that they see patients directly without the need for a medical referral. The chiropractor uses various methods of diagnosis, including a specialized history; general examination, including neurological and orthopedic tests; comprehensive static and motion palpation; and x-rays. The major therapy is manual adjustment or manipulation of the spine and extremities. Adjunctive therapies include the use of massage, heat, light, ultrasound, electrotherapy, specialized exercise programs, and nutritional advice.

Since most people with FMS experience a lot of musculoskeletal pain, chiropractic can play a significant role in helping a person to function better. By reducing spinal subluxations, chiropractic can be of benefit in treating symptoms of headaches, back pain, neck pain, and stiffness; shoulder, arm, or leg stiffness and pain; numbness in the hands or feet; and nervous tension. Many people report improved sleep after chiropractic treatment. Other benefits include pain reduction, increased mobility, and a general sense of well-being.

Since FMS is a complex condition, I have found that treating a person in cooperation with other health care providers has been beneficial. It is necessary to tailor treatment protocol to each individual. A person may be better able to tolerate more vigorous treatments on some days than others and the chiropractor must vary and change treatment style depending on the sensitivity and pain level of the individual on any given day. Most patients with FMS will need to receive chiropractic care on a regular basis. Since this condition can persist for years, maximum benefit is obtained from continued and consistent care.

Shiatsu Therapy
Fernando Cabrera, C.S.P., Vancouver, British Columbia

Fernando has been practicing shiatsu since 1992 and is a member of the Shiatsu Therapy Association of British Columbia. He is an instructor of shiatsu therapy and a clinical supervisor for the student training program.

Shiatsu is an ancient healing art based on the concept of energy flow through the body, and blocks to such flow. It has flourished in Asia for over five thousand years. *Shiatsu* is a Japanese word meaning precise finger pressure applied to specific parts of the body. It balances body and mind and triggers our own innate healing powers.

In traditional Oriental medicine, achieving and maintaining health depends on the strong and uninhibited flow of Qi, or vital force. Qi circulates to all parts of the body and mind through meridians, or energy channels. Disease, discomfort, fatigue, depression, and emotional distress can all be caused by blockage or interruption to the free flow of Qi energy. The finger pressure in shiatsu is applied over these channels or pathways and can unblock and stimulate the flow. Shiatsu can be used to restore balance and harmony, improve overall well-being, and enhance health.

In the treatment of fibromyalgia, shiatsu can help on several levels. Simply putting pressure on the specific points of the meridians can cause endorphin release and hence improve pain management. Several meridians are commonly found to be imbalanced in FMS: the triple heater, gallbladder, and spleen meridians. The triple heater meridian regulates the movement of Qi energy through all the other meridians. The gallbladder meridian is connected to the emotional attitudes of the individual; in particular, the emotion of anger. Imbalances of the gallbladder meridian cause fatigue and stiff muscles in the neck and shoulders. The spleen meridian is sensitive to damp environments, and certain health conditions may trigger imbalances or blockages in the flow of Qi through the spleen meridian. Such conditions are considered to be energetically cold and the patient often feels chilly and doesn't tolerate cold or damp climates.

These three meridians pass through the neck, shoulders, and upper back, all classic sites for FMS tender points. Often the shiatsu point is concurrent with an FMS tender point and shiatsu therapy can offer significant relief from tender-point pain. Shiatsu can also be helpful for treating headaches, low energy, stress, anxiety, neck and shoulder stiffness, insomnia, fatigue, and digestive disturbance.

Massage Therapy
Lori Johnson, R.M.T., Vancouver, British Columbia

Lori has been in private practice for ten years in Vancouver, British Columbia. She has studied pregnancy massage, craniosacral massage, and yoga therapy.

Massage has been used as a form of healing since the beginning of history. People from every part of the world have developed unique styles, but the final objective is the same—to enhance wellness. Swedish massage is one form that rehabilitates tissues by increasing blood circulation and flexibility, decreasing pain and spasm in the muscles, and calming the nervous system. Patients with FMS find that massage therapy is a very effective way of managing their muscle pain, fatigue, and stiffness. There are some specific techniques of massage to be employed when working with FMS. First, the therapist needs to take a complete case history to understand the patient's injuries and/or accidents. Pain tolerance should be discussed so both the therapist and the patient realize to what degree the client is suffering. It is important to move into the pain to a tolerable level and not to exceed that level, especially with FMS patients. Then the therapist will assess the client for range of motion, muscle tenderness, and posture. Based on the findings and information from the case history, the therapist will put together a treatment plan. The actual massage may include a variety of techniques, all of which will decrease symptoms and increase the health of the patient.

The first technique when working with FMS patients is a relaxing Swedish massage. This involves long strokes, circular movements, and squeezing and compressing the muscles. This helps to reduce spasm, increase circulation, improve flexibility, and prepare the body for deeper massage that will ultimately reduce pain, remove scar tissue, and allow nerve activity to regain its normal function. Heat is used to relax the muscles before deeper work.

Tender points are one of the characteristics that help to diagnose FMS. They are hypersensitive, palpable points in the muscle tissue. They can be active, meaning causing pain, or latent, meaning present but not causing pain. Tender points can become inactive by using a static, constant pressure directly on the point. By holding the point for six to fifteen seconds the pain will begin to subside. This technique can be intense for the patient, so the therapist should move into the tender point slowly so as not to cause too much pain. When receiving this kind of therapy the patient should take deep breaths directly into the hands of the therapist. This helps to keep the patient relaxed even though there is pain and it also calms the nervous system. Once tender points are resolved, often the pain in the muscle also subsides. Tender-point therapy is one of the main techniques to resolve FMS pain. Manual stretching is another technique. It is a simple procedure that involves taking the joint into all its possible ranges of motion and increasing the range by holding the joint to its limit until the muscles relax and then taking the joint a bit further into the stretch. By holding the body part securely, the muscles and nervous system relax.

Sometimes the patient may experience a reaction to the massage treatment, such as feeling sore, fatigued, or emotional. This is normal and the negative reaction should subside in a day or two, leaving the body with increased flexibility and vitality. Heat and stretching are effective ways of handling these reactions to massage. Massage is very beneficial for people suffering from FMS. These patients have often endured a trauma, emotionally or physically, that has disrupted the balance of the nervous system and muscular activity. With massage this balance is restored.

Craniosacral Therapy
Fred Samorodin, Vancouver, British Columbia

Fred holds a B.S. in rehabilitation therapy and is qualified in physical and occupational therapy. He took a one-year preceptorship in acupuncture and orthopedic medicine in the former Soviet Union and received a Certificate of Postgraduate Medical Studies (1977–78). He has operated a physical therapy clinic in Vancouver since 1980. Fred has extensive training in manual therapy, and particularly in craniosacral therapy with the Upledger Institute, from which he is certified as a clinical assistant in the teaching of craniosacral therapy techniques.

Craniosacral therapy is a light-touch bodywork technique developed by American osteopath Dr. John Upledger. He expanded upon the therapeutic principles developed by Dr. William Sutherland, D.O., the "father of cranial osteopathy." A craniosacral therapist palpates the inherent, natural "craniosacral rhythm" of the body that pulses at ten to twelve times per minute and applies gentle corrective touch to the skull, down to the tailbone. Craniosacral therapy enhances the body's natural healing processes by helping the body release myofascial restrictions. For nearly thirty years it has been shown to be effective for a wide range of medical problems associated with pain and the loss of function. The gentle nature of the therapy harnesses the subtle involuntary movements of the body to reduce tensions and stresses on the musculoskeletal system, as well as on the craniosacral system and the connective tissue surrounding the central nervous system.

Craniosacral therapists believe that stress patterns, habits of tension, poor posture, and misuse are stored in the fascia and other structural tissues of the body. Sheets of fascia may become inelastic and develop tender points and trigger points unless these torsions and tensions are allowed to unravel. By reestablishing the craniosacral rhythm and the proper flow of cerebrospinal fluid, the therapist can aid in relaxation of the entire body.

With FMS, a person experiences pain and discomfort over much of the body. There is an accompanying tendency toward sleep disturbance and reduced immune system functioning. Touch is recognized as having a relaxing effect on the body. When the touch is gentle and focused on helping the body balance out postural asymmetries, the benefits of the relaxation response are enhanced. The goal is to increase the parasympathetic tone of the body, away from the stresses of a fight-or-flight sympathetic nervous system bias. The contribution of craniosacral therapy to the management of FMS is to release more energy, enabling the patient to cope with the activities of daily living, and to improve the quality of sleep, leading to improved immune function.

Reiki
Jaime de la Barrera, MNIMH, Vancouver, British Columbia

Jaime is a reiki master in the Usui and Tera-Mai traditions and has taken the gendai reiki-ho masters training with Japanese reiki master Mr. Doi Hiroshi. Jaime has recently completed a four-year clinical phytotherapy program.

Reiki is a healing technique that makes use of the magic of touch. Originated thousands of years ago, reiki was rediscovered by Mikao Usui while meditating on the holy mountain of Kurama Yama in 1914. In several Asian cultures, healing disciplines such as reiki are applied to healthy people as a preventive method. Reiki may be used to help one return to a state of health or to achieve a healing balance. Reiki is both powerful and gentle; it is a wonderful energy that comes from the highest spiritual source. It is multidimensional and will aid in healing body, mind, and spirit. The reiki training is in three or four levels, but only the first level is needed to start using it on oneself, friends, and family.

Fibromyalgia causes great suffering, not only on the physical level but also in its emotional ramifications, as the disease is so poorly understood and so ineffectively treated by modern medicine. Reiki can help at both the physical and mental levels. On the physical level, the gentle but powerful reiki energy can help in coping with the daily pain, keeping it to a more reasonable and manageable level. Mentally, the benefits of reiki will be felt immediately as it will help not only with the emotional manifestations of disease, but also with the unbelievable obstacles faced by the patient during different stages of the disease. Reiki is very empowering and helps to make the individual more proactive and in control of his or her own situation.

Exercise

One of the diagnostic criteria of FMS, one that clearly differentiates it from chronic fatigue syndrome, is the improvement that is seen in FMS with mild to moderate exercise. Exercise is probably the simplest, cheapest, and most effective single thing that you can do to help yourself. You do not need memberships at gyms, personal trainers, expensive equipment, or fancy clothes. All you really need are some comfortable old sweats, a good pair of shoes, and a singular determination to make exercise a part of your life. If you like, you can use videos or take classes to learn some basic movements and refine your technique. Check out your local library before buying anything; try a few videos and find the ones you like.

A good exercise program will include stretching, strengthening, and aerobic components. Stretching provides flexibility and suppleness to the muscles, ensuring their relative elasticity and reducing chronic muscular tension. Yoga and Pilates are examples of good stretching exercises. Strengthening exercise, also called resistance exercise, supports energy production in the muscles and enhances stamina and endurance while reducing muscle fatigue and cramping due to lactic acid buildup. Lifting weights and using resistance bands are examples of strength training. Cardiovascular or aerobic exercise increases the heart rate and stimulates the circulation. Brisk walking, cycling, and swimming are examples of cardiovascular exercise.

An exercise program should be customized and personalized to suit your own particular needs. For people in chronic pain, the idea of exercising may seem like wishful thinking, but even a very small amount can be helpful. If you have been housebound for some time you may wish to start by walking to the garden gate and back, and even this, done regularly, will begin to make a difference. Once this much exercise is easy for you, try going to the end of the block and back, then around the block, then two blocks, and so on. Perseverance is the key here—exercise a little and often and consistently.

Research by both James Daly and Robert Bennet has confirmed that people with FMS produce excessive amounts of lactic acid in their muscles when they exercise and that this contributes to muscle fatigue and cramping. In this research, some of the patients also experienced elevated blood pressure as a result of this metabolic stress, and others exhibited erratic breathing patterns and low carbon dioxide levels when at rest, all indicative of hyperventilation, which is characteristic of FMS. Progressive aerobic training, slowly building up stamina and endurance, coupled with deep breathing exercises, can reduce these symptoms and improve exercise tolerance significantly. Regular, low-impact exercise can elongate muscle fibers, reducing chronic tension and contraction.

Benefits of Regular Exercise

- *Strengthening of ligaments, tendons, and muscles, and improved muscle tone.* Exercise increases blood flow to the connective tissues, enhancing delivery of oxygen for fueling energy production. In time this may lead to a strengthening of the "slow-twitch" muscle fibers that carry out aerobic respiration and provide sustained energy and stamina. Increased circulation also rapidly removes lactic acid produced by anaerobic respiration under times of heavier exercise and ensures an optimal cellular environment. Reduced injuries, more rapid healing, and increased stamina result from regular exercise.
- *Increased production of endorphins.* Pain-relieving and mood-enhancing endorphins are released from the hypothalamus under the influence of exercise. These are known to be deficient in patients with FMS and this may explain the mood elevation reported by people with FMS after exercise.
- *Increased production of serotonin.* Serotonin, which is known to be deficient in people with FMS, is boosted by exercise and the increased blood supply to the brain that occurs during a workout.
- *Increased production of T cells.* Killer T cells, an important, disease-fighting component of the immune system, are higher in number in people who exercise regularly. They enhance resistance to disease and improve overall immune function.
- *Improved joint metabolism.* Moderate exercise that does not strain the joints will improve the circulation of blood into and around the joints, bringing oxygen and nutrients to the joints, and removing metabolic wastes that would otherwise accumulate and predispose to an acidic environment and arthritic changes. Exercise also enhances movement of synovial fluid within a joint capsule, bringing nutrients to the avascular cartilage and removing metabolic wastes from it.
- *Increased cerebral circulation.* The increased circulatory dynamics seen during and after exercise enhance blood flow to the brain and may

reduce brain fog, improve memory and concentration, reduce depression and lethargy, and deepen sleep.

- *Weight management.* Exercise, coupled with sensible eating patterns, is the key to weight management. Many people with FMS struggle with their weight, partly due to the side effects of various prescription drugs, but largely as a result of their lack of exercise. Proper management of weight will decrease insulin resistance, protecting against Syndrome X and Type 2 diabetes. This can contribute to enhanced feelings of self-esteem and self-confidence, which can, in turn, improve the attitude and life experience of the person.
- *Increased bone strength.* One of the key components to the prevention of osteoporosis is regular, weight-bearing exercise. Because muscles are attached to bones, contraction of a muscle will pull on the bone and cause it to lay down more calcium to resist this pull. Over time, with repeated exercise, the bones become more dense and less prone to fractures.

How Much Is Enough?

There is no hard and fast rule regarding the "right" amount of exercise. The aim is to raise the resting pulse rate by at least 50 percent for twenty to thirty minutes at least three times a week. Many exercise physiologists and sports therapists recommend increasing the pulse rate by 60 to 80 percent, but this is unrealistic for many people with FMS and should only be attempted if you are already reasonably fit. If you are very unfit and have not exercised for a long time, then even very moderate exercise may achieve an adequate heart rate. As your fitness level rises, so will your exercise tolerance, and you will have to do progressively more exercise to achieve the desired elevation of the pulse rate.

This level of intensity in your exercise will ensure that you are achieving the training effect that is desirable. If you don't reach and sustain this level during your workout, you will miss out on many of the physiological benefits listed above. When you are exercising at this intensity you should feel slightly out of breath but be able to carry out a conversation. Monitor your resting pulse rate at the wrist and take it periodically during exercise to assess whether you have reached and are maintaining the appropriate pulse rate to ensure the training effect.

It is normal to feel some discomfort when commencing a new exercise program. Start very slowly, work out on alternate days to allow time for muscles to rest and recuperate in between, and stop if you experience prolonged or severe pain.

Tips to Make Exercise Easier

- Start very slowly, build up gradually, and never force yourself beyond your capacity. Begin with five minutes of stretching. When you are ready, add five minutes of walking. Over time you can add five minutes of light weights (use free weights that strap onto the wrists and ankles). This will provide the essential components of stretching, aerobic, and strength training. As your fitness level improves you can do each section for longer, then start mixing up the specific exercises so that you don't do too many repetitions at one time.
- If you are very weak and debilitated, then even lying down and sequentially contracting and releasing the large muscle groups several times will provide some exercise.
- Choose exercise that you enjoy. If you make it fun, you will be much more inclined to keep at it.
- Find an exercise buddy. It may be your spouse, your kids, or a friend, but making a commitment to another person will keep you motivated.
- Schedule your exercise at convenient times. Many people with FMS find they need to do some stretching in the morning before commencing activities for the day. However, you are also more vulnerable to

injuries then, when compared to later in the day after the muscles have warmed up a bit by normal movements. Aerobic activity should be done in the afternoon when injury is less likely.

- Try to do your exercise in a convenient location. Driving forty-five minutes to a one-hour class will sap your enthusiasm very quickly.
- Incorporate exercise into your daily routines. Take the stairs, not the elevator. Park the car or get off the bus a couple of blocks from your destination and walk a little. Go up and down the stairs at home as often as you can. Remember that housework, gardening, and even shopping are also forms of exercise.
- Vary your exercise routine so that all muscle groups are being used over the course of several days. Alternate two or three types of exercise through the week and don't get stuck with the same set of stretches or the same yoga routine all the time.
- Warm up well before doing any exercise. Even five minutes of stretching before a walk will improve muscle metabolism and reduce the risk of injury.
- Cool down properly after exercising. You need to allow time for the heart rate and breathing to return to normal and for muscles to relax. Don't forget to stretch again after exercise to encourage muscle elongation and ligament relaxation.
- Drink plenty of water while working out. Proper hydration will prevent slowing of the circulation as a result of fluid loss through sweating, and facilitate optimal blood supply to the muscles. In addition, proper hydration of cartilage, fascia, and other connective tissue makes it more fluid in nature, more resilient, and less prone to injury.
- Avoid sports drinks that are full of sugar, aspartame, artificial colors, and preservatives. If you need extra calories for sustenance during a workout, eat a protein bar, which will provide longer-lasting energy than a carbohydrate drink.
- When doing stretching exercises, never force the stretches and never bounce into them. Deep in the belly of a muscle are specialized fibers

called the muscle spindle, which measures the degree of stretch a muscle is undergoing and stimulates a countercontraction as appropriate. Bouncing or jerking into a stretch will initiate an impulse from the spindle that causes muscle contraction. Slow, sustained positions, held for three to ten seconds or even longer, will stretch the muscles without triggering countercontraction.

- Don't forget to breathe while you exercise! Delivery of oxygen to the bloodstream and removal of carbon dioxide that would otherwise acidify the body depends upon optimal exchange of air in the lungs. Stamina and endurance require plenty of oxygen for energy production.
- Avoid all high-impact sports and those where you are likely to fall. Football, aerobics, spinning, trail biking, skiing, and so on are not only probably too strenuous for people with FMS, but the chance of injury and consequent possible worsening of the condition is unacceptably high.
- Always wear good shoes for exercising. You can save yourself a lot of problems later on by ensuring you have well-fitted, supportive shoes with plenty of lift, bounce, and cushioning in them. Custom-fitted orthotics may be required to perfect your posture.
- Don't compare yourself to others and don't exercise competitively. Your exercise should be done for your own physical benefit only. Low intensity and longer duration is the preferred style.
- If you don't know how to begin exercising, then hire a personal trainer for just one or two sessions to set up a program for you. A qualified professional can also be helpful in checking occasionally that you are doing stretches correctly, or to inspire you with new variations if your routine becomes boring and repetitive.
- Schedule your exercise and stick to it. Make it a priority and don't let other demands upon your time squeeze it out. As with many things, setting the routine and keeping the discipline becomes easier with practice.

A Primer on
Herbal Medicines

It may well be better not to treat patients
with our well-known but hardly effective
armamentarium of drugs.
Treatments with antidepressants,
tricyclics, formal exercise programs—particularly
because they do not seem to work—
prolong medicalization and dependency,
the opposite of what
we should wish to accomplish.
Frederick Wolfe M.D.,
Journal of Rheumatology (1997)

How to Make Herbal Medicines

Three main methods of extraction are common: water extraction, solvent extraction, and fat extraction. Each method offers different properties, applications, and usefulness under various circumstances.

Water Extraction

For the amateur herbalist, and also in certain clinical situations, water extractions can be very useful. The methods employed are *infusions* and *decoctions*. These are very similar techniques.

An infusion is used for leaves, flowers, and other soft parts of the plant. The herbal material is placed in a suitable vessel and boiling water is poured over it. The infusion is steeped for five to fifteen minutes. A decoction is used for barks, roots, berries, and any hard parts of the plant. The herbal material is placed in a pan, covered with cold water, and brought to a boil. It is covered and allowed to simmer for five to fifteen minutes. To make a stronger tea, steep the herb longer, even overnight. An infusion or decoction may also be made cold. The plant material and water is allowed to stand at room temperature overnight before being strained off. This is useful where there are many volatile oils that may be lost if heat is used (for example, sweet flag) or where there is a lot of mucilage that would cause the end product to be very thick and glutinous (for example, marshmallow).

In both cases, the water acts as a solvent to extract only those constituents that are soluble in water. It may be usefully employed to extract tannins, bitters, and glycosides, but is not appropriate for extraction of resins, volatile and nonvolatile oils, or alkaloids. In the case of volatile oils, although they will not actually dissolve in water, they will evaporate in the heat, float on top of the water, and arise in the steam.

Advantages of water extraction are that it is quick, cheap, and easy; it requires no particular expertise nor any special equipment or ingredients. Disadvantages of water extraction are that it does not extract all therapeutically useful constituents, the resulting herbal remedy does not have a long shelf life (an infusion or decoction will last only about twenty-four hours in the refrigerator before bacterial contamination becomes a concern), and it is hard to have consistency in the end product. It is also worth noting that infusions and decoctions often taste unpleasant and this may reduce the compliance rate and hence the efficacy of the remedy. The taste can be improved by including peppermint, fennel, licorice, or other aromatic herbs in the blend. Taking them with a little juice can also help.

Infusions and decoctions can be drunk as teas, or used as a skin wash, douche, gargle, or soak.

Solvent Extraction

This is the method commonly employed by herbal practitioners. The herbal material (*marc*) is soaked for two weeks in an organic solvent diluted to a specific percentage with water (*menstruum*), after which the liquid is squeezed off to become the medicine and the herbal residue is discarded. Some solvents that may be used include:

1. Vinegar (*acetracta*)

This is about 4 percent acetic acid, which is excreted via the lungs, kidneys, and skin, where it acts as a mild expectorant, diuretic, and diaphoretic, respectively. An acetracta may be useful when administering herbs to a small child or a person with compromised liver function because vinegar is very gentle on the body. Vinegar is a reasonably good solvent, but the shelf life of an acetracta is only about three months. Because of the unpleasant taste the medicine is frequently mixed with honey; this mixture is called an *oxymel*.

2. Glycerine (*glycetracta*)

This is a colorless, odorless, viscous fluid with solvent capacities somewhere between alcohol and water. A glycetracta is commonly used to preserve fresh expressed plant juices (in the ratio of 1:1) and to make syrups. The taste is sweet and the shelf life is six to twelve months.

3. Alcohol (*tincture*)

For commercial preparations, an alcohol solvent is the most useful. Usually the alcohol used is ethyl alcohol (96.4 percent strength) diluted with water. Commercial ethyl alcohol is usually made from corn, to which many people are sensitive. Alcohol made from sugar beets may reduce the incidence of reactions to tinctures. Pesticide-free grape alcohol has recently become available as well. A tincture will extract all fat-soluble constituents, and because the tincture is also made with water, one can be reasonably sure of accessing all the useful parts of the plant. Note that the tincture must be at least 25 percent alcohol to ensure sterility and that different herbs require more or less alcohol to access the different constituents. For example, cayenne (*Capsicum minimum*) and ginger (*Zingiber officinalis*) both require 90 percent alcohol to provide maximum extraction of medicinal resins, but red raspberry (*Rubus idaeus*) and plantain (*Plantago lanceolata*) require only 25 percent alcohol to extract the water-soluble tannins. A tincture has the advantages that it extracts well, is convenient to dispense, is easy for the patient to use, and has a shelf life of up to three years.

Fat Extraction

Using fat as a solvent will extract those constituents that are soluble in fat or alcohol: gums, resins, fixed and volatile oils, waxes, and alkaloids. There are three methods used.

1. *Enfleurage.* Fresh plant material (usually flowers) is placed over a layer of fat with a low boiling point, such as cocoa butter, and allowed to stand for three days at room temperature. A mild organic solvent (alcohol) can then be used to extract the plant constituents from the fat.
2. *Digestion.* This is done in a similar way to enfleurage, but the fat is heated and kept warm for several hours to a few days. The warm oil digests the plant material and draws out the fat-soluble constituents. The oil is then squeezed out of the plant material.
3. *Infusion.* Plant material is placed in a jar with vegetable oil (usually almond or olive) and allowed to stand at room temperature for up to two weeks. The oil is then squeezed out of the plant material.

For most purposes the infusion method is preferred. It requires no solvents, and it involves no heat, thus preserving all the therapeutic properties of the plant. It is also easy to incorporate the resulting medicated oil into salves or liniments. The digestion method is advantageous when speed is important, because it can be made in twenty-four hours as compared to two weeks for an infused oil. The enfleurage method is used nowadays only for the extraction of a few extremely heat-sensitive volatile oils, such as jasmine, neroli, and rose.

Capsules

A final common method of preparing herbs for internal use is to make capsules. The herb is either air-dried or freeze-dried, ground, and used to fill gelatin capsules. This has the advantages of being inexpensive and convenient, but the shelf life tends to be fairly short with oxidation of the herb being a very real concern. Gelatin capsules and small filling machines are available from herbal stores.

How to Take Herbal Medicines

Having made an herbal extract with water, a solvent, or fat, it is then possible to incorporate the remedy into various mediums and apply them in various ways. For example, water extractions may be employed in a number of methods: the tea may be drunk, or it may be used as a mouthwash, gargle, compress, skin wash, eyewash, douche, enema, hair rinse, and so on. Tinctures may be diluted as internal medicines or may be used in all the same ways as a water extraction. Acetracta and glycetracta are almost exclusively used internally. Fat extractions are almost always applied externally in the form of skin oils or incorporated into ointments, lotions, and creams. A cocoa butter extraction may also be used as the base for suppositories. Infusions, decoctions, and solvent extractions may also be spray-dried and incorporated into tablets.

All these methods can be helpful, depending on the nature of the herb and what you are trying to achieve. For digestive and urinary spasms, a hot tea may be most helpful. For backache, muscle pain, and tension, a hot bath might be

Table A.1 Methods of Administration of Herbal Medicines

Route	Absorbing membrane	Form	Advantages	Disadvantages
Oral	Mucous lining of the gastrointestinal tract	Infusion, decoction, tincture, acetracta, glycetracta, capsule, tablet, or taken in the form of food	Convenient and painless. Remedy passes first to the liver where potentially toxic agents may be deactivated.	Absorption is slow, irregular, and unpredictable and thus is not suitable when a fast or precise response is important. Because the remedy passes first to the liver there is a possibility that useful constituents are broken down before reaching other parts of the body.
Sublingual	Mucous lining of the mouth	Lozenges, tablets, and/or spray	Uptake into the bloodstream is very rapid (usually within two minutes). Enters the systemic circulation directly without first passing through the liver.	Only a few remedies can be administered in this way. May be dangerous to avoid the first pass through the liver, which acts as a filter or screen for many toxic substances.
Rectal	Mucous lining of the rectum	Suppositories or enemas	Can be used in the vomiting, comatose, or uncooperative patient.	Bypasses the liver and enters the systemic circulation directly.

Table A.1 Methods of Administration of Herbal Medicines., *continued*

Route	Absorbing membrane	Form	Advantages	Disadvantages
			Useful for remedies that would cause nausea or vomiting if given orally.	Rectal route may be unacceptable to some sensitive patients.
Vaginal	Mucous lining of the vagina	Pessaries, creams, or impregnated tampons	Permits local treatment with very little being absorbed into the bloodstream.	May be messy or unacceptable to some patients. Not suitable during pregnancy.
Nasal	Mucous lining of the nose and upper respiratory tract, the alveolar epithelium	Sprays, aerosols, or inhalants	Uptake is almost instantaneous, and a very local effect may be obtained.	May be some absorption into the systemic circulation. The technique may be difficult for some patients.
Epidermal	Skin	Ointments, creams, liniments, powders, poultices, or plasters	A very local effect can be obtained. May be possible to get better access to a poorly vascularized area from the outside (e.g., a capsicum plaster over an arthritic joint).	Some absorption may occur into the systemic circulation, and this may be variable and unpredictable.

best. For memory loss and brain fog, a tincture might do the trick. Some herbal constituents, such as resins, saponins, and alkaloids, do not extract well into water. These are best taken as tinctures, where the alcohol acts as a solvent. Tannins, glycosides, and salicylates are readily extracted into water and are well suited to be taken in the form of teas. Essential oils should not be taken internally, but are ideal to use in massage oils, baths, and as inhalants.

Dosage and Frequency

Dosage and frequency depend upon several factors: the strength or concentration of the remedy, the severity of the symptoms, and the underlying physiological strength of the system or person. Thus, for example, a large, muscular man in generally good health but suffering from an acute head cold will tolerate and, indeed, need a much higher dose of herbal medicine than would a frail old lady with chronic arthritis or a five-year-old child with emotionally based asthma.

In general, acute conditions will require higher doses and/or stronger medicines than will chronic conditions. Likewise, a small body will require less than a large body. People with compromised liver function will metabolize their remedies differently and may need lower doses to prevent a cumulative action. The same is true for people with impaired kidney function, who may not be able to excrete remedies as fast as could otherwise be expected.

Children and the elderly are particularly at risk of liver or kidney insufficiency, but previous medical history, current complaint, other drugs or remedies being used, and alcohol and drug abuse should all be taken into account when determining the correct dosage.

Another factor to consider when estimating the dose is whether there is any concomitant constipation or diarrhea. If there is hypermotility of the gastrointestinal tract, then a remedy will pass rapidly through the system and not as much will be absorbed as in the case of hypomotility.

For specific dosages and safety parameters, refer to *The Botanical Safety Handbook* (CRC Press, 1997).

SOURCES AND RESOURCES

BOOKS

Fibromyalgia, Chronic Fatigue Syndrome, and Muscle Pain

These are the reference books I consulted. Some were more useful than others, but all contain some helpful information. More books on FMS are being written all the time and this list will surely expand in the future.

Cady, Roger, M.D., and Kathleen Farmer. *Headache Free.* Bantam Books, 1996.

Catalano, Ellen Mohr, and Kimeron Hardin. *The Chronic Pain Control Workbook.* New Harbinger Publications, 1996.

Chaitow, Leon. *Fibromyalgia and Muscle Pain.* Thorsons, 1995.

Chaitow, Leon. *The Natural Book of Pain Relief.* Harper Collins, 1993.

Conley, Edward J., M.D. *America Exhausted.* Vitality Press, 1999.

Dawber, Diane. *Lifting the Bull.* Quarry Health Books, 1997.

Dossey, Larry. *Prayer Is Good Medicine.* Harper, 1996.

Elrod, Joe M., M.D. *Reversing Fibromyalgia.* Woodland Publishing, 1997.

Fransen, Jenny, and Jon Russell, M.D. *The Fibromyalgia Help Book.* Smith House Press, 1996.

Goldberg, Burton. *Chronic Fatigue, Fibromyalgia, and Environmental Illness.* Future Medicine Publishing, 1998.

Goldenberg, Don, M.D. *Chronic Illness and Uncertainty.* Dorset Press, 1996.

Jacobson, Betsey, ed. *Multidisciplinary Approaches to Fibromyalgia.* Anadem Publishing, 1998.

Kabat-Zinn, Jon. *Full Catastrophe Living—Using the Wisdom of the Body and Mind to Face Stress, Pain, and Illness.* Dell Publishing, 1990.

Khalsa, Dharma Singh, M.D., and Cameron Stauth. *The Pain Cure.* Warner Books, 1999.

Pellegrino, Mark, M.D. *The Fibromyalgia Support Book.* Anadem Publishing, 1997.

Pollin, Irene. *Taking Charge: Overcoming the Challenge of Long-Term Illness.* Random House, 1994.

Skelley, Mari, and Andrea Helm. *Alternative Treatments for Fibromyalgia and Chronic Fatigue Syndrome.* Hunter House, 1999.

St. Amand, R. Paul, M.D. and Claudia Craig Marek. *What Your Doctor May Not Tell You About Fibromyalgia.* Warner Books, 1999.

Starlanyl, Devin and Mary Ellen Copeland. *Fibromyalgia and Chronic Myofascial Pain Syndrome.* New Harbinger Publications, 1996.

Teitelbaum, Jacob, M.D. *From Fatigued to Fantastic.* Avery Publishing, 1996.

Travell, Janet, and David Simons. *Myofascial Pain and Dysfunction: The Trigger Point Manual.* Williams and Wilkins, 1983, 1992.

Williamson, Miryam Ehrlich. *Fibromyalgia, A Comprehensive Approach.* Walker Publishing, 1996.

Williamson, Miryam Ehrlich. *The Fibromyalgia Relief Book.* Walker Publishing, 1998.

Nutrition and Diet Therapy

Some of these reference books are general and others are very specific. Few of them deal with FMS directly, but they all offer useful guidance on creating a balanced diet and optimal nutrition.

Balch, James, M.D., and Phyllis Balch. *Prescription for Natural Healing.* Avery Publishing, 1990.

Birkmayer, Georg, M.D. *NADH—The Energizing Co-enzyme.* Keats Publishing, 1998.

Clouatre, Dallas. *Glucosamine Sulphate and Chondroitin Sulphate.* Keats Publishing, 1999.

Colbin, Anne Marie. *Food and Healing.* Ballantine Books, 1986.

Colgan, Michael, M.D. *The Right Protein for Muscle and Strength.* Apple Publishing Company, 1998.

Crayhon, Robert. *The Carnitine Miracle.* Evans and Company, 1998.

———. *Nutrition Made Simple.* Evans and Company, 1984.

Fallon, Sally, Pat Connelly, and Mary Enig. *Nourishing Traditions.* Promotion Publishing, 1995.

Hartvig, Kirsten, N.D., and Nic Rowley, M.D. *10 Days to Better Health.* Piatkus Publishers, 1998.

Hartvig, Kirsten, N.D., and Nic Rowley, M.D. *You Are What You Eat.* Piatkus Publishers, 1996.

Jensen, Bernard, M.D. *Come Alive.* Self-published, 1997.

Krohn, Jacqueline, M.D., Frances Taylor, and Jinger Prosser. *Natural Detoxification.* Hartley and Marks Publishers, 1996.

Mindell, Earl. *The MSM Miracle.* Keats Publishing, 1997.

Moeller, Mary, and Joe M. Elrod, M.D. *The Fibromyalgia Nutrient Guide.* Woodland Publishing, 1999.

Murray, Michael. *Encyclopedia of Nutritional Supplements.* Prima Publishing, 1996.

Passwater, Richard, M.D., and Elmer M. Cranton, M.D. *Trace Elements, Hair Analysis, and Nutrition.* Keats Publishing, 1983.

Pitchford, Paul. *Healing with Whole Foods.* North Atlantic Books, 1993.

Sahley, Billie Jay. *Malic Acid and Magnesium for Fibromyalgia.* Pain and Stress Publications, 1997.

Sears, Barry. *Enter the Zone.* Regan Books, 1995.

Stolzfus, Meg, and Joanne Yount, eds. *The Low-Oxalate Cookbook.* The Vulvar Pain Foundation, 1997.

Werbach, Melvyn, M.D. *Nutritional Influence on Disease.* Keats Publishing, 1988.

Herbal Medicine and Natural Healing

These are the books I consulted as herbal references. I have dozens of other herbal books on my shelves, but these are the ones I have consistently found most informative and accurate.

Bartam, Thomas. *Encyclopedia of Herbal Medicine.* Grace Publishers, 1995.

Bone, Kerry. *Clinical Applications of Ayurvedic and Chinese Herbs.* Phytotherapy Press, 1996.

Bone, Kerry, and Simon Mills. *Principles and Practice of Phytotherapy.* Churchill Livingstone, 1999.

Bradley, Peter, ed. *British Herbal Compendium.* British Herbal Medicine Association, 1992.

Burns, David, M.D. *Feeling Good— The New Mood Therapy.* Signet, 1992.

Duke, James. *The Green Pharmacy.* Rodale Press, 1996.

Ellingwood, Finley, M.D. *American Materia Medica, Therapeutics, and Pharmacognosy (1919).* Eclectic Medical Publications, 1994.

Grieve, Maud. *A Modern Herbal.* Tiger Books, 1992.

Hutchens, Alma. *Indian Herbology of North America.* Merco, 1973.

Hylton, W. H., ed., *The Rodale Herb Book: How to Use, Grow, and Buy Nature's Miracle Plants.* Rodale Press, 1978. (OOP)

Lloyd, J. U., and H. W. Felter. *Kings American Dispensatory.* Eclectic Medical Publications, 1983.

Mills, Simon. *The Essential Book of Herbal Medicine.* Viking Arcana (Penguin) 1991.

Mowrey, Daniel. *Guaranteed Potency Herbs.* Keats Publishing, 1990.

Newall, C., L. Anderson, and D. Phillipson. *Herbal Medicines.* Pharmaceutical Press, 1996.

Tisserand, Robert, and Tony Balacs. *Essential Oil Safety—A Guide for Health Care Professionals.* Churchill Livingstone, 1995.

Weiss, Rudolph, M.D. *Herbal Medicine.* Beaconsfield Arcanum, 1988.

Willard, Terry. *Textbook of Advanced Herbology.* Wild Rose Publications, 1991.

Videotapes, Audiotapes, and CDs

Banyen Books and Sound
2671 West Broadway
Vancouver, BC
Canada V6K 2G2
604-732-7912
www.banyen.com

A huge selection of books and tapes on self-healing, as well as tapes of relaxation programs, nature sounds, and so on.

Body Pain Trigger Points Program (CD-ROM)
310-215-9816

Dr. R. Paul St. Amand and Claudia Marek (two videotapes, 1998)
Fibromeet
P.O. Box 461377
Escondido, CA 92046-1377

Effective Learning Systems (self-hypnosis audiotapes)
5255 Edina Industrial Boulevard
Edina, MN 55435
612-893-1680

Fibromyalgia—How You Can Help Yourself (audiotape)
Miryam Erhlich Williamson
P.O. Box 307
Orange, MA 01364

Fibromyalgia and You (videotape)
Jon Russell, M.D.
Fibromyalgia Information Resources
P.O. Box 690402
San Antonio, TX 78269

Fibromyalgia Exercise and *Fibromyalgia Fitness* (two videotapes)
Sharon Clark and Robert Bennet, M.D.
Oregon Fibromyalgia Foundation
1221 SW Yamhill, Suite 303
Portland, OR 97295

Fibromyalgia—The Path to Healing (audiotape)
90-minute presentation by Chanchal Cabrera

Medicines from the Earth Symposium 2000
Herbal Education Services
www.botanicalmedicine.org
800-252-0688

Gentle Fitness (videotape)
800-566-7780

Infomedix (sleep tapes)
12800 Garden Grove Boulevard, Room S
Garden Grove, CA 92643
800-367-9286

Serenity (relaxation tapes)
180 West 25th Street
Upland, CA 91786
800-869-1684

Stretching with Bob Anderson
800-315-1995

Tree Farm Communications (huge selection of audio- and videotapes on natural medicines)

23703 NE 4th Street
Redmond, WA 98053-3612
800-468-0464

Whole Person Associates (relaxation tapes)
P.O. Box 3151
Duluth, MN 55803
800-247-6789

WEB SITES

Web sites and cyber addresses change frequently. The information given below is current at the time of writing.

Acupuncture care and referrals
www.medicalacupuncture.org

Alternative health
www.healthy.net

American Association for CFS
www.weber.u.washington.edu/~dedra/aacfs1.htm

American Botanical Council
www.herbalgram.org

AMR'TA Natural Medicine
www.amrta.org/~amrta
www.geocities.com/Wellesley/5248/fms.html

Arthritis and rheumatism
www.rheumatology.org/ar/ar.html

British Columbia Fibromyalgia Society
www.alternatives.com/bcfms/default.htm

British Journal of Rheumatology
www.oup.co.uk/jnls/list/brheum.hdbl/

Chiropractic care and referrals
www.amerchiro.org

Discounted pharmaceuticals
www.institute-dc.org

David Nye, M.D.
www.alternatives.com/cfs-news/fm-md.htm

Emotional support group
http://fmpsc.poerpack.com/support.html

Fibromyalgia information page
http://prairie.lakes.com/~roseleaf/fibro/index.html

Fibromyalgia and myofascial pain syndrome (Devin Starlanyl)
www.sover.net/~devstar

Fibromyalgia Web site (Miryam Williamson)
www.shaynet.com/~wmson/

Fibromeet (Nancy Madeiros)
www.csusm.edu/public/guests/nancym/fibromt

FMS advocacy
www.cais.net/cfs-news/action.htm

FMS link collection site
www.hometown.aol.com/fibroworld/FMilyPages.html

Friends' Health Connection (a non-profit organization that links people with chronic or disabling diseases)
www.48friend.org

Gaia hypothesis
http://beep.roadrunner.com:80/~mkzdk/texts/gaia.html

Guaifenesin support group
www.geocities.com/HotSpringfs/
Spa/5252

Guaifenesin treatment
(Dr. R. Paul St. Amand)
www.fibromyalgiatreatment.com

Herb Research Foundation
www.sunsite.unc.edu/hrf/

Herbal medicine
www.botanicalmedicine.org

Journal of Rheumatology
www.jrheum.com/

Massage therapy care and referrals
www.amtamassage.org

National Fibromyalgia Research
Association
www.teleport.com/~nfa/

Naturopathic care and referrals
www.naturopathic.org

Oregon Fibromyalgia Foundation
(Robert Bennet, M.D.)
www.myalgia.com

Pain information
www.elsevier.com:80/inca/
publications/store/5/0/6/0/8/3/

Prescription medications information
www.rxlist.com

Rheumatoid arthritis and FMS
www.gen.emory.edu/medweb.rheum
atology.html

SLEEP journal
www.leland.standford.edu/dept/sleep/
journal/

USA Fibromyalgia Association
www.w2.com/fibro1.html

UK FM Association
www.community-care.org.uk/
charity/fmauk.html

ORGANIZATIONS

Support Groups and
Related Organizations

United States

American Academy of Allergy and
Immunology
611 East Wells Street
Milwaukee, WI 53202
414-272-6071

American Academy of Environmental
Medicine
P.O. Box 16106
Denver, CO 80216
303-622-9756

American Academy of Pain
Management
13943 Mono Way, Suite A
Sonora, CA 95370
209-533-9744

American Association for Chronic
Fatigue Syndrome
7 van Buren Street
Albany, NY 12206
518-482-2202

American Association of
Naturopathic Physicians
P.O. Box 20836
Seattle, WA 98102

American Chiropractic Association
1701 Clarendon Boulevard
Arlington, VA 22209

American Chronic Pain Association
P.O. Box 850
Rocklin, CA 95677
916-632-0922

American College of Rheumatology
60 Executive Park South, Suite 150
Atlanta, GA 30329
404-633-3777

American Holistic Medical
Association
6728 Old McLean Village Drive
McLean, VA 22101
703-556-9728

American Osteopathic Association
142 East Ontario Street
Chicago, IL 60611

Americans with Disabilities Act
Hotline
800-466-4232/800-949-4232

Arthritis Foundation
P.O. Box 19000
Atlanta, GA 30326
800-283-7800

Biofeedback Certification Institute of
America
10200 West 44th Avenue, Suite 304
Wheat Ridge, CO 80033

Fibromyalgia Alliance of America
P.O. Box 21990
Columbus, OH 43221-0990
614-457-4222

Fibromyalgia Alliance of America, Inc.
P.O. Box 16600
Washington, DC 20041-6600
202-310-1818

Fibromyalgia Association of Florida
P.O. Box 14848
Gainesville, FL 32604-6865
904-373-6865

Fibromyalgia Association of Greater
Washington
13203 Valley Drive
Woodbridge, VA 22191-1531
703-790-2324

Fibromyalgia Network
P.O. Box 31750
Tucson, AZ 85751-1750
520-290-5508

Food Allergy Network
4744 Holly Avenue
Fairfax, VA 22030-5647
703-691-3179

Hypoglycemia Association
P.O. Box 165
Ashton, MD 20861-4044
202-544-4044

International Foundation for Bowel
Dysfunction
P.O. Box 17864
Milwaukee, WI 53217
414-241-9479

Interstitial Cystitis Association
P.O. Box 1553
Madison Square Station
New York, NY 10159
212-979-6057

National Chronic Pain Outreach
Association
7979 Old Georgetown Road
Bethesda, MD 20814-2429
301-652-4948

National Depressive and Manic
Depressive Association
730 North Franklin, Suite 501
Chicago, IL 60610
800-826-3632

National Digestive Diseases
Information Clearing House
2 Information Way
Bethesda, MD 20892-3570

National Family Caregivers
Association
9223 Longbranch Parkway
Silver Spring, MD 20901

National Fibromyalgia Research
Association
P.O. Box 500
Salem, OR 97308
703-790-2324

National Headache Foundation
428 West St. James Place
Chicago, IL 60614
800-843-2256

National Sleep Foundation
729 Fifteenth Street NW, 4th Floor
Washington, DC 20005
888-394-7533

NIH/National Arthritis,
Musculoskeletal, and Skin Diseases
Information Clearing House
9000 Rockville Pike
Bethesda, MD 20892
301-495-4484

Restless Leg Syndrome Foundation
1904 Banbury Road
Raleigh, NC 27608

Sjogren's Syndrome Foundation
333 North Broadway
Jericho, NY 11753
800-745-6473

The TMJ Association
6418 West Washington Boulevard
Wauwatosa, WI 53213
414-259-3223

Vulvar Pain Foundation
P.O. Box Drawer 177
Graham, NC 27253

Canada

The Arthritis Society, BC Division
805 West 10th Avenue
Vancouver, BC V5Z 1L7
604-879-7511

Association de la Fibromyosité
du Québec
643 rue Notre Dame
Repentigny, PQ J6A 2W1

Fibromyalgia Association of BC
Box 15455
Vancouver, BC V6B 5B2
604-430-6643

Fibromyalgia Support Group of
Winnipeg
825 Sherbrook Street
Winnipeg, MB R3A 1M5
202-772-6979

Ontario Fibromyalgia Association
250 Bloor Street, Suite 901
Toronto, ON M4W 3P2

**Herbal and Natural
Medicine Associations**

American Association of Acupuncture and Oriental Medicine
4101 Lake Boone Tr., Suite 201
Raleigh, NC 27607
919-787-5181

American Botanical Council and
Herb Research Foundation
P.O. Box 144345
Austin, TX 78714-4900

American Herbalists Guild
1931 Gaddis Road
Canton, GA 30115
770-751-6021

Canadian Herb Society
VanDusen Botanical Garden
5251 Oak Street
Vancouver, BC V6M 4M1

The Canadian Herbal
Association of BC
7327 Kingsway
Burnaby, BC V3N 3C1

National Institute of Medical
Herbalists
56 Longbrook Street
Exeter, Devon
EX4 6AH United Kingdom

Professional Associations
Massage Therapist Association of
British Columbia
205–640 West Broadway
Vancouver, BC V5Z 1G4
604-873-4467/888-413-4467
Fax 604-873-6211

College of Massage Therapists of
British Columbia
103–1089 West Broadway
Vancouver, BC V6H 1E5
604-736-3404/877-321-3404
Fax 604-736-6500
www.cmtbc.bc.ca

Shiatsu Therapy Association of BC
www.shiatsutherapy.bc.ca
604-433-9495

PRODUCTS

Herbal Medicines and Essential Oils

Gaia Garden Herbal Dispensary
2672 West Broadway
Vancouver, BC V6K 2G3
604-734-4372
www.gaiagarden.com

*One of North America's largest
selections of herbal medicines,
aromatherapy supplies, and natural
health products. Custom blends
and mail-order service available.*

Nutritional Supplements

CFIDS and FMS Health Resource
1187 Coast Village Road, Suite 1-280
Santa Barbara, CA 93108-2794
800-366-6056

*Patient-owned organization that
donates proceeds to research into
CFIDS and FMS. Over two million
dollars donated so far.*

Tools for Easier Living

Adaptability
75 Mill Street
P.O. Box 515
Colchester, CT 06415-0515
800-566-6678

Enrichments
P.O. Box 5050
Bolingbrook, IL 60440-9973
800-323-5547

Intelli-Health Healthy Homes
960 Harvest Drive
Blue Bell, PA 19422
800-394-3775

Janice Corporation
198 U.S. Highway 46
Budd Lake, NJ 07828-3001
800-526-4237

Light for Health (full-spectrum lights)
942 Twisted Oak Lane
Buffalo Grove, IL 60089
800-468-1104

Nutri-Spec
RR #3, Box 384
Mifflintown, PA 17059
800-736-4320

*Suppliers of urine tensimometers
and charts for assessing biochemical
individuality, and of metabolically
balanced nutritional supplements.*

CONTRIBUTING PRACTITIONERS

Fernando Cabrera
SourcePoint Shiatsu Center
3261 Heather Street
Vancouver, BC V5Z 3K4
604-876-0042

Jaime de la Barrera
2672 West Broadway
Vancouver BC V6K 2G3
604-734-4372

Joanne Fallow
2672 West Broadway
Vancouver, BC V6K 2G3
604-734-4372

Cecil Herschler
207–2786 West 16th Avenue
Vancouver, BC V6K 3C4
604-732-7060

Lori Johnson
Soma Studio
213–1529 West 6th Avenue
Vancouver, BC V6J 1R1
604-738-1502

Else Larsen
204–3077 Granville Street
Vancouver, BC V6H 3J9
604-732-3422

Fred Samorodin
3618 Tanner Street
Vancouver, BC V5R 5P6
604-732-6323

HERBAL
MATERIA MEDICA

This section focuses on the plants used to treat fibromyalgia, including their holistic uses, contraindications, and beneficial combinations. Not all the herbs listed in the following categories are routinely or regularly used except by professional herbalists, but they are mentioned for completeness. In the interests of space, detailed information is given only for those likely to be in frequent use. Herbs marked by an asterisk (*) are not described in the text but for full information on all the herbs listed, for detailed references, and additional, valuable information see my Web site at www.gaiagarden.com.

Alteratives for the joints
Arctium lappa (Burdock)
Berberis vulgaris (Barberry)
Fucus vesiculosis (Kelp)
Galium aparine (Cleavers)
Guaiacum officinalis (Lignum vitae)
Harpagophytum procumbens
   (Devil's claw)
Rumex crispus (Yellow dock)
Urtica dioica (Nettle)

Diuretic/Uricosuric alteratives
Apium graveolens (Celery)
Betula alba* (Silver birch)
Filipendula ulmaris (Meadowsweet)
Petroselinum crispum (Parsley)
Plantago lanceolata (Plantain)
Urtica dioica (Stinging nettle)

Triterpenoid saponin anti-inflammatories
Bupleurum falcatum*
   (Chinese thoroughwax)
Glycyrrhiza glabra (Licorice)

Sulfur anti-inflammatories
Allium cepa (Onion)
Allium sativa (Garlic)
Armoracea rusticana (Horseradish)
Brassica niger/alba
   (Black/white mustard)

Resin anti-inflammatories
Boswellia carterii (Frankincense)
Bryonia dioica/alba* (White bryony)
Capsicum minimum (Cayenne)
Guaiacum officinalis (Lignum vitae)
Liquidambar orientalis* (Storax)

*Myroxylon balsamum** (Tolu balsam)
*Myroxylon pereirae** (Peru balsam)
Populus balsamifera (Poplar buds)
*Styrax benzoin** (Benzoin)
Zingiber officinalis (Ginger)

Salicylate anti-inflammatories
*Betula alba** (Silver birch)
Filipendula ulmaris (Meadowsweet)
Gaultheria procumbens (Wintergreen)
Populus spp. (Poplar)
Salix spp. (Willow)
*Viburnum opulus** (Cramp bark)
*Viburnum prunifolium** (Black haw)

Steroidal saponin anti-inflammatories
Dioscorea villosa (Wild yam)
Smilax spp. (Sarsaparilla)
Trigonella foenum-graecum
  (Fenugreek)
Yucca spp. (Yucca)

Essential fatty acid anti-inflammatories
Borago officinalis (Borage seed)
Oenothera biennis
  (Evening primrose seed)
Ribes niger (Black currant seed)

Volatile oils anti-inflammatories
Achillea millefolium (Yarrow)
*Betula alba/lenta** (Silver/Sweet birch)
Chamomilla recutita (Chamomile)
Cinnamonum zeylanicum
  (Cinnamon)
Curcuma longa (Turmeric)
Guaiacum officinale (Lignum vitae)
Juniperus communis (Juniper)

*Melaleuca leucadendron** (Cajuput)
*Myristica fragrans** (Nutmeg)
Rosmarinus officinalis (Rosemary)
Tanacetum parthenium (Feverfew)
Zingiber officinalis (Ginger)

Cerebral circulatory stimulants
Centella asiatica (Gotu kola)
Ginkgo biloba (Ginkgo)
*Myristica fragrans** (Nutmeg)
Rosmarinus officinalis (Rosemary)
Vinca major/minor (Periwinkle)

Warming tonic circulatory stimulants
Marsdenia condurango
  (Condor plant)
Myrica cerifera (Bayberry)

Central circulatory stimulants
Achillea millefolium (Yarrow)
Capsicum minimum (Cayenne)
Zingiber officinalis (Ginger)

Peripheral circulatory stimulants
Achillea millefolium (Yarrow)
Capsicum minimum (Cayenne)
*Corydalis ambigua** (Yan hu suo)
*Paeonia lactiflora** (White peony)
Rosmarinus officinalis (Rosemary)
Zanthoxylum spp. (Prickly ash)
Zingiber officinalis (Ginger)

Adaptogens/Tonics
Astragalus membranaceous
  (Milk vetch)
Borago officinalis (Borage)
*Bupleurum chinense** (Chai Hu)
Eleutherococcus senticosis
  (Siberian ginseng)
Glycyrrhiza glabra (Licorice)

Oplopanax horridum (Devil's club)
Panax quinquefolium
   (American ginseng)
Panax ginseng (Korean ginseng)
Pfaffia paniculata (Suma)
Schizandra chinensis (Wu Wei Zi)
Withania somnifera (Ashwagandha)

Connective tissue tonics
Centella asiatica (Gotu kola)
Crataegus oxycanthoides (Hawthorn)
Equisetum arvense (Horsetail)
Plantago major/lanceolata (Plantain)
*Polygonum multiflorum** (He shou wu)
Vaccinium myrtillus (Blueberry leaf)

Sedative nervines
Eschscholzia california
   (Californian poppy)
Lactuca virosa (Wild lettuce)
Passiflora incarnata (Passionflower)
Piscidia erythrina
   (Jamaican dogwood)
Valeriana officinalis (Valerian)

Gentle, calming nervines
Chamomilla recutita (Chamomile)
Melissa officinalis (Lemon balm)
Nepeta cataria (Catnip)
Scutalleria lateriflora (Skullcap)
*Zizyphus jujuba** (Sour date seed)

Tonic nervines
Avena sativa (Oats)
Bacopa monniera (Brahmi)
Borago officinalis (Borage)
Centella asiatica (Gotu kola)
Hypericum perforatum
   (St. John's wort)

*Polygonum multiflorum** (He shou wu)
Verbena officinalis/hastata
   (Blue vervain)
Vinca major/minor (Periwinkle)

**Nervines that have a
muscle-relaxing effect**
Cimicifuga racemosa (Black cohosh)
*Paeonia lactiflora** (White peony)
Piper methysticum (Kava)

Gentle sedative analgesics
Chamomilla recutita (Chamomile)
Humulus lupulus (Hops)
Hypericum perforatum
   (St. John's wort)
Lavandula officinalis (Lavender)
Melissa officinalis (Lemon balm)
Passiflora incarnata (Passionflower)
Scutalleria lateriflora (Skullcap)

Muscle-relaxing analgesics
*Cannabis sativum** (Marijuana)
Lobelia inflata (Lobelia)
Piper methysticum (Kava kava)

**Stronger analgesic herbs
with a CNS effect**
*Corydalis ambigua** (Yan hu suo)
Eschscholzia california
   (California poppy)
Lactuca virosa (Wild lettuce)
Piscidia erythrina
   (Jamaican dogwood)
Valeriana officinalis (Valerian)

Topical muscle relaxants
Lobelia inflata (Lobelia)
*Viburnum opulus** (Cramp bark)

Warming muscle relaxants
Rosmarinus officinalis (Rosemary)
Zanthoxylum spp. (Prickly ash)
Zingiber officinalis (Ginger)

Antispasmodic herbs
for the urinary tract
Achillea millefolium (Yarrow)
Viburnum opulus* (Cramp bark)

Demulcents for the urinary tract
Agropyron repens (Couch grass)
Althea officinalis (Marshmallow)
Plantago lanceolata/major (Plantain)
Zea mais* (Corn silk)

Antispasmodic herbs
for the digestive system
Chamomilla recutita (Chamomile)
Humulus lupulus (Hops)
Lavandula officinalis (Lavender)
Lobelia inflata (Lobelia)
Melissa officinalis (Lemon balm)
Mentha piperita (Peppermint)
Myristica fragrans* (Nutmeg)
Verbena officinalis/hastata
   (Blue vervain)
Viburnum opulus* (Cramp bark)

Demulcent herbs
for the digestive system
Althea officinalis (Marshmallow)
Plantago lanceolata/major (Plantain)
Ulmus fulvus (Slippery elm)

Astringent tonics
for the digestive system
Filipendula ulmaris (Meadowsweet)
Myrica cerifera (Bayberry)
Plantago lanceolata/major (Plantain)

*Anti-***Candida** *agents*
Calendula officinalis (Marigold)
Tabebuia spp. (Lapacho/Taheebo/
Pau d'Arco)

Achillea millefolium (Yarrow)
FAMILY: Asteraceae
PART USED: Flower and leaf
A common weed now cultivated as a
garden ornamental, yarrow has long
been used in medicine. The flowers
are an effective diaphoretic, inducing
perspiration and gentle detoxification
through the skin. This is especially
useful in the early stages of a cold or
flu. A cup of yarrow tea, drunk hot,
will raise the core body temperature,
which reduces microbe activity and
induces immune function. It will
enhance the body's natural efforts to
sweat out the infection.

The flowers contain a volatile oil,
one component of which is chamazu-
lene, a notable anti-inflammatory.
In cosmetic use the volatile oil is
employed as a skin regenerator.
The volatile oil is partially excreted
through the kidneys where it
increases local blood flow and hence
increases diuresis. The flowers also
increase circulation into the pelvic
region, reducing stagnation and congestion of the tissues. This exerts a
gentle but effective tonic and normalizing effect on women's reproductive
organs and the menstrual cycle. The
leaves are quite strongly astringent
and can be used to reduce mucous

membrane secretions and excess bleeding. The leaves can also be used to treat sinus congestion and rhinitis in colds and flu, bleeding of the upper digestive tract, mucus colitis, vaginal discharge, nephritis, and cystitis. Additionally, they are effective in reducing endometrial overgrowth and can be used to treat endometriosis, fibroids, leucorrhoea, dysfunctional uterine bleeding, and the sequelae of miscarriage, termination, and labor.

Clinical Applications in Fibromyalgia
I prescribe yarrow especially as a warming, anti-inflammatory, pelvic decongestant, and antispasmodic for symptoms of urinary spasms and interstitial cystitis. It combines well with ginger and cramp bark for this purpose. I also use it for *Candida* overgrowth, leaky gut syndrome, and symptoms of irritable bowel syndrome, where both the bitterness and the astringency are helpful. It combines well with calendula, plantain, licorice, and slippery elm for this purpose. The astringency extracts best into a tea, but the bitterness is unpalatable, so I often combine it with something sweet such as spearmint, licorice, or stevia.

Actea racemosa (Black cohosh)
Family: *Ranunculaceae*
Part used: Root
Indigenous to the eastern Appalachi-ans, this atypical buttercup was a favorite herb of the Eclectic school of practitioners in the late 1800s, second only in popularity to echinacea.

Black cohosh is a traditional sedative nervine and antispasmodic. It is used with good results in anxiety, hysteria, panic attacks, imaginary worries, muscle cramps, and stiffness. It also relieves spasmodic coughs, menstrual cramps, and vascular spasms leading to hypertension or impaired local perfusion. It has been shown to have hypotensive and peripheral vasodilating properties. Black cohosh is an anti-inflammatory and antirheumatic, probably due to the presence of salicylates. A bitter glycoside stimulates appetite and digestive function, including hepatic and pancreatic stimulation.

Black cohosh has a particular balancing effect upon the female hormonal system and has been used with good results in chronic dysmenorrhea, breast pain, menopause, threatened miscarriage, migraines of menstrual origin, and ovarian pain. It binds to estrogen receptors in the tissues and suppresses luteinizing hormone from the pituitary gland without affecting follicle-stimulating hormone. This makes it a useful remedy when treating certain types of infertility, polycystic ovary syndrome, and ovarian tumors. Interestingly, the estrogenic effect of black cohosh has been shown to have a paradoxical inhibitory effect on estrogen-dependent breast tumor cell growth.

Clinical Applications in Fibromyalgia
This is a wonderful herb for the person with FMS. It alleviates symptoms of muscle stiffness and soreness, sciatica, neuralgia, rheumatism, and arthritis. It combines well with warming herbs such as prickly ash and ginger, and with muscle relaxants such as cramp bark for this purpose. It is especially helpful where anxiety contributes to muscle tension.

Agropyron repens
(Couch/Twitch Grass)
FAMILY: *Graminae*
PART USED: Rhizome
This pervasive perennial grass is a common and pernicious weed found widely throughout temperate zones. The rhizome is rich in polysaccharides as well as the sugar mannitol. It also contains a trace of volatile oil mostly comprising monoterpenes and sesquiterpenes. In addition the ash contains up to 30 percent silica, which actively contributes to wound healing and exerts a regenerative effect on the parenchyma of the lungs and kidneys. Absorbed sugars pass from the bloodstream into the glomerular filtrate of the nephron where they exert an osmotic pressure and tend to hold water in the nephron. Thus couch grass is considered an osmotic diuretic that does not actually increase renal filtration but does prevent reabsorption of water from the filtrate. This serves to increase the urinary volume and dilute urinary solutes, thus protecting against precipitation of minerals and the formation of kidney or bladder stones. The sugars are also demulcent in the kidney and reduce irritation and inflammation. There is also a broad antibiotic activity exhibited by the volatile oil.

Clinical Applications in Fibromyalgia
I use couch grass as a demulcent diuretic in interstitial cystitis and to relieve symptoms of bladder spasms. It combines well with corn silk, cramp bark, and ginger for this purpose. The sugars extract well into water and it tastes sweet and bland, so it is easily taken as a tea.

Allium cepa (Onion)
FAMILY: *Liliaceae*
PART USED: Bulb
Traditionally incorporated in foods around the world, this common vegetable is a powerhouse of nutrition. It is rich in sulphur compounds, much like garlic and several other members of the family, such as shallots, leeks, and chives. Sulphur has been likened to the match or spark that lights the fire of all metabolism. It is critical to health, most particularly to the detox-

ification processes in the liver. Just one or two generations back it was traditional to use sulphur (brimstone) to cure infections and various skin afflictions, and molasses has long been known as a source of sulphur. Raw onions have a mildly diuretic effect, probably through renal stimulation from the volatile oils, and they are a good source of vitamin C. Hot poultices of onion can be applied over swollen glands, toothache, earache, and sore throats.

Onion skins yield quercitin, a bioflavonoid that promotes structural integrity of the blood vessel lining, tensile strength of connective tissue, and increased resistance to inhaled allergens and microbes. This can be extracted by boiling and using the resulting fluid in soups or juices. The fluid can also be applied topically to soothe skin irritations.

A homeopathic preparation of *Allium cepa* can be used for a runny nose and head colds, as well as for colic in infants and bladder pain with reddish, smarting urine. Onion is used for preventing cataracts and heart disease and for treating allergies, asthma, burns, colds, diabetes, hypertension, hypercholesterolemia, HIV, inflammatory bowel disease, insect bites and stings, pneumonia, scabies, TB, varicose veins, and yeast infections.

Clinical Applications in Fibromyalgia
I often prescribe onion soup as part of a cleansing protocol because the sulphur compounds aid in hepatic detoxification processes and promote tissue cleansing. I also recommend it for *Candida* overgrowth and bowel flora disturbances associated with leaky gut syndrome.

Allium sativa (Garlic)
FAMILY: *Liliaceae*
PART USED: Bulb
A close relative of the onion, and likewise rich in antimicrobial sulphur, garlic is especially indicated for acute infections, blood poisoning, elevated cholesterol, atheroma, thrombosis, and arteriosclerosis. It also shows great promise against cancer. Much of the medicinal value of garlic lies in the essential oil. When you cook with garlic the whole house smells wonderful, but there is precious little of the aromatic, volatile compounds left in the food. It is better to add the garlic just at the end of cooking to preserve the medicinal effects.

The optimum way to take garlic is raw. Over the years I have perfected a technique for taking raw garlic (and still having friends). I call it socially responsible garlic medication! The secret is to avoid chewing it because then the volatile compounds don't get a chance to lodge in the pores of the mouth where they can linger for hours. Peel and chop a clove or two of garlic and put it on a teaspoon. Use this to set the garlic at the back of the throat and simply swallow with water like a pill. If you do this at night, by the morning you won't even know you took it. If your stomach burns with raw garlic, then make sure to eat a little food before taking it.

Clinical Applications in Fibromyalgia
I recommend garlic as part of a tissue cleansing protocol because the sulphur compounds aid in hepatic detoxification processes. It is also helpful for *Candida* overgrowth and bowel flora disturbances associated with leaky gut syndrome. Garlic is best taken fresh. Any processing will reduce the content of volatile oils that carry the active constituents.

Althea officinalis (Marshmallow)
FAMILY: *Malvaceae*
PART USED: Root and leaf
This is a large perennial plant related to hollyhock and hibiscus. It is very rich in mucilage and also contains starch and simple sugars, as well as pectin, asparagine, various phenolic acids, and a trace of volatile oil. Marshmallow is demulcent when taken internally and emollient when applied topically. It is also a soothing expectorant. To reduce extraction of the starch it should be infused without heat (soaked for twelve hours in cold water). It has traditionally been used for gastric and enteric

irritation and inflammation, peptic ulceration, respiratory catarrh and cough, cystitis, urethritis, and kidney and bladder stones. Topical uses involve a drawing action, being beneficial in abscesses, boils, and varicose ulcers. Marshmallow also exhibits antimicrobial activity, and a marked hypoglycemic action has been demonstrated in animal studies.

Clinical Applications in Fibromyalgia
I prescribe marshmallow in the form of a tea as a soothing and demulcent diuretic in interstitial cystitis or spasms of the bladder. It combines well with corn silk, cramp bark, and couch grass for this purpose. The mucilage and polysaccharides are best extracted into water; tinctures and other solvent extracts do not work as well as the simple tea.

Apium graveolens (Celery)
FAMILY: *Apiaceae*
PART USED: Seed, stems, and leaves
A common green vegetable, this plant has a long folk medicine tradition as a blood purifier. It is incorporated into detoxification programs, especially those dealing with arthritis and rheumatoid complaints. Celery aids the body in the removal of uric acid through the kidneys. The seeds are found to be the strongest, and a tea or extract is commonly prescribed. Celery has potent antiplatelet activity, reducing blood clotting as well as

being a vasodilator and thus of benefit in reducing hypertension. Celery and some other members of the *Apiaceae* family contain chemicals that act as calcium channel blockers and may enhance the antihypertensive effect. The traditional Chinese use of celery for dizziness may be attributed to this hypotensive effect.

Clinical Applications in Fibromyalgia
I recommend celery frequently as a cleansing, alterative diuretic to aid in the removal of acid wastes from the tissues. It is especially useful in arthritic conditions and has traditionally been used as part of a spring cleanse. Juicing the stems is a good way to take it, but the tincture is made from the seeds and is considerably stronger. Using celery seeds in cooking is also beneficial.

Arctium lappa (Burdock)
Family: *Asteraceae*
Part used: Root
This large biennial weed is common on roadsides and disturbed soil. It puts out a basal rosette of leaves in the first year and a flowering spike in the second, giving rise to numerous burrs or seed heads, the stickiness of which is accorded by millions of tiny hooks and which is said to have been the original inspiration for Velcro. The root is cultivated as a vegetable called *gobo* in Japan where it is slivered and stir-fried

or boiled in soups. In herbal medicine the root is considered an excellent alterative and is traditionally used for eruptive skin conditions and for arthritis, rheumatic conditions, cancer, and liver dysfunction. It contains a bitter compound that promotes digestive function, including secretion of digestive enzymes, hydrochloric acid, and mucus, as well as liver and pancreatic function, and peristalsis. It has bacterial and fungicidal properties. The root also contains up to 45 percent inulin, which is a complex polysaccharide that serves to slow the absorption of sugars from the gut and so reduces and aids in balancing blood sugar. Burdock can be used to lower blood sugar and is helpful in treating diabetes and hypoglycemia.

Clinical Applications in Fibromyalgia
This is one of my favorite herbs as an alterative for the joints to aid the removal of metabolic wastes from the tissues and to promote optimal liver and bowel function. It combines well with yellow dock, cleavers, nettle, and barberry for this purpose. It is also useful to balance and stabilize the blood sugar and combines well with licorice and blue vervain for this purpose. Some grocery stores or Oriental food markets carry the root as a vegetable and this can be juiced as part of a cleansing protocol.

Armoracea rusticana (Horseradish)

FAMILY: *Cruciferae*

PART USED: Root

This root, cultivated for use as a condiment, has been traditionally used as a strong rubefacient and kidney stimulant. It contains a mustard oil glucosinalate that gives the "bite" to horseradish sauce. This is another sulphur compound, heating and antimicrobial like onion and garlic.

The glucosinalates, about seventy of which are known to date, mostly come from the *cruciferae* or mustard family, including black radish, white and black mustard, nasturtium, and shepherd's purse. They all need water to be activated, so aqueous preparations are best. Topically they have an irritant effect, which is rubefacient to vesicant. This makes them a useful poultice for rheumatic and other inflammatory conditions. Unlike other poultices, which are applied very hot, glucosinalate-containing poultices should be made no hotter than 45° C to avoid the production of toxic nitriles. Taken internally, glucosinalates are mildly irritant, causing digestive stimulation similar to bitters. Taken in large doses, they will cause gastric inflammation and nausea. The glucosinalates are excreted via the kidneys where their irritation causes diuresis, and via the lungs where their irritation enhances expectoration. They are also somewhat antibacterial and antifungal, and act as a circulatory stimulant.

Many glucosinalates exhibit an antithyroid effect through an inhibition of thyroid gland uptake of iodide as well as an inhibition of conversion of iodide to iodine. Thus there is a potential for using them to treat hyperthyroidism and, conversely, they are probably best avoided in cases of hypothyroidism. In clinical practice this means that vegetables of the mustard family, such as cabbage, broccoli, kale, turnips, and cauliflower are excellent for people suffering from hyperthyroidism, but should be avoided by people suffering from hypothyroidism. This thyroid-lowering effect is minimized by cooking.

The most recent research into the glucosinalates has focused on their apparent anticarcinogenesis effect. Hepatic enzyme induction by *Cruciferae*, particularly brussels sprouts, cauliflower, and cabbage, appears on in vivo testing to offer some considerable protection against carcinogens. In 1982 the National Research Council Committee on Diet, Nutrition and Cancer recommended that everyone increase their consumption of these foods as a preventive measure. In people with low thyroid function, supplementing with iodine is probably appropriate.

Clinical Applications in Fibromyalgia

This is not an herb I use often because it is so powerful and it is possible to burn the skin if you're not careful. Occasionally, though, I recommend it as a warming topical application for muscle stiffness and local inflammation. Taken internally it provides sulphur that enhances a cleansing protocol and increases renal circulation which also aids in elimination of toxins.

Astragalus membranaceous (Milk Vetch)

FAMILY: *Leguminosae*

PART USED: Root

This plant, closely related to licorice, has a long tradition of use in traditional Chinese medicine where it is believed to tonify the spleen and lung meridians and support the protective Qi energy (roughly equivalent to the immune system in Western medicine). Much of the modern research into the plant has been carried out on animals and in vitro, so extrapolation to human effects are not always easy.

No single active constituent has been identified. The root contains many triterpenoid saponins as well as flavonoids, isoflavonoids (which impart a yellow color considered to be an indicator of quality), sterols, amino acids, and numerous polysaccharides.

The polysaccharides and saponins have demonstrated significant immune-modulating activity in vitro, including improved lymphocyte responses, enhanced natural killer cell activity, and potentiation of mono-cyte activity. Whole root extracts have also demonstrated marked immune-modulating effects, including increased phagocytic activity and increased superoxide dismutase (a potent cell antioxidant) production with oral ingestion in mice, increased immunoglobulin levels, and some antiviral action attributed to enhanced interferon production.

Astragalus has long been known as a tonic and adaptogenic herb. Studies have shown enhanced cell growth, metabolism, and longevity in tissue cultures, as well as memory improvement and protection of the liver and kidneys against toxins. A cardiotonic, positive inotropic, and hypotensive effect has been observed in animal studies.

Traditional Chinese formulas including *Astragalus* have been used for fatigue, irritability, poor healing sores, organ prolapse, excessive uterine bleeding, numbness, pain or swelling of the extremities, excessive or inappropriate sweating, and symptoms of nephritis. Modern Western herbalists recognize it as one of the preeminent tonics for chronic immune deficiency, as well as for congestive heart failure and kidney failure.

Clinical Applications in Fibromyalgia

I use this herb extensively when the immune system is compromised and the patient suffers from frequent colds and infections. In FMS, where there is often concurrent leaky gut, food allergies, and immune dysfunction, it is very helpful for long-term use, with the added benefit of being an adaptogen.

Avena sativa (Oats)

FAMILY: *Graminae*

PART USED: Unripe grain, ripe grain, and stem

Oats are an ancient grass, indigenous to northern Europe and now widely grown as a food crop. They are considered a powerful balancing and normalizing agent to the nervous system, being either a stimulating tonic or a sedative tonic, as required. Most commercial medicinal products are made from the stem or straw. This is left behind when the grain is threshed and is consequently very cheap. However, the superior medicine, and the one most practitioners use, is made from the whole, unripe grain heads, harvested when they are in the milk stage. At this time the grain is still green and squeezing the grain head causes it to exude a milky fluid. The top 6 to 8 inches of the plant should be processed fresh for maximum preservation of the active constituents. Oats are a nerve tonic, restorative, antidepressant, and tranquilizer, as well as a rich source of minerals with a nutritive specificity for the brain. Oats are traditionally recommended for epilepsy, nervous depression, and, particularly

with black cohosh and skullcap, for trembling, spasms, and twitching.

Rolled oats or oatmeal may be used as a skin softener and to reduce redness, itching, or irritation. Put 1 cup of oatmeal or 2 cups of oat flakes into a muslin bag or old cotton sock. Tie securely and drop into a warm bath. Swirl around till the water is milky, then submerge the body or the affected part.

Oats have a very low level of gluten, and oat flour can be substituted for wheat flour in many recipes. Rolled oat flakes are not as nutritional as steel cut oats because the steaming and rolling damages cell membranes and causes the loss of B vitamins and other nutrients. To make real Scottish porridge, which is much more nutritious, take 1 cup of coarse oatmeal or steel cut oats and soak in 3 cups of water overnight. Simmer for a few minutes, stirring frequently, until the oats are thick and soft. Flavor as desired with honey, milk, butter, cinnamon, dried fruit, or chopped nuts. Note that a tablespoon of oat bran daily can promote regular bowel function and reduces cholesterol.

Clinical Applications in Fibromyalgia
This is a wonderful opportunity to eat your medicine! I most commonly prescribe it in the form of porridge as a nutritive nerve tonic and fortifying relaxant, to aid sleep, and to reduce

anxiety and stress. It combines well with chamomile, passionflower, hops, catmint, and skullcap for this purpose. It is also effective in a bath for the itching and irritated skin that often accompanies FMS.

Bacopa monniera (**Brahmi**)

FAMILY: *Scrophulariceae*

PART USED: Aerial parts

This is an annual, succulent, creeping plant found throughout the Indian subcontinent and often confused with gotu kola, which sometimes also shares the name *brahmi*, meaning "king" or "leader." It is the leading nerve tonic of Ayurvedic medicine, being used to treat epilepsy, schizophrenia, depression, mania, hysteria, and insanity, and to improve memory and mental acuity. Recent clinical trials have confirmed the memory-enhancing action of this herb and have shown improved motor coordination, more rapid learning, anticonvulsant, and sedative properties. The sedative action allows brahmi to be used to calm and relax the mind without dulling it like most sedatives, herbal or pharmaceutical. Because of the paradoxical action of sedation and improved learning and retention, brahmi shows promise in the treatment of attention deficit hyperactivity disorder, as well as in treating nervous exhaustion and nervous breakdown. Brahmi also has some

anti-inflammatory action without risk of gastric irritation.

Clinical Applications in Fibromyalgia

I recommend this herb for brain fog, confusion, memory loss, and reduced concentration. It combines well with ginkgo, gotu kola, periwinkle and rosemary for this purpose.

Berberis vulgaris (**Barberry**)

FAMILY: *Berberidaceae*

PART USED: Root

A common northern temperate shrub, now cultivated in many gardens for its bright yellow flowers, colorful leathery leaves, and dark purple berries, barberry was listed in Gerard's herbal of 1633, has been widely used in Europe and Russia, and was known by the Blackfoot, Navaho, Paiute, and Shoshone Indians. The root contains several alkaloids, notably berberine, which has a powerfully antimicrobial action. Isolated berberine sulphate has shown significant activity against a host of bacteria, fungi, and viruses. Berberine has also demonstrated immunostimulant, anticonvulsant, sedative, hypotensive, and cooling activity. It increases circulation to the spleen, the largest organ of the lymphatic system, and increases macrophage activity. Berberine is seen to have stronger antimicrobial activity in regions of high acidity, such as occur at the sight of infection and inflammations. In higher doses berberine may depress myocardial activity, slowing the heart beat and respiration.

The root is quite bitter and serves as an effective digestive stimulant, with a tissue specificity for the liver and biliary system. It has traditionally been used for its blood cleansing effect and for treating arthritis and chronic eruptive skin conditions. Tannins in the root, possibly combined with the effect of the berberine, provide a strong tonic action on mucous membranes throughout the body, regulating the quality and quantity of mucus and hence providing enhanced immune protection.

Clinical Applications in Fibromyalgia
I use barberry as an alterative with a tissue specificity to the joints and connective tissue, to aid in elimination of metabolic wastes and environmental toxins. It combines well with burdock, yellow dock, and nettles for this purpose. Much of the therapeutic activity is triggered by the bitter compounds that must be tasted in order to stimulate the digestive and eliminative functions. Hence a tea or tincture is preferred and capsules will not be effective. It is also effective as a tonic for the lining of the intestines, to reduce bacterial overgrowth and *Candida albicans,* and for leaky gut and irritable bowel syndromes. It combines well with yarrow, calendula, plantain, and licorice for this purpose.

Borago officinalis (Borage)
Family: *Boraginaceae*
Part used: Leaf, flower, and seed
Traditionally called the herb of courage, this has long been a remedy for brightening the mood, reducing depression and apathy, and gladdening the heart. Pliny, Dioscorides, Parkinson, and Gerard all recommended it for melancholy. Originally from southern Europe, it is now naturalized around the world. The bright blue star-shaped flowers are delightful when crystallized for cake decorating, scattered on a salad, or frozen in individual ice cubes to float in a summer drink. The leaves have a faint cucumber smell and may be steeped with water and flavored with lemon and honey to make a refreshing cold drink.

The leaves contain up to 11 percent mucilage, which has a demulcent and diuretic effect, drawing mucus secretions from the kidneys, and having a soothing and cleansing effect on the urinary tract. They also exhibit a diaphoretic or cooling action, reducing fevers and inducing perspiration. The leaves have a soothing expectorant effect on the lungs, encouraging the release of mucus and aiding in clearing congestion from the lungs. Additionally, they have traditionally been used as a tonic and balancer for the adrenal glands.

In human trials, an extract of borage leaves was found to increase task performance ability while reducing cardiovascular reactions to stress, systolic blood pressure, and the heart rate. Borage is used as a tonic adaptogen, nourishing and strengthening the adrenal glands and regulating sympathetic and parasympathetic influence.

The leaves contain between two to ten parts per million of pyrrolizidine alkaloids, primarily an unsaturated alkaloid with minimal toxicity. Saturated pyrrolizidine alkaloids, such as those found in *Symphytum officinale* (comfrey), another member of the *Boraginaceae* family, are notably toxic, causing hepatic veno-occlusive disease after prolonged use in certain sensitive individuals. There is no conclusive proof of harm from the use of borage, only theoretical arguments about likelihoods and probabilities, but common sense and caution suggest that it should be avoided during pregnancy, with any preexisting hepatic dysfunction, and for longer than four weeks without a few weeks' break. The American Herbal Products Association recommends it for external use only.

As a topical application, it is normally the expressed fixed oil that is used. This may also be taken internally. It is especially rich in gamma-linolenic acid, as is also found in evening primrose and black currant seed oils, and with equally impressive anti-inflammatory and prostaglandin-balancing effects.

Clinical Applications in Fibromyalgia
Internally the oil may be used as a source of gamma-linolenic acid (GLA), which is anti-inflammatory and promotes the formation of beneficial prostaglandins. I prescribe the foliage and flowers internally as an adaptogen to protect and spare the adrenal glands and reduce the stress response and associated depression. It combines especially well with licorice, Siberian ginseng, and blue vervain for this purpose.

Boswellia carterii (Frankincense)
FAMILY: *Burseraceae*
PART USED: Gum-resin
This herb has an ancient and noble history. It was burned at nightfall by the Egyptians as an offering to Ra, the sun god, to ensure the return of the sun with the new morning, and they used it in embalming, where its powerful germicidal properties helped to preserve the bodies. It was brought as a gift to the baby Jesus by the wise men, along with myrrh and gold. Greeks, Romans, and Persians all used frankincense as a ceremonial and domestic incense and air purifier. In older texts it is sometimes referred to as *Olibanum*. The tree is indigenous to north Africa and parts of the Indian subcontinent, sometimes forming small forests; over twenty-five species are medicinal. In the heat of the day the essential oil evaporates into the dry air and the tree may appear to

shimmer in the heat. This allows the tree to cool itself and protect itself from the fierce sun, without sacrificing precious water. It is harvested by incising the trunk and collecting the resin that exudes. This is allowed to dry on the tree for up to three months before being scraped off as clear yellow to brown crystalline "tears."

The medicinal resin contains about 8 percent volatile oil as well as up to 35 percent gum. The medicinal action may be employed as a tincture in 90 percent alcohol, or as a distilled essential oil. Internally the tincture is stimulating, strongly antiseptic, and anti-inflammatory with a tissue specificity for the mucous membranes (the lining tissues of the gut, respiratory, urinary, and reproductive organs). Here it is employed to increase phagocytosis and reduce infection, and as an anti-inflammatory to increase microcirculation to the membranes, regulate mucus secretions, and tonify the tissues.

For topical cosmetic applications the essential oil may be used for bacterial and fungal skin infections, boils, poorly healing wounds, acne, and mature or aging skin.

Because of its traditional use as a ritualistic and ceremonial incense, frankincense is considered to enhance meditation and spiritual practices and promote a sense of calm and peace.

Clinical Applications in Fibromyalgia
I use frankincense as an anti-inflammatory and antimicrobial for inflammations and irritations of the gut, including *Candida albicans* and diarrhea. It combines well with licorice, calendula, and plantain for this purpose.

Brassica niger/alba (Black/White Mustard)

FAMILY: *Cruciferae*
PART USED: Seeds
This is a small, weedy annual, indigenous to northern and central Europe and now widely cultivated. It has a long tradition of use as a rubefacient, counterirritant, diaphoretic, diuretic, and stimulant. Like many other members of this family, mustard is rich in sulphur-containing glucosinalates, or mustard-oil glycosides. Therapeutically, these all have similar properties, being strongly rubefacient and even blistering if applied too long. When used carefully, plasters of ground mustard seed can be counterirritant, warming, and anti-inflammatory.

A traditional folk remedy from the north of England for bronchitis and wheezy coughing is to apply goose grease over the chest, apply a plaster of ground mustard seeds mixed to a paste with water, and then cover with brown paper and red flannel. Presumably the paper prevents the plaster from drying, which would inactivate the enzymes responsible for breaking the glycosides into active compounds, and the flannel keeps everything warm. The goose grease is to protect the skin and aid rapid removal of the plaster, but any oil will work. Perhaps the red is symbolic of the heat that will be generated, but I am only guessing here. The same remedy is also effective for pleurisy, pneumonia, and intercostal neuralgia.

A similar plaster can be applied over stiff or arthritic joints. Mustard oil is also available from Asian foods stores, and makes an excellent massage oil. It can be easily blended with essential oils and applied as a friction rub, liniment, or massage oil. A foot bath can be made using 1 tablespoon of powdered mustard in 1 liter of hot water. This is an effective preventive at the onset of a cold or flu, warming the entire body and aiding the immune response to the microbe. For chronically cold feet, the powder can be sprinkled into shoes and socks. Mustard is occasionally used internally, as tea made with ¼ teaspoon of powdered seeds per cup, for the treatment of hypothermia and at the onset of a cold or flu.

Clinical Applications in Fibromyalgia
I use mustard as a counterirritant, warming, and anti-inflammatory for topical application. I sometimes suggest to patients that they have their massage therapist use mustard oil in a treatment, being careful to avoid the face and other sensitive areas. Mustard plasters are cheap and easy to make and very effective for stiff and sore muscles. Simply mix mustard powder to a paste with warm water and apply over the affected area. Cover with plastic wrap and a warm towel. Leave on as long as it is comfortable. Be aware that some people have more sensitive skin than others and may burn.

Calendula officinalis (**Marigold**)
FAMILY: *Asteraceae*
PART USED: Flower
This pretty, bright orange flower was named after the Latin word *calends*, meaning "day," for its habit of closing tight at the end of the day. It is native to the Mediterranean area but has been widely cultivated in gardens around the world.

It is noted as an anti-inflammatory and wound-healing herb with a long history of use. It is an antifungal, antiprotozoal, antibacterial (especially against *staphylococcus* and *streptococcus*), cholagogue, emmenagogue, lymphatic stimulant, decongestant to the tissues, anticancer agent, and menstrual regulator. Additionally, it protects against the effects of radiation and protects the brain tissue from the deleterious effects of anaesthesia. The anti-inflammatory and wound-healing action is seen with direct contact on the affected tissue. Thus it is not effective for arthritic-type inflammation but makes an excellent remedy for inflammations and lesions of the digestive tract, vaginal tissue, and skin.

Clinical Applications in Fibromyalgia
This is one of the most useful herbs in treating inflammations of the large intestine, as can occur with FMS and leaky gut syndrome. In particular, it is useful for treating *Candida albicans* overgrowth. It exerts direct action against the yeast cells, as well as reduces inflammation of the bowel wall caused by yeast by-products and heals lesions that may permit entry of yeast and other pathogens into the bloodstream. I frequently combine it with lapacho for treating *Candida.*

Capsicum minimum/fructescens and others (Cayenne)
FAMILY: *Solanaceae*
PART USED: Fruit
Commonly known as chili pepper, there are a great many varieties, all with the typical pungent heat, and many that are eaten as a condiment. Brought to Britain from India in the mid–sixteenth century, cayenne was named after the Greek "to bite" in allusion to the powerful heat it contains. Today it is found worldwide and sometimes cultivated as an ornamental or a house-plant. It is considered to be a stimulant, tonic, carminative, sialogogue, stom-achic, alterative, astringent, antispas-modic, sudorific, emetic, antiseptic,

antirheumatic, anodyne, and analgesic. Cayenne has long been regarded in herbal medicine as an excellent stimu-lant, producing a natural warmth, opening the peripheral blood vessels, and equalizing circulation. It is a pow-erful antioxidant, rich in iron, and accelerates oxygenation of tissues, thus increasing available energy.

Modern use has focused on the resin, and especially its content of capsaicin. When applied topically over a site of pain, capsaicin is shown to first increase then rapidly deplete the level of Substance P in sensory nerves serving the affected area. Substance P is a potent mediator of the pain response and reducing its availability has the effect of reducing the sensation of pain. Thus topical use of cayenne, in a cream, ointment, or plaster, can be effective in reducing the pain of inflammation in joints or muscles. It is also known to reduce the pain of shingles, toothache, migraines, and herpes.

Additionally, cayenne used inter-nally significantly lowers both plasma cholesterol and triglycerides, and the LDL:HDL ratio.

Clinical Applications in Fibromyalgia
This is a wonderful herb used topically to reduce sensations of pain in joints and muscles and as a warming, rube-facient, and anti-inflammatory. I usually recommend using a propri-etary cream that has a precisely cali-

brated dose that won't burn the skin. It is also a good idea to use cayenne liberally in cooking.

Centella/Hydrocotyl asiatica (Gotu Kola)

FAMILY: *Apiacae*

PART USED: Stem and leaf

This is an herb with a long tradition of use that has recently enjoyed a sudden surge in popularity. It is sometimes eaten like a green vegetable in India and is used as a general tonic and tissue healing agent. In traditional Chinese medicine, it is reputed to improve memory and mental acuity and to promote longevity. Gotu kola contains flavonoids, terpenoids, and volatile oil, as well as three key terpene compounds. These compounds regulate the regeneration of collagen and hence promote tissue healing and the last stages of injury resolution. It was traditionally used in India for the treatment of leprosy. Modern research has demonstrated its effectiveness at speeding the resolution of eczema, wounds, lacerations, varicose or pressure ulcers, surgical wounds, gangrene, and skin grafts. Gotu kola also improves circulation into the extremities—the legs, feet, and head. This contributes to its healing properties by delivering vital oxygen and nutrients to the tissues, and providing white blood cells for immune

function. The circulatory stimulation also contributes to the enhancement of memory and concentration. It is used to boost energy and stamina, clear the head, and promote mental sharpness.

Clinical Applications in Fibromyalgia

This is a very good herb for people with FMS because it helps several problem areas at once. I prescribe it for promoting mental acuity, memory, and concentration, and to reduce brain fog, often in combination with rosemary, gingko, and periwinkle. I also use it to improve the circulation to toes and fingers in combination with ginger, cayenne, and prickly ash. In addition, as a collagen and connective tissue tonic, it may be helpful in treating mitral valve prolapse, loss of cartilage or lubricating fluids in joints, and possibly in improving the structural integrity of fascia. Note that this latter use is based on supposition and clinical experience and has not been proven in laboratory experiments or clinical trials. It also heals leaky gut and increases integrity of mucous membranes.

Chamomilla recutita (Chamomile)

FAMILY: *Asteraceae*

PART USED: Flowers

There are many species of chamomile that grow all over the northern temperate zones, and the recorded history of its medicinal use goes back to the times of the ancient Egyptians. It was traditionally used as a strewing herb in medieval times, and when planted between the cracks of paving stones or on garden paths, it gives off a rich but delicate perfume when walked upon.

Several species have been used medicinally. German chamomile (*Chamomilla recutita*) is generally preferred, although Roman chamomile (*Anthemus nobilis*) is also commonly used. The part used in herbal medicine is the flower head, picked just as it comes into bloom and dried carefully to prevent browning. It has a sweet scent and taste with just a hint of bitterness.

Chamomile is widely used in folk medicine around the world. The main therapeutic attributes are anti-inflammatory and relaxing (to both nervous and smooth muscle tissue). It is also bitter and has a pronounced inhibitory effect upon allergic sensitivities.

The anti-inflammatory action is best seen in topical application (as a compress, soak, or cream) but is also very effective in the whole digestive system. Thus it can be used as an eye-wash for any minor eye inflammations or irritations; as a skin wash or a cream for eczema, psoriasis, or varicose veins; as a douche for all vaginal infections or inflammations, and for leucorrhoea; or it may be taken orally for ulcers, inflammatory bowel disease, or minor hepatic inflammations.

The antispasmodic effects of chamomile are pronounced. It relaxes smooth muscle, which surrounds the entire digestive, respiratory, reproductive, and urinary systems. It does this by inhibiting the transmission of nerve impulses that would otherwise activate muscle function. Chamomile relieves spasmodic conditions such as allergic asthma, bronchitis, constipation, biliary dyskinesia, menstrual cramps, and bladder spasms.

Chamomile also has a strong sedative effect in the brain. It helps in the treatment of anxiety, stress, and sleep disturbance. It has long been known as one of the most gentle yet effective sedatives available—even Peter Rabbit was given chamomile by his mother after an escapade in Mr. MacGregor's garden! It is safe for children, even very small babies who are fretful or distressed. A very pleasant way to extract the sedative properties is to place a cup of chamomile flowers in a muslin bag and steep it in the bath. This will release all the volatile oils so that you can inhale the aroma, and the flower water will soften your skin. Try adding half a cup of oatmeal or mixing chamomile with rose petals or lavender for variety.

A traditional remedy for pain was to crush together equal parts of chamomile flowers and poppy heads and either drink the strong tea or apply it as a poultice.

The bitter action of chamomile is interesting because it stimulates all aspects of digestive function. The peristaltic movements are made smoother, digestive juices are released, and nervous tension in the bowel is eased. Combined with the strongly carminative effect of the volatile oil, this makes chamomile an ideal herb to use in cases of inflammatory bowel diseases such as ulcerative colitis or Crohn's disease, as well as for gas, indigestion, peptic ulcers, and irritable bowel syndrome.

Chamomile also has significant effects upon the immune system. The volatile oil has been shown to have marked antibacterial effects, especially against *staphylococcus aureus,* a common skin pathogen, as well as being active against *Candida albicans yeast.* Additionally, chamomile makes the mucus membranes less reactive to allergen exposure. Coupled with the anti-inflammatory action, this makes chamomile a very useful herb to include in any formula for inhalant or ingested allergies.

The essential oil of chamomile is one of the safest and mildest of all oils. It can safely be used on the skin undiluted and will not cause irritation or sun sensitization. For internal use, the tea or the tincture forms are preferred. In the tincture the volatile oils are dissolved out into alcohol and in the tea they are evaporated into steam that is inhaled; either way the results are equally impressive. Chamomile may also be used as a cool compress or in a spritzer for redness, broken capillaries, bruising, or any irritation of the skin. It is especially useful for treating acne rosacea, which usually has an underlying low-grade bacterial infection as part of the problem. The antibacterial and the anti-inflammatory effects are both important here.

Clinical Applications in Fibromyalgia
This is one of my favorite remedies for a host of ailments. I recommend its use internally as a gentle, non-habit-forming sedative for sleep disturbance and as an anxiolytic. It combines well with skullcap, passionflower, valerian, and other sedative and relaxant herbs for this purpose. As a spasmodic carminative it is very helpful for gas, cramping, and the symptoms of irritable bowel syndrome. It combines well with calendula, hops, blue vervain, lavender, ginger, and cinnamon for this purpose. It can be applied topically in the form of a wash, bath, compress, or cream for itching or irritation of the skin. It combines well with lavender and chickweed for this purpose.

Cinnamomum zeylanicum (Cinnamon)

FAMILY: *Lauraceae*

PART USED: Bark

A tree reaching up to 30 feet high and often growing only in sand, cinnamon prefers a constant supply of rain and warmth. It is indigenous to Sri Lanka but has been cultivated commercially for over 200 years in Sumatra, China, India, Mauritius, Brazil, Jamaica, and other hot, moist climates. Securing a supply of cinnamon was the cause of the colonization of Ceylon (Sri Lanka) first by the Portuguese, then the Dutch, and lastly the British. Widely used in baking and cooking, it is commonly adulterated with *Cinnamomum cassia,* which is easier and cheaper to grow but has less of the key active constituents. The volatile oil is used in perfumery and soaps. Synthetic vanilla is made from eugenol isolated from the volatile oil.

The bark contains tannins, which make it an effective astringent for nosebleeds, uterine bleeding, and enteric bleeding. Tannins provide an antimicrobial effect, useful in cleaning wounds and reducing infection. Cinnamon has demonstrated activity against *E. coli, Staph. aureus* and *Candida albicans.* Cinnamon bark also has mucilage, which makes it a demulcent, soothing and healing tissues. The bark is rich in volatile oil, sometimes as high as 10 percent, and mainly comprising eugenol, cineol, cinnamaldehyde, and terpenes. Good- quality oil distilled from the bark should be 50 to 75 percent cinnamaldehyde and only 4 to 10 percent eugenol. If oil is adulterated with cheaper leaf distillate then there may be up to 90 percent eugenol and only 3 percent cinnamaldehyde. The presence of small volumes of eugenol in cinnamon bark volatile oil protect against skin irritation by cinnamaldehyde. Cinnamaldehyde has been shown to reduce hepatic glutathione and eugenol is a known liver toxin. For this reason cinnamon oil is not recommended for internal use. Some authorities recommend using N-acetyl-cysteine concurrently when taking extracts of cinnamon to boost hepatic glutathione levels.

Cinnamon may be taken in the form of a decoction or a tincture in hot water for its warming and stimulating effect. Little volatile oil is extracted this way and liver toxicity is very unlikely. Cinnamon is considered to equalize the circulation and increase the core body temperature. This is useful in the early stages of a cold or flu, when raising the core temperature stimulates the immune response. It may also be applied topically as a poultice or liniment for muscle stiffness, aching, cramping, and arthritis.

Cinnamon has powerful tonic properties and is especially useful for promoting the appetite and encouraging recovery from chronic debility or during convalescence. It is an antispasmodic, relieving menstrual and digestive cramps, and is a carminative that aids indigestion, belching, and flatulence. It is also considered to invigorate the senses and to be an aphrodisiac.

Clinical Applications in Fibromyalgia
This herb is used as a warming and invigorating tonic for weakness and debility. It combines well with tonic adaptogens such as licorice, Siberian ginseng, and ashwagandha for this purpose. It tastes good and the tea can be taken long-term without adverse effects. It is also useful for the spasmodic colicky pain of irritable bowel syndrome, in combination with chamomile, cramp bark, and ginger.

Crataegus oxyacantha/monogyna/laevigata
(Hawthorn)
FAMILY: *Rosaceae*
PART USED: Spring shoots, flowers, and fruit
This is a shrubby tree found commonly in English hedgerows and often planted as an ornamental for its lovely blossoms and bright red fruits. The flower buds, spring twig tips, and ripe berries are harvested for medicine. Active constituents include a variety of

flavonoids of various types, which are all strongly antioxidant and tonic to connective tissue. They promote tissue healing, reduce oxidative stress, and may inhibit carcinogenesis. The berries contain citric, ascorbic, and tartaric acids, which contribute to the antioxidant effect.

The Eclectics described hawthorn as specific for angina, tachycardia, valvular deficiency with or without enlargement, rheumatic valvular damage, cardiac insufficiency or heart failure, and difficulty breathing. It regulates all functions of the heart, increasing or decreasing the heart rate, as needed. Hawthorn dilates the coronary blood vessels and is especially indicated in enlargement of the heart with oppressed breathing.

Hawthorn has been shown to increase oxygen utilization by the heart and increase energy metabolism in the heart. It is also useful as a diuretic in cases of cardiac edema. Hawthorn is used specifically for arrhythmias, degenerative heart disease (especially in the elderly), coronary heart disease, hypertension, tachycardia, and weakness of cardiac function secondary to infectious disease such as pneumonia or influenza. It has traditionally been used to increase the strength of the heart without raising the blood pressure, to dissolve mineral deposits and remove plaque, as a sedative for the nervous system, and as an excellent nourishing tonic for the heart.

Due to the very high presence of flavonoid compounds, hawthorn is a excellent antioxidant and provides improved tensile strength and structural integrity to collagen, which makes up connective tissue. This supports its traditional use as a strengthening tonic for the heart valves, vascular wall, and other connective tissue in the body, including muscles, tendons, ligaments, joint capsules, and hyaline cartilage in the joint cavity.

Clinical Applications in Fibromyalgia

This is the herb of choice as a strengthening tonic for the heart valves where there is mitral valve prolapse or symptoms of palpitations, oppression in the chest, shortness of breath, or faintness due to cardiac weakness. It combines well with motherwort and linden as a general cardiac tonic, and with horsetail and gotu kola for mitral valve prolapse. The connective tissue tonic effect may be beneficial in strengthening and tonifying fascia, muscle, and joint tissues. The active constituents of hawthorn extract well into water and the taste of the infusion is pleasant.

Curcuma longa (Turmeric)

FAMILY: *Zingiberaceae*
PART USED: Underground stem or rhizome

A native of southern and eastern Asia, and widely cultivated as a spice in China, India, and Indonesia, the bright yellow-orange pigment of turmeric is used as a strong dye. The alcoholic extract of the root is noted as an aromatic, warming stimulant, alterative, stomachic, carminative, cholagogue, choleretic, anti-inflammatory, detoxifier and regenerator of liver tissue, and anticarcinogenic. It also exhibits strong antimicrobial properties, especially against gram-positive bacteria and salmonella.

Many of the therapeutic properties are carried in the volatile oil and resin, so a solvent is required, or the powdered root may be taken in capsules. A decoction is not as effective. The volatile oil fraction and the curcumin have demonstrated powerful anti-inflammatory effects, comparable to hydrocortisone and phenylbutazone in acute inflammation, but without the significant side effects of these prescription drugs. Curcumin has been shown to be more effective in animals where the adrenal glands are intact and functioning normally, indicating that it may work in part by increasing the sensitivity of receptor sites to adrenal hormones. Turmeric inhibits the formation of pain-mediating prostaglandin by regulating the enzyme's cascade, much as aspirin does.

Turmeric is traditionally used as a remedy for biliousness, gallstones, liver disease, and jaundice. Modern research has shown it to be powerfully antioxidant to the liver cell membranes and to be a hepatic protective and rejuvenator akin to milk thistle or artichoke. Turmeric has shown promise in the treatment of arthritis, rheumatism, bursitis, tendinitis, gout, fungal infections, lice, and scabies.

Clinical Applications in Fibromyalgia
I use turmeric extensively as an alterative that promotes detoxification while also protecting the liver from oxidative stress. Being a warming herb, it may counteract the cooling effect of bitters traditionally used for liver stimulation and detoxification (for example, yellow dock and barberry) that may be too cooling if used alone in FMS. It is also effective in reducing inflammation of joints, especially in combination with licorice and devil's claw; and the gut, in combination with calendula and althea.

Dioscorea villosa (Wild yam)
FAMILY: *Dioscoreaceae*
PART USED: Root
Many types of wild yam grow throughout northern Central America, the United States, and southern Canada, and there are Asian species as well. *Dioscorea villosa*, the preferred medicinal variety, has a long history of traditional use as an antispasmodic, anti-inflammatory, muscle relaxant, cholagogue, especially for intestinal

inflammation and spasms, and for rheumatism.

Wild yam has been heavily harvested as a source of the starter materials for synthetic steroids, notably progesterone for the manufacture of the birth control pill. This compound is a steroidal saponin called diosgenin, many times smaller than analogous endogenous hormones, yet it appears to act in a similar fashion. It is found in other herbs with apparent hormonal action, including fenugreek and false unicorn. The postulated mechanism of action is that the tiny plant steroid interfaces with the receptor site on the target tissue and initiates a subthreshold response that "primes" the receptor site for faster or more pronounced action when the endogenous hormone enters the same receptor site.

Other traditional uses include diaphoretic, relaxant or sedative, antiemetic, and antihypertensive. It has been used against arthritis, rheumatism, muscular stiffness or inflammation, colic, inflammatory bowel disease, irritable bowel disease, diverticulosis, gallstones, adrenal exhaustion, persistent nausea, angina, and hypertension. It is especially indicated in menopausal conditions where it seems to regulate progesterone and estrogen and reduce symptoms such as hot flashes, palpitations, and vaginal dryness.

Clinical Applications in Fibromyalgia
This is a wonderful herb for people with FMS because it has several overlapping beneficial actions. I prescribe it as an anti-inflammatory for the joints for treating arthritic pain in combination with white willow, turmeric, devil's claw, and other anti-inflammatories. I also use it extensively as an antispasmodic and relaxant to the large intestine in treating irritable bowel syndrome. It combines well with cramp bark, ginger, and chamomile for this purpose.
I also combine wild yam with black cohosh, kava, and lobelia to potentize the muscle-relaxant effect.

Eleutherococcus senticosus (**Siberian Ginseng**)
FAMILY: *Araliaceae*
PART USED: Root
This northern relative of ginseng has been extensively researched and found to share many of the same adaptogenic properties. It is a general tonic to the body, acting to increase the body's resistance to stress and to increase vitality. It has been widely used by athletes and those engaged in heavy manual labor and has proven to be safe and effective.

Scientific research has demonstrated a blood sugar–balancing effect, as well as a tonic, restorative, relaxant effect on the nervous system that provides calmness with increased alertness. Other proven effects include immune regulation and stimulation, improved stamina and endurance, antithrombotic and antiedematous action, enhanced fertility, improved liver healing, increased resistance to radiation, and reduced wound-healing time.

Overall, Siberian ginseng can be considered a tonic and normalizer of body function. It is not a stimulant as is Korean ginseng, and is safe for long-term use.

Clinical Applications in Fibromyalgia
Most of my patients with FMS end up taking this herb at some point in their treatment and often throughout the herbal program. I recommend it especially as an adaptogen and general tonic that is safe for long-term use. It helps to build energy and reduce the physiological response to stress. It combines well with licorice, ashwagandha, and blue vervain for this purpose.

Equisetum arvense (**Horsetail**)
FAMILY: *Equisetaceae*
PART USED: Aerial vegetative parts
This is a very primitive plant, looking today almost as it did in the time of the dinosaurs, sixty-five million years ago, but very much smaller. Back then it reached as tall as a tree and is today, in its fossilized form, a major component of coal and oil. The modern plant grows between 2 and 4 feet high and, due to its prolific underground

stems, can be a major pest in the garden. Its closest living relatives are the ferns and, like them, horsetail reproduces by means of spores, without flowers. Horsetail accumulates silica in the stem and branches, the ash being up to 70 percent silica.

Medicinally, horsetail is considered a very cooling plant, used as a diuretic and cleansing agent for the kidneys and employed in gravel or stones of the kidneys and bladder. It has a reputation for rebuilding the tissue of the kidneys after chronic infection or inflammation. Horsetail is a powerful astringent, and is especially useful in the kidneys and lungs for bleeding conditions and loss of tissue tone. It is considered to be an excellent connective tissue regenerator, providing a strengthening and nourishing action to connective tissue, especially the kidneys, lungs, joints, bones, and nervous system. The silica content is believed to impart an increased tensile strength to connective tissue, improving the elasticity and reducing tissue damage.

Horsetail also aids in the absorption, distribution, and utilization of calcium by the tissues, and aids in the removal of uric acid via the kidneys. It has an special reputation as a tonic to the bladder, being prescribed for incontinence, bed-wetting, urethritis, mucus in the urine, and excessive frequency of urination. Administra-

tion of horsetail invokes a transient increase in circulating white blood cells, indicating an immune-stimulating effect. Additionally, it is antimicrobial against *staphylococcus aureus* and *streptococcus pyogenes*, as well as several mycobacteria.

Clinical Applications in Fibromyalgia
This herb is commonly prescribed as a tonic and regenerator of connective tissue, to strengthen and tonify the joints and rebuild cartilage. It combines well with glucosamine sulphate and MSM supplements for this purpose, and hawthorn and gotu kola may augment this action. Horsetail also tones the bladder and produces a gentle diuretic action that alleviates symptoms of interstitial cystitis.

Eschscholzia california
(**California Poppy**)
FAMILY: *Papaveraceae*
PART USED: Aerial parts
This attractive, brilliant orange member of the poppy family is usually harvested in full bloom, the entire aerial parts being medicinally active. The therapeutic applications of California poppy are similar to morphine or opium, but the effect is milder and not narcotic. It is especially indicated for anxiety and nervous tension, as well as for insomnia, overexcitability, hyperactivity, hysteria, fear, and all sorts of pain. Like opium, it also has

an antitussive and antispasmodic effect. The extract may be made from fresh or dried plant material, but the fresh is generally considered to be stronger. It is considered to be safe for children and not habit forming.

Clinical Applications in Fibromyalgia
I recommend this herb for anxiety and nervous tension, as well as for insomnia. It combines well with chamomile, valerian, skullcap, and other sedatives for this purpose. For the management of pain, it combines well with Jamaican dogwood, corydalis, or wild lettuce.

Filipendula ulmaris (Meadowsweet)
Family: *Rosaceae*
Part used: Aerial parts and root
This atypical member of the rose family grows prolifically in the English countryside, preferring moist areas and light shade. There are several other types of this genus around the world, in temperate zones. All are astringent, but only *F. ulmaris* is widely used as a medicine.

Like all members of the rose family, this plant is rich in tannins and hence is quite astringent. The tissue specificity of meadowsweet is for the upper digestive tract, with a pronounced effect on gastric and duodenal bleeding. It is also rich in various salicylates that have a pronounced anti-inflammatory effect. The drug aspirin was originally sourced from

white willow but named after the old name for meadowsweet, which was *Spirea ulmaris*. The herb has traditionally been used for arthritis, gout, and rheumatism.

Meadowsweet acts to reduce high fevers and regulate temperature; it is also a diaphoretic, an antacid, and an antibacterial. It is especially indicated in rheumatic and arthritic disorders where there is excessive accumulation of uric acid in the joints and tissues, and in gastrointestinal hyperacidity. It exhibits some mild diuretic action with an astringent tonic effect in the urinary system.

Clinical Applications in Fibromyalgia
This is one of my favorite herbs for arthritic pain in joints and to reduce uric acid in the system. It combines well with devil's claw, licorice, and turmeric for joint pain and with silver birch, celery, and parsley to remove acid wastes, which is especially useful in treating the tender points of FMS.

Fucus vesiculosis
(Kelp/Bladder Wrack)
Family: *Fucaceae*
Part used: Thallus
This is a large seaweed, forming vast underwater forests in the cold northern seas. The large, flat fronds are used as a medicine and food supplement. Kelp has long been used as a rich source of minerals for fertilizing soil.

Kelp is rich in iodine, which acts as a stimulant of thyroid activity. It can be used to tonify and strengthen a weak thyroid gland and is used to treat hypothyroidism and obesity induced by low metabolic rate. It is also effective for people who tend to be cold, slow, and sluggish and have dry skin or hair, heavy menstruation, abnormal growth of facial or body hair, or who tend to be constipated or have dry, hard stools, even though they may not test positive for low thyroid function. Kelp is considered to be an alterative and antiarthritic and to be of benefit in the removal of metabolic wastes from the tissues. It has been traditionally used both internally and topically in the form of plasters to treat arthritic joints. Anecdotal evidence suggests that kelp is beneficial to the sensory nerves, meninges, spinal cord, and brain tissue.

Kelp is markedly rich in alginates, which provide a bulking and demulcent action in the large intestine, aiding constipation and inflammatory bowel disease, including ulcerative colitis, Crohn's disease, irritable bowel syndrome, and diverticulitis. In particular, kelp contains a large amount of sodium alginate, which reduces the absorption of radioactive strontium into the thyroid gland. Kelp may be useful against radiation exposure, such as from x-rays or environmental pollution. The polysaccharides are responsible for the marked protective effect against breast cancer and the

notable stimulation of T-cell function and enhanced immune response.

Kelp is also known to be active against many gram-positive and gram-negative organisms.

Clinical Applications in Fibromyalgia
This herb can be eaten in soups and stews or ground roughly and sprinkled over food as a condiment. It is, however, hard to eat sufficient quantities to get significant therapeutic benefit, so an extract or capsules are preferred. It is especially helpful where sluggish thyroid function contributes to chilliness, menstrual disturbance, lethargy, lassitude, and fatigue. I also recommend it frequently as an alterative for the joints and muscles.

Galium aparine (Cleavers)
FAMILY: *Rubiaceae*
PART USED: Aerial parts
This is a common hedgerow or woodland plant, related to coffee and henna. It is characterized by a creeping square stem with whorls of two true leaves and four leaflike stipules occurring at intervals, and tiny, inconspicuous white flowers. The stems are weak and fragile and climb by means of tiny hooked barbs on the leaf and stem surface, which attach to adjacent plants and so enable the cleavers to reach up to the light. Coumarins that ferment on drying give a sweet grasslike scent. It is rich

in enzymes and has been used to curdle milk when making cheese. Dioscorides, almost 2,000 years ago, reported the stems being used to fashion a rough sieve, and the seeds may be collected, roasted lightly, and then ground as a coffee substitute.

Cleavers is known as a depurative, aiding lymphatic flow, easing glandular congestion, and reducing fluid retention or edema. It contains glycosides that reduce the tone of the smooth muscle in the renal pelvis and urinary tract, thus acting as an effective yet gentle diuretic. The presence of several phenolic acids provides for some antimicrobial activity, with a tissue specificity for the urinary tract. Other components give a mild laxative effect. Cleavers has traditionally been used as an alterative for swollen lymph glands, arthritis, gout, rheumatism, cancer, eczema, psoriasis, and other eruptive skin conditions. It is used as a slimming agent in obesity and is effective for increasing and enriching the milk supply in nursing mothers. A cooling skin wash may be made from the fresh juice or an infusion of the fresh plant. This is useful for sunburn or other burns, and for itching, red skin rashes.

Clinical Applications in Fibromyalgia
I recommend this herb extensively as part of a cleansing and detoxification program. By stimulating lymphatic flow and diuresis, it draws toxins and metabolic wastes from the tissues and reduces acid accumulation that can contribute to arthritis and tender points. It is best taken as a tea or by juicing the fresh plant. It combines well with bitter alteratives such as barberry and burdock. Topical applications of the tea or the fresh plant juice may be useful to reduce itching, redness, and irritation of the skin.

Ganoderma lucidum (Reishi)
FAMILY: *Basidiomycetes/Fungi*
PART USED: Fruiting body and mycelia
One of the most ancient and venerated herbal medicines of Asia, this shelf or bracket fungus ranks along with ginseng as one of the great panaceas. It has a range of beneficial effects that cause it to be classified as one of the best invigorating, tonic herbs. It has many other names, reflecting its widespread usage among indigenous peoples. Some of these names include Auspicious Herb, Holy Mushroom, Herb of Spiritual Potency, Ling Chi, and Ling Zhi. The Latin name translates as "lustrous skin." Its recorded use goes back over five hundred years to ancient Chinese dynasties.

Probably the most significant active constituents, among many useful chemicals in the plant, are the polysaccharides that provide an immunological effect and support the functioning and regulation of the whole immune system. These are water-soluble constituents, and this may account for the traditional use of reishi in teas and soups as an immune-enhancing herb. Triterpenes are also clinically active, especially in the cardiovascular system. These are not readily water soluble and hence have not been utilized clinically until more recent times.

Various polysaccharides act synergistically in the immune system to regulate and normalize its functions, thus supporting the healing process at its very core. Reishi has specifically been shown to increase the function of macrophages and to stimulate T-cell formation. Some of this may be due to a powerful antioxidant capability, which also contributes to its reputed use as an herb of longevity. The polysaccharides are also responsible for the antitumor effect and for blood sugar balancing.

The triterpenes inhibit angiotensin-converting enzyme in the lungs and thus serve a similar purpose to the ACE inhibitor class of antihypertensive drugs. They have the added advantage that, unlike the drug, the plant terpenes also regulate platelet aggregation and thus prevent the formation of blood clots, and strengthen and tone the walls of the erythrocytes, thus preventing their early demise. The triterpenes regulate hepatic cholesterol synthesis and can be very effective in cases of hyper-lipoproteinemia, especially of the familial type where standard dietary restrictions do not help.

The steroidal components of reishi have been shown to collectively offer great support in cases of hepatotoxicity and liver cancer. They also serve to reduce mast cell lysis and histamine release, thus reducing allergic and inflammatory responses.

Traditional Chinese medical texts call for up to 9 g of reishi powder daily. This may be taken stirred into hot water as a broth or simply added to soups and gravies where it serves as something of a flavoring agent as well, imparting a rich, woody, smoky flavor to foods. It has more recently been made into tinctures because the use of alcohol facilitates the extraction of steroidal and triterpene compounds.

Animal experiments have shown no side effects after thirty days of consuming more than 5 g/kg body weight—equivalent to some 350 g/day in an average adult. When commencing treatment, many people experience transient cleansing reactions such as pimples, sore muscles, dizziness, bowel disturbance, and itchy skin. These pass within a few days as the toxins are eliminated from the body, and can be controlled by regulating the daily dose.

Clinical Applications in Fibromyalgia
Reishi is a wonderful herb for long-term use in FMS. I prescribe it as an adaptogenic tonic and energy booster, and to balance blood sugar, protect the liver, and reduce mood swings. It also has some antioxidant and anti-inflammatory action. I usually use capsules in order to achieve the high doses required, and have recently been experimenting with the tincture, which seems stronger.

Gaultheria procumbens (Wintergreen)

FAMILY: *Ericaeae*
PART USED: Leaves and essential oil
This is a low-growing, evergreen shrub in the heather family, related to bearberry and pipsissewa. Like most of its relatives, wintergreen has some diuretic and urinary disinfectant properties.

Wintergreen leaves are rich in volatile oils, which are mostly excreted through the kidneys where they are slightly irritating and exert a diuretic and antimicrobial effect. An extract of the leaves is used to treat kidney and bladder stones, cystitis, urethritis, and nephritis. It is also somewhat astringent, which contributes to the antimicrobial effect and provides improved tone in the renal tubules, reducing inflammation and exudation.

The distilled volatile oil should not be used internally but is very effective when applied topically as a treatment for arthritis and rheumatism. The oil is very rich in methyl salicylate, which has a powerful rubefacient, analgesic, and anti-inflammatory effect on inflamed joints and muscles. It is beneficial in treating rheumatoid arthritis and other joint inflammations, muscle pain, gout, backache, lumbago, sciatica, sprains, and intercostal neuralgia. Due to a tendency to cause skin irritation, true volatile oil of wintergreen is now usually substituted by a synthetic methyl salicylate product or by volatile oil of *Betula lenta* (sweet birch), which is equally anti-inflammatory and analgesic but nonirritating.

Clinical Applications in Fibromyalgia
I use the volatile oil of wintergreen, or sweet birch, as a topical application for muscle stiffness, soreness, and inflammation. It is warming and pain relieving, and combines well with mustard oil as a carrier.

Ginkgo biloba (Ginkgo)

FAMILY: *Ginkgoaceae*
PART USED: Leaf
This tree is an example of a living fossil, having survived unchanged for millions of years. It is the sole survivor of its whole genus. It is indigenous to China but is now widely spread around the world in temperate zones as an ornamental. It is very resistant to pollution, so is often used in city plantings. The leaves are harvested in the late fall as they turn color.

In traditional Chinese medicine, the seed was used to dispel dampness from the lungs and relieve wheezy productive coughing. In modern Western phytotherapy, the leaf is used and there is a tremendous body of literature on the therapeutic effects of the leaf extract.

The leaves contain a variety of different flavonoids, which are all antioxidant and anti-inflammatory. They also contain diterpenes. In clinical research and in commerce this herb is often used as a standardized extract. It is standardized to 24 percent flavonoglycosides, of which 10 percent should be quercitin.

The ginkgolides are probably the major active constituent. They competitively inhibit the binding of platelet-activating-factor (PAF) receptors in the mucous membrane lining of the blood vessel wall. They have been shown to increase perfusion and oxygenation of the cardiac muscle; reduce thrombus formation; inhibit lipid peroxidation (the primary precursor to atherosclerosis); inhibit platelet aggregation; stabilize the blood-brain barrier, thus regulating what gets into and out of the brain; increase circulation to the limbs and the head; and reduce inflammatory histamine responses, including weal, flare, and asthma.

Ginkgo extract produces a significant increase in dopamine synthesis and the release of catecholamines. This is achieved through reactivation of norepinephrine and beta receptors, which causes dilation of the airways and dilation of the peripheral blood vessels. This can be helpful in cases of memory loss, Alzheimer's, Parkinson's, dizziness, and decreased alertness. The high quercitin content appears to be responsible for the marked antioxidant effect and the inhibition of platelet aggregation. It may also contribute to the formation of beneficial prostaglandins and may increase perfusion of the retina. Ginkgo increases the number of cholinergic receptor sites in the brain. This stimulates the release of endogenous relaxation factors such as prostacyclin in the arterial endothelium, which allows for peripheral vasodilation and a hypotensive effect. It is effective for senile macular degeneration, diabetic retinopathy, tinnitus, vertigo, reduced auditory acuity, and labyrinthitis.

Clinical Applications in Fibromyalgia
This herb provides excellent results in treating memory loss, confusion, and brain fog. It enhances learning ability and facilitates concentration. It combines well with rosemary and periwinkle for this purpose. Occasionally, a sensitive individual may experience full or throbbing headaches and visual disturbances, in which case the herb should be reduced in dosage or discontinued. Palpitations, anxiety,

panic disorders, and high risk of hemorrhagic stroke are contraindications for ginkgo. I generally do not use the standardized and highly concentrated product but just a simple tincture, and it does give good results.

Glycyrrhiza glabra (Licorice)
FAMILY: *Leguminosae*
PART USED: Rhizome

This plant has a long tradition of use, going back about 3,000 years, including promoting longevity in ancient Chinese medicine and as a sweetening agent in the time of the Egyptians. It was named by Dioscorides almost 2,000 years ago after *glukos* (sweet) and *rhizo* (root).

The major active constituent of licorice is a triterpenoid glycoside called glycyrrhizin. This is fifty times sweeter than sucrose and has a powerful demulcent and expectorant effect, stimulating the production of a thin mucous in the respiratory passages that is easily coughed out. This mucous stimulation also occurs in the stomach, where it coats the gastric mucosa with a protective coating that reduces the incidence and severity of peptic ulceration in the stomach and duodenum. The drug carbenoxalone, frequently prescribed to treat peptic ulcers, is derived synthetically from glycyrrhizic acid.

Glycyrrhizin has a pronounced effect on adrenal function. It is widely used as a tonic, adaptogenic adrenal agent, promoting energy production while nourishing and replenishing the glands. It is also noted to have significant anti-inflammatory effects, presumably due to some glucocorticoid activity that enhances cortisol activity. A mineralocorticoid effect is seen in some sensitive individuals, resulting in fluid retention and elevated blood pressure. If this is problematic, then processing can remove the glycyrrhizin (resulting in deglycyrrhizinated licorice or DGL, which seems to be still effective, raising questions about the actual active constituents).

Glycyrrhizin in high doses binds with and blocks estrogen receptors, but in lower doses isoflavones in the herb potentiate estrogen activity. Another flavonoid protects against many complications of diabetes , including peripheral neuropathy, cataracts, retinopathy, and nephropathy. Licorice has demonstrated a liver protective effect, possibly by regulation of the cytochrome P450 pathway. Flavone glycosides exert an antispasmodic action, reducing coughs, cramps, asthma, and spastic constipation. Licorice is especially indicated in cases of chronic bronchitis, bronchiectasis, asthma, adrenal exhaustion, chronic immune impairment, arthritis, and chronic fatigue. Additionally, licorice has demonstrated significant antimicrobial activity against Epstein-

Barr and other viruses, *Staphylococcus aureus, Mycobacterium smegmatis,* and *Candida albicans.*

Clinical Applications in Fibromyalgia

Licorice is one of my favorite herbs in treating FMS. It promotes normal adrenal function, regulates cortisol activity, and promotes energy, while also being notably anti-inflammatory in the joints. It also protects the gastric mucosa from the irritant effects of analgesics. It is safe for long-term use, providing there is no history of hypertension or edema. Licorice is pleasant tasting and may be used to disguise the taste of other, less palatable herbs.

Guaiacum officinalis (**Lignum vitae**)

Family: *Zygophyllaceae*
Part used: Resin
The heartwood of this tree from tropical Central and South America is exceptionally hard and dense and rich in resins, making it very resistant to rot. Because of this, it has significant commercial value. The resin is collected by heating the wood or by making an alcohol extract of the wood, which is then slowly dried, yielding the resin residue.

This herb has fallen out of favor with modern practitioners and there is little clinical research available. Formerly it was used to treat venereal disease and the side effects of the mercury remedies.

Lignum vitae is considered an excellent alterative with a tissue specificity for the joints. If taken hot, it will increase the circulation and warm the extremities; it is diaphoretic and aids in the removal of toxic wastes through the skin. If taken cool, it is a cleansing diuretic and aids in the removal of heat and swelling from the fingers and toes. Phenolic lignans are responsible for the marked antirheumatic and antiarthritic effects. It is reputed to be able to break down fibrous tissue and enhance elasticity of the tissues.

Lignum vitae is well known for treating rheumatoid and osteoarthritis, gout, or tendon contracture after an injury. It is traditionally used also for pustular skin afflictions and is a mild laxative.

Clinical Applications in Fibromyalgia

I like to use this herb in combination with other anti-inflammatories such as devil's claw and licorice to treat painful inflammation of the joints. While this is not always necessary in treating FMS, many people with concurrent arthritic changes will find it helpful.

Harpagophytum procumbens (**Devil's Claw**)

Family: *Pedaliaceae*
Part used: Tubers
This plant is native to southern Africa and has traditionally been used by

native people for duodenal and upper intestinal inflammations, as well as for arthritis and rheumatism. The major active constituent is a group of iridoid glycosides, which are bitter and stimulate digestive function, although they are somewhat deactivated by gastric juice, so enteric-coated products are preferred. Additionally, devil's claw contains triterpenes, phytosterols, aromatic acids, and flavonoids. In vitro and in vivo experiments have shown devil's claw to possess bitter tonic action as well as anti-inflammatory, antirheumatic, and analgesic properties.

Analgesic and anti-inflammatory activity appears to be greatest in chronic rather than acute conditions. The tissue-decongesting and antispasmodic activity of this herb are equivalent to that of the drug *phenylbutazone*. The mode of action of the anti-inflammatory effect is not well understood, but has been shown not to involve mediation of prostaglandin synthesis. Injection of devil's claw extract results in localized, dose-dependent analgesia equivalent to that provided by aspirin.

Devil's claw extract has demonstrated cardioactive properties, including protection against induced arrhythmias. Low doses either slow or increase the heart rate, while higher doses have a markedly slowing effect with a reduction in coronary blood flow.

Devil's claw also has some antifungal activity, as well as being a hepatic stimulant, a cholagogue, and a stomachic and lymphatic agent. It is traditionally used for arthritis, rheumatism, gout, lumbago, sciatica, fibrositis, fibromyalgia, polymyalgia rheumatica, neuralgia, liver disorders, biliousness, duodenal and upper intestinal inflammations, gallbladder disease, hemorrhoids, and liver congestion.

Clinical Applications in Fibromyalgia
I use this herb extensively to treat FMS where there is concurrent joint damage, preferably in the form of enteric-coated capsules or tablets. It is effective for arthritic and rheumatic pain and has particular benefit where chronic use of nonsteroidal anti-inflammatories has caused sensitivity or lesions of the gastric lining.

Humulus lupulus (Hops)
Family: *Cannabinaceae*
Part used: Female flowers
The hops plant is a nonwoody climbing perennial that carries the flowers on separate male and female plants. It is closely related to both stinging nettle and marijuana. The female flowers and the strobiles or fruits are the preferred therapeutic part, and most especially the golden orange lupulin, or hop flour, which is a glandular

secretion that forms in the strobile and falls out like a dust when the fruits are shaken.

In folk medicine, beer has long been known as a tried and true remedy for stimulating urinary flow and for insomnia, as well as both internally and as a skin wash to remove blemishes. Hops have been used to treat anxiety, insomnia, and restlessness for over 1,000 years in Europe. The earliest known record of the plant is in the *Tang pen tsao* herbal by Lu-tsao in China in A.D. 659. It was also noted by Gerard in 1597, Burton in 1624, and appears in most herbals published in Europe since the Elizabethan era.

Hop flowers contain up to 1 percent volatile oil, up to 5 percent tannins, plus various bitter resins.

In laboratory research hops have been shown to inhibit the action of several neurotransmitters, including acetylcholine, atropine, papverine, and histamine, and this may contribute to its sedative and soporific qualities. They appear to both shorten the time taken to fall asleep and to deepen the slumber. The folk tradition of sleeping on a hops pillow neatly demonstrates how much the old wives really knew. The warmth from one's head will cause the slow release of volatile compounds into the air, and the nose will be ideally situated to receive the aroma all night. Hops may also be helpful for hysteria,

anxiety, panic, mania, or obsessive or compulsive behavior, and any situation of stress.

Controversy exists over the presence and significance of estrogen-like compounds in hops. Older books claim that there are phytoestrogen compounds in the glandular secretion of hops, which may bind to our cellular receptor sites and "prime" them to respond more rapidly and efficiently to endogenous estrogen. This may be clinically beneficial where the body's own estrogen is lowered; for example, in early menopause, anovulatory infertility, and delayed menarche. Certainly in the days when hops were picked by hand, only women would do the work because the men, if exposed to high levels of the hop flour, would develop feminizing features (change in voice, body hair growth patterns, development of breasts, loss of libido). For this reason, hops have been traditionally prescribed as an anaphrodisiac in men and a hormone balancer in women. However, more recent research has failed to confirm the presence or activity of estrogenic compounds.

Hops are bitter and, as always with bitters, they stimulate digestive activity. Tasting the bitterness in the mouth will stimulate a nerve reflex response that enhances all aspects of digestive function, including salivation; production of all digestive juices, including enzymes and acids; promotion of liver function; and peristalsis. This digestive stimulation may be helpful in cases of persistent indigestion, impaired absorption of foods, liver sluggishness manifesting as difficulty digesting fats, and in cramping, griping, or colic. Because it can take twenty minutes after ingestion for the bitter effect to occur, there may be something to be said for that beer before supper—just make sure it is a bitter variety. The stimulation of liver function serves to improve the filtering of the blood and the removal of impurities. This lends strength to the traditional folk use for clearing a blemished complexion and treating skin diseases.

Hops are found to be generally antispasmodic to smooth muscle, easing constriction of the bronchioles in asthma, the blood vessels in hypertension, and the bladder in urinary retention.

Because of their relatively high tannin content, hops are mildly astringent. This may be useful in bleeding conditions of the digestive system especially where there is also cramping and spasmodic pains; for example, in Crohn's disease, ulcerative colitis, and peptic ulceration. Tannins are also somewhat antimicrobial due to their astringent effect on the protein coats of microbes.

Hops are especially indicated therapeutically for nervous indigestion, digestive cramping and spasms, digestive ulcerations, irritable bowel, insomnia, excitement, mania, and menopause. However, hops may worsen depression.

Clinical Applications in Fibromyalgia
I use hops occasionally to treat FMS when I want both a sedative and a bitter action. They are useful in cases of irritable bowel syndrome, which is aggravated by stress and where the bitter digestive stimulation and the spasmolytic action is indicated. Hops are almost specific in cases of restless leg syndrome, where sleep is disturbed by an inability to relax the legs. I am careful to avoid using hops where there is any depression.

Hypericum perforatum
(St. John's Wort)
Family: *Guttiferae*
            (*formerly Hypericaceae*)
Part used: Aerial parts
This is a perennial plant, originally from southern Europe but now growing prolifically in warm temperate climates, including California, eastern and central United States and Canada, and much of Europe. It is characterized by tiny "perforations" on the leaves and flowers, which are actually oil glands. The flowers exude a red stain when squeezed, and this was considered to represent the blood

of John the Baptist because the plant reputedly flowers on Saint John's Day (June 24). The infused oil of *hypericum* has long been known as an effective topical treatment for burns and scalds, as well as for the pain of shingles, and the tea is an excellent vulnerary. More recently the extract has been shown effective against depression.

The red pigment carried in the dark glands mostly consists of dianthrone derivatives. An essential oil, carried in the white glands on the leaves and flowers, contains monoterpenes and sesquiterpenes. Many flavone compounds are also present.

Hypericum has a tissue specificity for nervous tissue and the bladder, where it acts as a tonic and regenerator. It appears to have a specific regenerative effect upon the nervous supply of the outlet of the bladder, where it serves to improve nervous control of the voiding reflex. Other recognized actions of the herb include anti-inflammatory, cell wall and capillary strengthening, diuretic, antibacterial, wound healing, cholagogic, coronary dilation, tumor inhibition, and sedation. This herb also exhibits some astringent activity and may be styptic and antidiarrheal. Hypericin has also shown significant antitumor activity, although how this translates into therapeutic application is not yet clear. The dianthrone derivatives exhibit a marked antiviral activity, especially against enveloped retroviruses such as herpes, shingles, cytomegalovirus, and HIV. This antiviral effect is enhanced by exposure to light.

Several constituents appear to contribute to the marked antidepressant effect of St. John's wort. Extract of the whole plant has been shown to regulate neurotransmitters in the brain, including inhibition of synaptic uptake of noradrenaline, serotonin, and dopamine, and gamma-aminobutyric-acid. Additionally, there is up-regulation of central serotonergic receptors, and possible inhibition of monoamine-oxidase activity. Suppression of interleukin-6 may assist in deactivating the hypothalamic–pituitary–adrenal (HPA) axis and reducing elevated corticotrophin-releasing factor. This could contribute to the antidepressant effect and may be particularly beneficial in fibromyalgia, where there is chronic up-regulation of the HPA axis and elevated CRH (corticotropic-releasing hormone). In addition, St. John's wort has been shown to increase nocturnal melatonin plasma concentrations.

Recent evidence suggests that St. John's wort may induce a number of enzymes in the liver that speed the elimination of metabolic wastes. This partially explains its traditional use as a liver stimulant and blood cleanser.

However, as more and more people use the herb, practitioners are beginning to observe some potentially dangerous side effects from this liver enzyme induction. Specifically, Saint John's wort is known to induce activity of enzymes in the cytochrome P450 series. Certain drugs are also processed by these enzymes, and concurrent use of Saint John's wort may cause reduced blood levels of the drugs and reduced efficacy. Caution should be used when taking St. John's wort concurrently with prescription medications. High doses of St. John's wort may also lead to photosensitivity and transient skin rashes after exposure to sunlight.

Clinical Applications in Fibromyalgia
This is an excellent herb to use where there is mild to moderate depression, anxiety states, impaired sleep, and overactivity of the HPA axis. It is almost a specific for FMS. It combines well with other sedative and relaxant herbs as a bedtime remedy and with other nerve tonics such as oats and blue vervain for daytime use. It can be used in weaning off prescription antidepressants, but a qualified herbalist should supervise this process.

Juniperus communis (**Juniper**)
FAMILY: *Cupressaceae*
PART USED: Cone
This is an evergreen, shrubby plant with prostrate stems, closely related to Virginia cedar. The cone is often

misidentified as a berry. It matures slowly over two to three years and is harvested when ripe and dark purple in color. Juniper has long been known as an aromatic cooking spice, being used to reduce the greasiness of ham and duck. It is known in folk medicine for its disinfectant properties, and a berry was routinely held in the mouth of physicians when tending the sick to ward off evil vapors. Clothes, linens, and instruments were washed in juniper tea and the boughs were boiled or smouldered in the sick room to purify the air.

The cones are rich in volatile oil, up to 2 percent, almost half of which comprises monoterpene alcohols, which are tonifying, antiseptic, antiviral, and immune stimulating. The volatile oil also contains a uterine irritant and is potentially abortifacient.

The volatile oil is excreted through the kidneys and lungs, where it exerts a disinfectant and antimicrobial effect in treating infections. There is a slight irritation of the renal mucosa, which causes increased glomerular filtration rate and hence diuresis. Because of this irritation, juniper volatile oil should not be used internally nor should the tincture be taken for longer than six weeks without a two-week break before recommencing. Albuminuria is the first sign of juniper-induced renal damage and the herb should be discontinued if this occurs.

Juniper is bitter, and hence a gastric and intestinal stimulant. It increases the flow of gastric acid and digestive enzymes and is a carminative and an antimicrobial agent in the gut.

The volatile oil in a carrier oil, or the infused oil, may be applied topically as a warming liniment, being rubefacient and stimulating. It has long been recognized as one of the best topical counterirritants and anti-inflammatories for arthritis and rheumatism. Do not apply the volatile oil undiluted.

Clinical Applications in Fibromyalgia
I love this herb as a volatile oil or infused oil, as a topical application for sore, stiff, aching muscles, and for poor peripheral circulation leading to sensations of chillness and cold fingers or toes. It smells great and has the added benefit of a marked antimicrobial action. I do not use it internally.

Lactuca virosa (Wild Lettuce)
Family: *Asteraceae*
Part used: Stem and leaf (latex is preferred but rarely available in commerce)
This is a very common member of the daisy family. It grows prolifically on wastelands throughout the Northern Hemisphere and most species seem to have some medicinal value, with the true *virosa* species being preferred. The name *lactuca* refers to the milky fluid the cut plant exudes, and the name *virosa* refers to its poisonous nature. The medicinal part of the plant is this milky latex, which is harvested by repeatedly cutting into the stem rather in the manner of tapping a maple tree. The latex is taken up onto a cotton cloth or sponge, which is then soaked in alcohol to remove the latex. The alcohol is then evaporated away, the resultant *lactucarium* being the medicinal product. The best time for cutting the stem is just before the peak of flowering.

The constituents of the *lactucarium* are sesquiterpene lactones plus various related triterpenes. In the expressed juice of the *Lactuca* are many other compounds, including flavonoids and traces of sugars.

Lactucopicrin and lactucin are bitter substances in the latex, and their effect upon the body is to inhibit the excitability of the nervous system, specifically, the motor division. The vegetable drug is sometimes known as *lettuce opium* for its similarity of effect, although *Lactuca* does not exhibit constipating or narcotic effects and will not cause habituation. It is specifically indicated for insomnia, restlessness, excitability, and other symptoms of an overactive nervous system. Similar to codeine, *Lactuca* is also an antitussive and is thus effective for persistent or debilitating coughs, although it is not sufficiently strong for acute or severe coughs. It has some antispasmodic action and may be helpful in colic, dysmenorrhea, and rheumatism. There are no known contraindications and it is entirely safe for children and for long-term use.

Clinical Applications in Fibromyalgia
This is a much underrated and underused herb. I prescribe it for restlessness, anxiety, panic disorders, and insomnia. In treating FMS it combines well with sedative and relaxant herbs such as skullcap and chamomile for daytime anxiety and with stronger sleep aids such as valerian or Jamaican dogwood at night for insomnia.

Lavandula officinalis (Lavender)
FAMILY: *Lamiaceae*
PART USED: Flower and essential oil
A small perennial plant, lavender is indigenous to the Mediterranean and widely cultivated in Europe, especially France and England, for the perfume industry. Highly aromatic, it was formerly used as a strewing herb and to protect stored clothes and linens from mustiness. The name comes from the Latin *lavare*, meaning "to wash" and indicates its long tradition as a bathing herb. It is highly regarded in cosmetic use, being soothing and anti-inflammatory to the skin and having a mildly antiseptic action as well. It is an excellent remedy for burns and wounds, as it promotes skin healing and reduces scarring.

Lavender flowers are rich in volatile oil, which also occurs to a lesser extent in the leaves and stem. This oil is best extracted by distillation or by making a tincture; if infusing the plant, then the steam should also be inhaled for maximum efficacy. It exhibits an antispasmodic as well as a marked sedative and relaxing effect, finding great use in the treatment of anxiety, restlessness, disordered thoughts, insomnia, hysteria, and fright. The oil is also carminative, relieving digestive spasms and easing the passage of gas. An extract of the herb is mildly bitter, so stimulating to all digestive functions; is a notable choleretic and cholagogue; and is astringent, which provides improved tone to the digestive mucosa. Thus it is indicated in cases of indigestion and dyspepsia, as well as in chronic inflammatory bowel disease and irritable bowel syndrome, especially where there is a marked stress component.

Additionally, lavender may be used for hypertension, migraines, tension headaches, peptic ulcers, depression, and neurasthenia. It has a long tradition of use topically as a rub for rheumatism, where the antispasmodic action probably contributes to relief of stiffness, aching, and pain.

Clinical Applications in Fibromyalgia
This is one of my favorite herbs. I encourage patients to grow it in their gardens, or even in a small pot on a window sill or balcony so that they can have the pleasure of smelling the fresh flowers. Wearing a flower stalk in one's buttonhole is a lovely way to obtain the medicinal effects. The volatile oil can be used in a bath or a room diffusor, dropped onto a handkerchief and carried in the pocket, sprinkled onto the collar of clothing (don't worry, the pure oil will evaporate and leave no stain), or even dropped onto chairs, car seats, or carpets. Lavender is one of the very best remedies for stress, tension, anxiety, fear, persistent unwanted thoughts, and disturbed sleep. Taken internally, it is also helpful for disordered digestion associated with stress, specifically, irritable bowel syndrome. It can be used daily with no risk of side effects and does not interfere with any other medications.

Lobelia inflata (Lobelia)
FAMILY: *Campanulaceae*
PART USED: Aerial parts
Traditionally known as pukeweed or Indian tobacco, this plant was a preferred remedy of the herbal practitioners of the early 1800s, who prized it for its emetic properties. It contains many alkaloids closely resembling nicotine. On ingestion, these cause an initial and transient stimulation of the autonomic ganglia, causing a sense of overall stimulation, much like nicotine, followed by widespread, generalized autonomic depression, causing muscle relaxation and depression of the vasomotor center in the brain stem, thus lowering the blood pressure. At the same time the vagus nerve is depressed, thus dilating the airways and increasing the rate and depth of respiration. This makes it a very valuable remedy for the treatment of acute asthma. Lobelia is also an irritant to the gastric mucosa, and thus by nerve reflex a stimulating expectorant, activating the mucociliary escalator and aiding in the removal of waste matter from the lungs.

Lobelia is an appetite suppressant and an adrenal stimulant, inhibits platelet aggregation, and shows moderate antimicrobial activity against gram-positive and gram-negative bacteria. In larger doses lobelia is a powerful emetic and this protects against accidental overdose and excessive autonomic depression. Lobelia is also useful to reduce the cravings for nicotine and assist in quitting smoking.

Topical application of lobelia provides a significant muscle-relaxing effect, reducing cramps and spasms and having some analgesic action.

Clinical Applications in Fibromyalgia
This is one of the very best muscle-relaxant herbs when applied topically to skeletal muscle spasms and also

when taken internally for smooth muscle spasms. I prescribe it in carefully controlled doses for internal use in treating spasmodic pain in the digestive system as a result of irritable bowel syndrome, and for spasmodic pain in the bladder as a symptom of interstitial cystitis. In topical use it is very helpful for relieving stiffness and cramping of skeletal muscles. It makes an excellent liniment in combination with cramp bark and a warming and penetrating oil, such as mustard oil or infused oil of juniper.

Marsdenia condurango
(Condor Plant)
Family: *Asclepidaceae*
Part used: Bark
This vine is native to Ecuador and supposedly used by condor birds to weave their nests. It was traditionally used to treat syphilis and cancers of the digestive tract. It is extremely bitter and is considered an excellent restorative tonic to the upper digestive system, regulating the production of all digestive enzymes as well as mucous and hydrochloric acid. It promotes the appetite and enhances the digestive capability. It is especially indicated in cases of debility and convalescence after a long sickness. Recent research has confirmed the traditional use for early-stage cancers of the stomach and breast.

Clinical Applications in Fibromyalgia
This herb is rarely used today, but shows great promise in treating the debility and weakness of FMS. Chronic pain and disease takes a toll on the appetite and digestive function through long-term sympathetic dominance, leaving a person more vulnerable to digestive deficiencies and consequent nutritional deficiencies and bacterial/yeast disturbances in the gut. This bitter herb, with its special application to convalescence and debility states, is clearly indicated in treating the digestive weakness that often accompanies FMS.

Melissa officinalis (Lemon Balm)
Family: *Lamiaceae*
Part used: Leaves and volatile oil
This is a highly aromatic member of the mint family, commonly grown in herb gardens and used to make flavorful teas, either fresh or dried. The name comes from the Greek *mel* meaning "honey," in reference to the sweet smell, and "balm" is a corruption of balsam, also referring to the smell. Ancient Romans and Greeks used it as an antidepressant, to drive away melancholy, and to aid the languishing patient.

The major active constituent is a volatile oil rich in monoterpenes. There are also a small amount of tannins and a bitter. In modern herbal medicine *melissa* is highly regarded as a carminative, sedative, antispasmodic, mild diaphoretic, and antidepressant. Recent research has indicated a potent antiviral activity, specifically against retroviruses such as those involved in AIDS, shingles, and herpes. This is brought about by polyphenols that preferentially occupy receptor sites on the cells and prevent the adherence of the virus. It is also rich in antioxidant compounds, which enhance overall immune function. *Melissa* has long been used to treat the symptoms of hyperthyroidism. It has been shown to decrease serum and pituitary levels of TSH (thyroid-stimulating hormone) after injection, although whether oral ingestion is equally effective in reducing thyroid activity has not yet been determined.

The volatile components of lemon balm have been shown to concentrate in the hippocampus of the limbic system in the brain, that part of the central nervous system that governs and controls the autonomic system and physiological responses to stress. It is considered a restorative and rejuvenating tonic to the entire central nervous system and the German Commission E monographs endorse *melissa's* traditional use for tension headaches.

The volatile oil of *melissa* is prohibitively expensive and often adulterated with lemon grass and other oils rich in citronellal, which reduces the benefits. Aromatherapists use the pure volatile oil to treat indigestion, hypertension, muscle spasms and cramping (both skeletal and intestinal), menstrual pain, infertility, shock, anxiety, depression, nervousness, insomnia, and palpitations.

Clinical Applications in Fibromyalgia
This herb, which makes a sweet and refreshing tea, is a particular favorite of mine. I find it invaluable in treating stress and anxiety, especially where there is associated digestive disturbance or impaired sleep. It combines particularly well with chamomile, hops, and blue vervain for this purpose. I also find lemon balm very helpful as part of a protocol for mitral valve prolapse with palpitations and sensations of oppression in the chest. When using *melissa* as a tea, the steam should be inhaled for maximum efficacy.

Myrica cerifera (**Bayberry**)
FAMILY: *Myricaceae*
PART USED: Root bark
This is an attractive ornamental shrub, indigenous to northeastern America, with berries that persist throughout the winter. The berries are covered with a whitish aromatic wax that can be used to make candles. This gives rise to the folk names of candle bush, wax myrtle, and wax berry.

A decoction of the root bark yields a strongly warming, stimulating, astringent action, specifically tonifying to the mucous membranes. The major active compounds are a group of triterpenes, a flavonoid, tannins, and an astringent resin containing a saponin, which, when taken internally, is very useful in cases of mucous colitis, diarrhea, dysentery, cholera, candidiasis, ulcerative colitis, and Crohn's disease. It is a notable anti-inflammatory to the mucus membranes lining the gut with therapeutic value in treating autoimmune disease and arthritis associated with leaky gut syndrome. It can also be employed where there is chronic laxity of the uterus with mucous secretions and habitual miscarriage. It may be used as a douche for leucorrhoea and as a mouthwash for gum disease and canker sores. In the form of an inhaled snuff, bayberry is useful for nasal polyps and chronic rhinitis. As a sitz bath it can help hemorrhoids or anal fissures. It can also be used as a skin wash for wounds, abrasions, and indolent ulcers.

Bayberry is an excellent diaphoretic peripheral vasodilator, opening the small blood vessels, distributing circulation to the periphery, and warming the body. It is very helpful in treating persistently cold hands and feet and to promote sweating at the onset of a cold. For this purpose it has long been a key ingredient of Composition Formula, first made famous by Samuel Thomson in the early 1800s. As long as 2,000 years ago, Galen mentioned the berries for cold and rheumatic conditions, an infused oil being applied as a friction rub over the affected part. Bayberry is also bactericidal, a bitter choleretic, and an anthelmintic.

Clinical Applications in Fibromyalgia
I prescribe this herb for internal use as a warming peripheral circulatory stimulant for cold extremities. I also use it internally where there is low-grade inflammation of the gut with mucus in the stool and possibility of leaky gut. The resin is one of the key active constituents, so a tincture is preferred over a decoction for maximum extraction. I also like to make it into an infused oil to be included in a warming liniment with mustard oil, infused oil of juniper, and rubefacient volatile oils such as cajuput and marjoram. This is an excellent treatment for stiff, sore, aching muscles and for rheumatic inflammation.

Nepeta cataria (Catnip/Catmint)
FAMILY: *Lamiaceae*
PART USED: Aerial parts
This is a rough-textured, dull green member of the mint family, with a distinct odor that intoxicates cats. It is indigenous to Europe and was introduced to America, where it has spread widely.

Catnip is useful in raising fevers and thus effectively cooling the body, acting first as a diaphoretic and then as a febrifuge. It is carminative, reducing abdominal gas, griping, and colicky spasms. It is also somewhat astringent and may be useful in managing diarrhea. It is traditionally used as an enema for colicky babies where the sedative action is also helpful. Catnip is a gentle but effective relaxing agent, producing a sense of calm and well-being. Little scientific research has been done on this herb, but the sedative effects are thought to be due to a volatile oil component structurally similar to the valepotriates found in valerian. It may be used to treat stress headaches, migraines, anxiety, nightmares, and depression. It is especially useful for digestive disturbance due to anxiety or stress.

Clinical Applications in Fibromyalgia
This is a particularly useful herb because it grows easily and prolifically and is readily available. I prescribe it in FMS as a tea for stress, tension, and anxiety states where the sleep is disturbed. It also helps to equalize the body temperature and reduce chills.

Oenothera biennis
(**Evening Primrose Seed**)
FAMILY: *Onagraceae*
PART USED: Flowers and the oil from the seeds
This is a beautiful garden plant, reaching 3 to 4 feet tall, with large yellow flowers that open in the evening and emit a delicate fragrance. The flowers have been used in folk medicine as a soothing emollient in salves

and baths. The roots are sometimes eaten in salads where they impart a peppery taste. The seeds are collected for commerce and the pressed oil is sold in capsules.

The seed oil contains up to 15 percent gamma-linolenic acid (GLA) and 65 percent linoleic acid. GLA is a precursor of the inflammatory prostaglandin E2 (PGE2) series via arachidonic acid, and of the anti-inflammatory prostaglandin E1 (PGE1) series. Actions attributed to the PGE1 series include anti-inflammatory, immunoregulatory, and vasodilatory properties, as well as inhibition of platelet aggregation and cholesterol synthesis, and elevation of cyclic adenosine monophosphate (AMP) resulting in up-regulation of cellular energy production. Dietary supplementation with GLA increases arachidonic acid synthesis slightly and markedly promotes production of the PGE1 series.

A great deal of clinical research has been done on evening primrose oil and it has generally proven to have remarkable clinical benefits. It may be useful against atopic eczema, premenstrual syndrome, elevated cholesterol, alcoholism, Sjogren's syndrome, attention deficit hyperactivity disorder, hypertension, diabetes, fibrocystic breast disease, postviral fatigue disorders and chronic fatigue syndrome, schizophrenia, platelet aggregation and vascular blockage, inflammations including rheumatoid arthritis, systemic lupus erythematosus, and multiple sclerosis.

Clinical Applications in Fibromyalgia
The fixed oil extracted from the seeds of evening primrose is very beneficial in long-term use for many symptoms of FMS, including skin rashes and itching, joint and other tissue inflammations, fatigue, dry mouth, and premenstrual problems. In order to maintain the optimal balance of the various essential fatty acids and prostaglandins, it is recommended to take evening primrose oil with fish oils, which provide eicosapentanoic acid.

Oplopanax horridum (Devil's Club)
FAMILY: *Araliaceae*
PART USED: Root bark
This spiny shrub, growing only in a narrow coastal mountain zone in the Pacific Northwest, is related to ginseng and has been revered as a sacred plant by many generations of American Indians. It grows 3 to 10 feet high, with stems that are savagely armed with spines that cause festering sores if they pierce the skin. The leaves reach an impressive size of up to 20 inches across. Spikes of small, whitish-green flowers appear in June and give way to a striking show of bright red berries in the fall.

Traditionally, the devil's club root was harvested in the spring or fall as the sap rose and fell. Because it grows quite prolifically in its particular ecological niche, and because both roots and stems can reproduce into a new plant, it is possible to harvest quite heavily. As long as the regrowing plant is given time to mature, a stand of devil's club can continue to produce a harvest indefinitely. The roots are dug and then scrubbed clean. The inner bark is peeled off with a sharp knife and cut into quills. These are air-dried, then stored in an airtight container. It is recommended that the bark be used as soon as possible and that it not be stored for more than six months because it will lose potency.

The chemical components of this plant have not been identified, but it has been known as a powerful medicinal agent for many generations. In modern times its primary use is as an hypoglycemic agent and blood sugar regulator. It seems to have a synergistic effect with insulin, thus lowering the required dose of the drug, and it also seems to have an amphoteric effect on blood sugar to keep it within normal homeostatic parameters. It has traditionally been used during fasts and vision quests, where it may help to curb hunger pangs as well as possibly providing some psychospiritual effects.

Devil's club has traditionally been used by many native peoples for the treatment of arthritis, by oral ingestion and in the form of poultices, ointments, and washes. The root bark burned to a white ash was applied to open sores and wounds to prevent infection and reduce inflammation. It is effective for constipation and skin afflictions due to poor liver function. Tuberculosis, pneumonia, bronchitis, and other chest infections were traditionally treated by oral ingestion of the root bark and by inhalation of the steam or smoke from the boiled or burned plant. It was used as a post-parturition tonic and regenerative, providing strength and sustenance to the new mother and aiding in reestablishing the normal menstrual rhythm. It was also used as an anti-galactogogue. A strong decoction was used to wash the hair in cases of lice and nits.

Traditionally this herb was used as an adaptogenic or stress reducer by warriors preparing for battle, by hunters preparing for a chase, or by people undertaking a long journey by foot or canoe. The fresh root serves to reduce the sensations of fatigue and physical pain and to improve stamina and endurance. It also has some mood-altering properties that were traditionally used to access the sub-conscious states. Frequently taken before ritual fasting, vision quests, and sweat lodges, it opens the mind and reduces inhibitions. It seems particularly to aid in contacting the Nature spirits and the rooted ones.

Another traditional attribute of the plant is as a purifier and protector from evil spirits. The dwelling of a powerful shaman might be constructed from devil's club boughs, so that he would be protected from all evil influences. Its emetic properties were sometimes employed as a purifying technique as well. The smoke from smoldering devil's club was used as incense to cleanse the air. Pieces of the bark are still sometimes tied around the necks of children as amulets to ward off evil spirits. These may be pithed out to form beads which are often painted and decorated.

Clinical Applications in Fibromyalgia
I use a strong tea or a tincture of this herb as an adaptogen to increase energy, stamina, and endurance. It is also useful to balance blood sugar where hypoglycemia contributes to mood swings and loss of energy.

Panax ginseng
(Korean Ginseng)/
Panax quinquefolium
(American Ginseng)
Family: *Araliaceae*
Part used: Root
Both of these closely related species have similar constituents and therapeutic actions. Korean ginseng has long been known in the Far East as a great tonic elixir, reputed to promote longevity and cure all ills. American ginseng was not widely used by

American Indians but has been popularized more recently as a result of modern research looking for analogues to Korean ginseng. Both types of ginseng are now widely cultivated and are used as adaptogens to reduce responses to stress, and as tonics and aphrodisiacs. The name comes from the Greek *panacea,* meaning "that which heals." Red ginseng is cured (cooked) and is considered to be more warming and stimulating than the raw white root. Traditional indications include chills, digestive weakness, palpitations, neurosis, anxiety, debility, sexual inadequacy, asthma and dyspnea, sweats, organ prolapse, and prostration.

The Rb1 group of saponins, most abundant in American ginseng, tend to have a depressant effect on the central nervous system. This makes American ginseng very useful as an anticonvulsive, analgesic, and tranquilizer, and to reduce hypertension, anxiety, stress response, and psychosis. American ginseng is also noted for its anti-inflammatory activity.

The Rg1 group of saponins, more prevalent in Korean ginseng, have a slightly stimulating effect on the central nervous system, combating fatigue and enhancing memory and concentration. They are slightly anabolic, increasing protein and lipid synthesis.

When the two ginsengs are taken together there is a synergy of action resulting in improved stamina,

endurance, and performance; reduced recovery time; and reduced injury rate. They promote stability of the blood sugar; reduce allergic reactions; tonify the sexual organs and functions of men and women; and regulate the heart force, heart rate, and blood pressure. Ginseng increases the body's response to short-term or immediate stress, while reducing physiological disruption and disturbance due to chronic stress. Ginseng improves oxygen uptake from hemoglobin and improves muscle strength, recovery time, and aerobic performance. Memory, mood, and mental performance are also benefited by use of ginseng.

Clinical Applications in Fibromyalgia
From the above description it seems that ginseng would be a very useful herb in treating FMS. Indeed, this is the case, but there are significant cautions that must be observed. In fact, I almost never prescribe *Panax* (Korean) ginseng and only rarely use the American ginseng; I prefer to rely on Siberian ginseng, devil's club, licorice, or ashwagandha for the adaptogenic and tonic effects so beneficial in FMS. The reason for this is that I find Korean and, to a lesser extent American, ginseng to be too stimulating for most people with chronic debility. Ginseng can certainly be useful when patients need a quick pick-me-up, for example, if they know they will have to attend a

function, take an exam, go on a journey, or carry out some other short-lasting but stressful and draining activity. Ginseng taken for a few days before such events can be remarkably helpful, but I encourage patients to cease use after the event is over, or switch to a less stimulating adaptogen. Some sensitive patients have been known to develop palpitations and insomnia when taking ginseng, and it should never be used in conjunction with other stimulants. Ginseng also tends to lower blood sugar, which may aggravate symptoms of hypoglycemia.

Passiflora incarnata (Passionflower)
FAMILY: *Passifloraceae*
PART USED: Stem and leaves, harvested after maturation of fruits
This is a vinelike perennial with beautiful, large, showy flowers and fruits the size and shape of an egg that are edible when ripe. It is often grown as an ornamental.

The aerial parts contain a small amount of indole alkaloids, which are mildly hallucinogenic. Whether or not they are the active constituents is unclear and some authors believe that flavonoids may be equally or possibly even more active. The whole plant extract acts as a depressant of motor activity and the central nervous system, as well as raising the pain threshold. Passionflower reduces arterial pressure and increases the rate of res-

piration, thus encouraging adequate oxygenation of the tissues. It is widely used as a sedative, sleep inducer, antispasmodic, and anticonvulsant. It is especially noted for nervous tension, anxiety, hysteria, nervous excitability, hyperactivity, constrictive headaches, twitching of the limbs, senile tremor, and Parkinson's disease. It is also noted for benzodiazepine, alcohol, and narcotic withdrawal, and as a pain reliever.

Passionflower has traditionally been used for hypertension, especially where there is a stress component, and to strengthen the cardiac muscle, increasing the efficiency of the beat. It is useful in angina, palpitations, and arrhythmias.

Clinical Applications in Fibromyalgia
This is an exceptionally useful herb in treating sleep disturbance, anxiety, nervous tension, and acute or chronic pain. I prescribe it in low doses for daytime use and higher doses at night. It combines well with other sedative nervines and analgesics. I also use passionflower to treat palpitations and other symptoms of mitral valve prolapse.

Petroselinum crispum (Parsley)
FAMILY: *Apiaceae*
PART USED: Root, leaves, and seeds
This is a common herb sold as a garnish and flavoring agent. It was mentioned by Homer and named by

Dioscorides almost 2,000 years ago. The ancient Greeks dedicated the herb to Persephone and it was used in funeral rites. The leaves are rich in boron, which helps to metabolize calcium, and they are also rich in calcium in a very bioavailable form. This makes parsley a useful salad vegetable that can aid in maintenance of normal bone density. It is also rich in zinc, making it useful for the immune system and the prostate gland, and in chlorophyll, which can aid the body in ridding itself of environmental toxins.

Parsley seed oil stimulates hepatic regeneration, which makes it valuable as part of cleansing and detoxification program. Myristicin in the volatile oil (as well as in nutmeg oil) is mildly hallucinogenic and is structurally related to amphetamine and the sympathetic amines. It may compete for monoamine oxidase (MAO) enzymes and thus exert an MAO inhibition effect that will aid in reduction of blood pressure. Parsley is also diuretic, and these two actions may reduce blood pressure quite effectively. The diuretic action is also helpful in treating kidney stones and flushing them through the system. Parsley is officially approved for use in Germany for this purpose. Parsley is specifically helpful in removing uric acid wastes from the tissues and this makes it effective in treating arthritis, rheumatism, and gout. Parsley is also a uterine stimulant and is not recommended in large amounts during pregnancy.

Parsley has traditionally been used to reduce swelling and tenderness of the breasts and to dry up the milk after weaning of an infant. Parsley inhibits the secretion of histamine on exposure to allergens and thus reduces the severity of an allergic reaction. It may be useful in treating hay fever, asthma, and eczema. Parsley is carminative, antispasmodic, and mildly alterative and antioxidant. Parsley extract also has moderate antimicrobial activity. It has traditionally been used as a brain tonic, for wasting and excessive weight loss, and as a mild stimulant of the adrenal and thyroid glands.

Clinical Applications in Fibromyalgia
One of the benefits of this herb is that it can be eaten as a green vegetable. Indeed, this is perhaps the best way to ingest it because the seed and the volatile oil extracted from it may cause photosensitivity in high doses. I prescribe parsley to be eaten daily in salads to aid renal elimination and protect the liver. It has a long history of use in treating acid imbalance in the body, which can contribute to tender points and trigger points.

Pfaffia paniculata (Suma)
FAMILY: *Amaranthaceae*
PART USED: Root
This is a Brazilian shrub, commonly named *para todo*, meaning "for every-

thing," indicating its wide range of uses. Although it has no relation to ginseng, suma is sometimes referred to as Brazilian ginseng because of its remarkable adaptogenic properties. It improves resistance to stress and disease, increases stamina and endurance, and reduces recovery time after illness or injury. It is considered a nerve and glandular restorative and tonic. It is also a stimulant to the immune system, increasing resistance to pathogens and greatly aiding tissue healing and wound resolution. Suma is a hormone balancer, sometimes called "the female ginseng," and used with good results in treating symptoms of infertility, premenstrual syndrome, menopausal hot flashes, and vaginal atrophy. It is indicated for extreme stress situations, physical or mental exhaustion, hypotension, loss of appetite, and loss of libido or sexual debility. It is widely recognized as a treatment for cancer, due in part to its many vitamins and minerals, including germanium. Additionally, it aids in regulating blood sugar and shows promise in treating both diabetes and hypoglycemia.

Clinical Applications in Fibromyalgia
This herb has only fairly recently become readily available and I do not have extensive experience with it. I have used it mostly as an alternative to Siberian ginseng for the tonic and adaptogenic properties and have found it to be effective without any observed side effects.

Piper methysticum (Kava Kava)
FAMILY: *Piperaceae*
PART USED: Rhizome
Indigenous to the South Pacific, the rhizome of this plant from the pepper family has traditionally been used by the South Sea islanders to prepare an intoxicating drink. Chewed and fermented, it is used in ceremonial rites and to calm the mind and relax the body.

It first entered the Western *materia medica* as an effective antimicrobial for the genitourinary system, being especially indicated for sexually transmitted diseases with mucus discharges. Recent research has revealed the presence of a number of lactones that act on the reticular formation of the brain, inhibiting spontaneous motor activity without interfering with deliberate or desired motor function. This makes kava an effective treatment in muscular stiffness, twitching, and cramping and for feelings of tension in the muscles, without affecting power, endurance, or stamina. Kava lactones have a local anesthetic effect equivalent to cocaine. They are also spasmolytic, especially in the bladder; thus kava is an excellent remedy for cramping pains and spasms of the bladder.

Kava is a potent anxiolytic, reducing anxiety, nervous tension, restlessness, and tension headaches without loss of mental acuity or clarity of thought. It also has some sedative action and may be used in withdrawal of benzodiazepine therapy. Kava extract exhibits marked antifungal activity, though not against *Candida albicans.*

Clinical Applications in Fibromyalgia
This herb is especially useful when muscle tension interferes with sleep. It is beneficial in treating tension, stress, and anxiety, especially when they lead to muscle tension and possibly headaches. Chronic high consumption can lead to a dry, scaly skin condition, possibly due to interference with cholesterol metabolism. Dopamine antagonism has been reported, and kava should not be used in patients undergoing dopamine therapy (for example, patients being treated for Parkinson's). Occasionally, a paradoxical effect is seen with kava and there can be increased muscle tension, palpitations, and anxiety. I am one of those unfortunate few to whom this happens. The first (and only) time I used kava on myself I was awake all night, sitting bolt upright with my muscles rigid. Three hot baths through the night failed to relax me and the next morning I felt unbelievably stiff and sore. If you are using kava for the first time, I advise a small dose and careful observation of the effects. Recent evidence suggests a potential toxic effect in the liver when extracts are made in a non-traditional

way. High-potency capsules and tablets are best avoided until this controversy has been resolved.

Piscidia erythrina
(**Jamaican Dogwood**)
FAMILY: *Leguminosae*
PART USED: Root bark
This is a small tree indigenous to the West Indies the root bark of which is traditionally used, not only as a medicine, but as a fish poison as well. Pieces of the bark are placed in a basket, which is then swirled through the water. Active compounds are released into the water and fish become stunned, rise to the surface, and are easily gathered. In larger doses there may be a narcotic effect upon humans as well.

The medicinal value of *piscidia* lies in its painkilling and sedative effect. Hypotensive, antitussive, anti-inflammatory, and antipyretic actions have also been observed. The therapeutic indications for *piscidia* include disorders of sleep; neuralgia and other nerve pain; dysmenorrhea; inflammatory fevers; intestinal, cholecystic, or renal colic; spasmodic coughing; hysteria; overexcitability of the mind; and pain.

Unpleasant effects may occur with injudicious dosing. These may include headache, vomiting, and convulsions. Very high doses may cause heart failure or respiratory arrest. It is contraindicated in bradycardia, pregnancy, and cardiac insufficiency.

Clinical Applications in Fibromyalgia
Due to the unpleasant effects of high doses, this herb has fallen from favor in recent times. I find this a pity, as it is exceptionally useful in certain cases. I prescribe it when the mind cannot be quieted, when the thoughts are racing and sleep is elusive. It is of great value in treating pain, especially that due to nerve entrapment such as neuralgia or sciatica, but also pain due to excessive tension in the muscles. It combines well with kava and cramp bark for muscle tension and with valerian, wild lettuce, or California poppy for impaired sleep.

Plantago major/lanceolata (Plantain)
Family: *Plantaginaceae*
Part used: Leaves
Two species, the broad leaf and the ribwort plantain, are used interchangeably and often grow adjacent to each other, typically on disturbed soil. The basal rosette form allows repeated cutting or grazing without harming the plant and it is a tenacious weed. Sometimes called "white man's footsteps," it has spread from Europe all over the world.

Plantain contains enzymes that cause browning of the leaf when it is bruised. This is considered undesirable and the best plantain is hand-harvested to avoid leaf damage. Due to these enzymes, plantain leaves can be used to curdle milk when making cheese.

A high percentage of mucilage provides a demulcent and emollient effect. Applied topically as a fresh green poultice, plantain has a drawing action and can be used to draw out bees' stingers, insect bites, and splinters, or to draw grit and dirt from a wound. Made into an infused oil, or as a skin wash from the dried leaves, plantain is soothing and cooling to skin irritations, reducing redness, stinging, burning, and itching. It is especially noted for eczema where there is cracking and weeping of the skin. Taken internally as a tea, it is soothing for throat irritations, dry coughs, and hoarseness, and also serves as a potent tissue regenerator in the lungs and kidneys.

Plantain contains allantoin, a cell proliferent also found in comfrey, egg white, and placental fluid. It encourages cell regeneration and accounts for the remarkable wound-healing properties of the plant. Additionally, plantain contains vitamin A, vitamin C, zinc, chlorophyll, and tannins, all of which promote tissue healing. This makes plantain very useful in healing skin wounds, indolent ulcers, and gastrointestinal ulcers. Plantain is helpful in treating diarrhea, the tannins being astringent and drying and the mucilage being soothing and anti-inflammatory. It is also noted as an effective remedy in treating gastric and duodenal ulcers. It has an anticatarrhal effect in the kidneys and urinary tract, as well as the upper respiratory system. In this context it does not necessarily reduce mucus production, but rather it appears to improve the overall functioning of the mucus membranes and to regulate the stickiness of the mucus.

Studies suggest that plantain extract is a bronchodilator with value in treating spasmodic symptoms of asthma and bronchitis, where the mucilage is also soothing and expectorant for the associated lung congestion. Other documented effects include hypotensive, cholesterol- and triglyceride-lowering, mild laxative, and liver-protective actions.

Clinical Applications in Fibromyalgia
This herb is one of the most widely used in herbal medicine. In treating FMS it is helpful as a topical remedy for itching and rashes, in the form of a skin wash or an infused oil. Taken internally it is beneficial in treating irritation and lesions of the gut lining. In cases of irritable bowel syndrome, *Candida albicans* overgrowth, bacterial disturbance, food allergies, and leaky gut, plantain tea or extract can help in healing the damaged gut wall, regulating mucus production, and reducing unwanted passage of food particles into the bloodstream. Plantain is especially soothing and anti-inflammatory for the symptoms of interstitial cystitis.

Populus balsamifera (Balsam Poplar)
FAMILY: *Salicaceae*
PART USED: Spring buds and bark
This is a small tree, preferring moist ground, with male and female flowers borne on separate trees. Various species are found throughout the northern temperate zone, frequently hybridizing. *Populus candicans* (cottonwood), *P. alba* (white poplar), and *P. nigra* (black poplar) are used interchangeably with *P. balsamifera.*

The bark is rich in glycosidal salicylates and has similar properties to the willow to which it is related. It was traditionally used to reduce excessive fevers and sweating, being considered equal to cinchona in treating malarial fevers. Unlike the salicylates in aspirin, poplar extract does not cause gastric irritation.

The resin from *P. balsamifera* makes an excellent aromatic, warming, stimulating chest rub, which helps to thin the mucus secretions of the lung mucosa. It is rich in volatile oils, which are absorbed across the skin, then excreted through the lungs where they have a stimulating expectorant effect, aiding in the removal of waste materials from the lungs. The resin may also be used as a warming and anti-inflammatory liniment for arthritic joints and muscular rheumatism.

Individuals with a known hyper-sensitivity to aspirin or salicylates should not use poplar, nor should people with asthma, diabetes, gout, hemophilia, attention deficit hyperactivity disorder, and kidney or liver disease. Concurrent administration of poplar with other salicylate-rich substances should be avoided. Possible salicylate-drug interactions may occur with anticoagulants, methotrexate, metoclopramide, phenytoin, probenacid, spironolactone, and valproate. People taking guaifenesin should also avoid poplar.

Clinical Applications in Fibromyalgia
I have found over the years that extracts of willow have a stronger and more reliable anti-inflammatory effect than poplar when taken internally. However, I do use the infused oil of poplar spring buds in warming liniments and embrocations. It smells wonderful and has a pronounced anti-inflammatory action when applied to arthritic joints. The infused oil is also warming and relaxing to stiff or sore muscles. It combines well with other warming or counterirritant herbs for topical application, such as infused oil of juniper, mustard oil, or essential oil of ginger or cajuput.

Ribes niger (Black Currant Seed)
FAMILY: *Rosaceae*
PART USED: Oil from seeds
This thorny shrub is cultivated exten-sively for the delicious berry. The root was traditionally used as an astringent specific for the lower bowel, being effective in treating diarrhea and loose stools. Now the major therapeutic application is of the oil extracted from the seeds. This is very rich in gamma-linolenic acid (GLA), as is found in the seeds of evening primrose and borage. Thus it is anti-inflammatory and useful in all cases of reduced or impaired delta-6-desaturase enzyme and disturbances of prostaglandin formation.

Rosmarinus officinalis (Rosemary)
FAMILY: *Lamiacae*
PART USED: Leaves/volatile oil
Although rosemary is indigenous to the Mediterranean area, it also grows quite well in North America, preferring light soil and sunny, sheltered positions. Like all members of the mint family, rosemary contains volatile oils which are, in fact, the main active constituents.

Probably the main effect of rosemary is on the nervous system, where it has both a tonic and a stimulating action. It is considered an excellent thymoleptic, raising the spirits and reducing depression without creating overexcitation of the thoughts. This makes it an appropriate remedy for nervous debility and exhaustion. Another major action of rosemary is to stimulate the circulatory system. It is especially effective at enhancing the blood supply to the hands, feet, and head, and is therefore very effective in the treatment of cold hands and feet and other problems associated with poor circulation.

By stimulating the blood flow to the head, rosemary has developed a reputation for strengthening the memory, and it was on this basis that Shakespeare immortalized rosemary in *Hamlet* as the herb of remembrance. In the time of the Roman empire, students used to wear rosemary wreaths on their heads to improve their memories. In medieval Europe rosemary was known as the herb of fidelity and was used as a token of esteem between lovers or friends, signifying that they would not forget each other. The improved cerebral circulation can be effective in treating headaches and cold-type migraines with a constrictive or tight headache, as well as problems such as ringing in the ears, glaucoma, and reduced retinal circulation. Rosemary also contains compounds that inhibit the breakdown of acetylcholine, the major parasympathetic neurotransmitter, and it may offer some protection against the onset or progression of Alzheimer's disease and presenile dementia.

Rosemary, and especially the volatile oil, contains powerful antioxidants with a potency equivalent to BHA and BHT, which are widely used as preservatives in the food and cosmetics industries. Potential carcinogenicity of BHA and BHT has led to intensive research into suitable alternatives and rosemary is considered an excellent candidate for this purpose. Antibacterial and antifungal activity of rosemary oil has marked activity against gram-negative and gram-positive bacteria, as well as several molds including *Candida albicans.*

Taken as an infusion, rosemary is useful in mild cases of gastroenteritis or food poisoning, and can be used as a mouthwash and gargle for sore throats, mouth ulcers, and gum disease. As a skin wash, rosemary can be used to treat cuts, wounds, and skin infections. Rosemary also has beneficial actions in the digestive system where it is an excellent remedy for indigestion, flatulence, and diarrhea. It exerts a marked carminative or spasmolytic effect, induced by the volatile oil, while the bitter taste stimulates the flow of digestive juices and smooth peristalsis. Rosemary also has a warming and slightly analgesic effect when used as a skin wash or in a liniment, and this action can be useful in treating stiff muscles, arthritis, bursitis, or muscle cramps.

Clinical Applications in Fibromyalgia
Rosemary is one of my favorite remedies in treating FMS. The volatile oil or an infused oil from the leaves

can be used as a warming and pain-relieving topical application. It combines very well with other rubefacient and analgesic herbs such as mustard oil, horseradish, infused oil of juniper, and volatile oil of ginger for this purpose. Taken internally, rosemary extract is invaluable in treating memory lapses, confusion, brain fog, depression, listlessness, and general lowered vitality. The carminative properties can be beneficial in irritable bowel syndrome, while the antimicrobial and especially the antifungal action is helpful in treating bowel flora disturbances.

Rumex crispus (Yellow Dock)

FAMILY: *Polygonaceae*
PART USED: Root
This plant is well known as a general alterative tonic, being slightly laxative and a cholagogue (stimulating the flow of bile from the gallbladder). Bowel flora balance is critical to yellow dock's proper laxative activation, and herbalists often prescribe it along with garlic and *lactobacillus acidophilus* to promote optimal bowel flora activity.

The laxative action of yellow dock provides an alterative effect. It is considered especially effective in clearing chronic dry and itchy skin conditions, including eczema, pruritus, and shingles, as well as for eruptive conditions such as cystic acne and boils. Yellow dock is also reputed to clear morbid waste material from the joints and is used, frequently in combination with burdock, as an alterative for arthritis, rheumatism, and gout.

However, long-term use or very high doses of yellow dock may cause some abdominal cramping. It is also possible that long-term use will lead to habituation. Yellow dock also contains tannins, which tend to astringe the gut wall and reduce the laxative properties somewhat as well as tone a flaccid bowel wall.

Yellow dock exhibits some antibacterial action. It is reputed to concentrate iron from the soil and to be an excellent source of bioavailable iron in anemia.

Clinical Applications in Fibromyalgia

I commonly prescribe this herb as part of a cleansing and detoxification program. It has traditionally been used in spring cleanses and combines very well with burdock, dandelion root, stinging nettle, barberry, and cleavers for this purpose.

Salix spp. (Willow)

FAMILY: *Salicaceae*
PART USED: Bark and leaves
There are a great many species of willow and they all appear to be medicinally active although the black (*S. nigra*) and white (*S. alba*) are most commonly used. Their therapeutic effect is much like that of poplar bark, being rich in phenolic glycosides that

yield salicylates and hence cause antipyretic, analgesic, antirheumatic, and anti-inflammatory actions. Tannins contribute to an astringent effect. Willow was the original source for salicylic acid from which aspirin was made.

Salicylic acid is known to act upon the enzymes that control prostaglandin formation, promoting the PG1 and 3 series, which are generally anti-inflammatory, while inhibiting the PGE1 and 2 series, which tend to be inflammatory. Salicylates in whole plant extracts, and the salicin they yield, are not irritating to the gastric lining, as is aspirin. Plant-derived salicylates do not exhibit the anticoagulant properties seen in aspirin and cannot be used as a substitute to prevent blood clotting.

Indicated uses for willow include feverish conditions such as colds and influenza, as well as arthritic and rheumatoid conditions and pain from musculoskeletal disorders. Collagen disorders with inflammatory changes are a specific indication. Individuals with a known hypersensitivity to aspirin or salicylates should not use willow, nor should people with asthma, diabetes, gout, hemophilia, attention deficit hyperactivity disorder, kidney or liver disease, and those taking guaifenesin. Concurrent administration of willow with other salicylate-rich substances should be avoided. Possible salicylate-drug interactions may occur with anticoagulants, methotrexate, metoclopramide, phenytoin, probenacid, spironolactone, and valproate.

Clinical Applications in Fibromyalgia
Willow is a very useful herb for the treatment of FMS, both on a long-term basis and for short-term applications for acute pain situations. For chronic musculoskeletal pain willow is best combined with warming herbs to reduce its cooling properties, which may be too strong in a person with FMS, who already tends to feel chilly. Ginger, turmeric, and prickly ash are useful for this purpose. For a quicker-acting analgesic effect in cases of inflammation, combine willow with Jamaican dogwood, wild lettuce, California poppy, or other analgesic herbs.

Schizandra chinensis
(Wu Wei Zi/Chinese Magnolia)
FAMILY: *Schisandraceae*
PART USED: Fruit and seed
This herb is widely used in traditional Chinese medicine, where it is said to enter the lung and kidney meridians and to be useful to reduce coughing and tonify deficient kidneys, thus being used for nocturnal emissions, spermatorrhoea, leucorrhoea, and excessive urination. It is also used for excessive perspiration, night sweats, insomnia, and forgetfulness.

Schizandra is considered an adaptogen, reducing the physical response to stress while also serving as a stimulant and energy restorer. It is beneficial to athletes, improving endurance, stamina, and power, and reducing recovery time. Individual components have a depressant effect on the central nervous system, but the whole fruit extract shows a stimulant effect. Inhibition of the dopamine system has been suggested and stimulation of cholinergic receptors in the parasympathetic system has been demonstrated. Learning ability, concentration, memory, and recall are all improved with *schizandra*. Fine coordination is also improved and tactile sensitivity is increased.

Active constituents include a group of lignans, as well as triterpenes and volatile oil. The lignans show considerable promise in protecting the liver from toxic damage. They stimulate the microsomal concentration of cytochrome P450, the major detoxifying enzyme system of the liver, and they inhibit lipid peroxidation. Liver cell regeneration is increased and hepatocyte membrane stability is increased by schizandrin B. Additionally, there is an increase in liver glycogen synthesis, protein synthesis, and hepatic enzyme activity after ingestion of *schizandra,* which has exhibited a strong anti-inflammatory and anticancer action in animal studies.

Clinical trials using *schizandra* have shown promise in treating mild spastic paralysis following stroke, Parkinson's disease, Ménière's disease, and cerebellar ataxia. *Schizandra* is known to be a uterine stimulant and should be avoided during pregnancy, but can be helpful to induce cervical dilation and proper contractions in childbirth.

Clinical Applications in Fibromyalgia
This is an herb I have only recently introduced to my clinical practice and I am using it more and more frequently. As a warming adaptogen with a specific action on mental processes and a tonic and protective action on the liver, it is particularly useful in treating FMS where allergies and environmental toxins aggravate the problem. As a parasympathomimetic it is helpful in treating people stuck in the sympathetic/adrenalin response pattern, which is classic in FMS. I combine it with other adaptogens such as licorice and Siberian ginseng for a long-term tonic action and with sedative herbs such as blue vervain and passionflower for disturbed sleep.

Scutalleria lateriflora (Skullcap)
FAMILY: *Lamiaceae*
PART USED: Aerial parts
This smallish, perennial plant, indigenous to North America, has pretty, pale blue flowers. It has traditionally

been used as a sedative and anticon-vulsant to treat epilepsy, Saint Vitus' dance, hysteria, nervous tension, and anxiety.

Skullcap contains a bitter flavone glycoside, which may be responsible for the observed parasympath-omimetic effect in the gut. This vagal stimulation causes secretion of hydrochloric acid, and mucous and digestive enzymes; promotes smooth and regular peristalsis; and activates the liver. This makes skullcap a valu-able remedy in treating symptoms of irritable bowel disease. As well as being markedly relaxing and sedative, skullcap has significant tonic proper-ties and is especially indicated where there is mental exhaustion, distress after excessive work or stress, in chronic fatigue syndrome, and for persistent unwanted thoughts and an inability to quiet the mind.

Clinical Applications in Fibromyalgia
I prescribe skullcap as a very effective sedative, gentle but powerful. I use it in combination with other relaxing nervines such as chamomile and *melissa* for daytime use in treating anx-iety, panic attacks, disordered thoughts, and oversensitivity to stress. At night I use it with other sedative nervines such as hops and passionflower to promote deep and restful sleep.

Serenoa repens/serrulata
(**Saw Palmetto**)
FAMILY: *Palmae*
PART USED: Fruit
Saw palmetto is a small, scrubby tree growing in swampy areas of the southeastern United States, especially Georgia and Florida. It is the oil-rich berries that are used medicinally. These were traditionally eaten by the males of the indigenous tribes of the area, being considered a powerful male tonic. Later they were fed to cattle, which demonstrated improved weight gain, glossier coats, and healthier offspring when compared to animals not fed the berries. Based on these observations the first research and clinical trials into saw palmetto were carried out.

This is a plant that has been rapidly gaining popularity among professional and lay herbalists for its unique actions upon the male reproductive organs. It is considered to be one of the best tonic and restorative herbs and to be very effective in regulating abnormal growth of the prostate gland. Over twenty double-blind placebo-controlled studies have demonstrated that saw palmetto extract affords sig-nificant improvement of all the symp-toms of benign prostatic overgrowth. In many cases the studies have demon-strated that saw palmetto is signifi-cantly more effective at symptom management than are the standard prescription drugs.

The berries resemble an olive in size and shape and are purplish black, with a strong, acrid smell and taste. They are harvested when ripe, from October through December. The berries contain up to 1.5 percent oil, comprising both saturated and unsaturated fatty acids and a variety of sterols that may be used by the body to support the formation of a variety of steroid-based hormones.

Traditionally, saw palmetto berries have entered the *materia medica* as an effective agent for a variety of inflammatory disorders of the mucous membranes, including inflammation of the uterine lining, peritonitis, appendicitis, and pelvic inflammatory disease, and for laryngitis, bronchitis, and whooping cough. They have also been found useful as a tonic food in convalescence, anorexia, or severe debilitation. Additionally, older herbals describe saw palmetto's use in ovarian pain, underdevelopment of female or male sexual organs, and for menstrual cramps. Its major role, though, has been in the treatment of male reproductive disorders, specifically, impotence, infertility, and benign prostatic hyperplasia.

Saw palmetto also exhibits some estrogenic influence, and this may explain the traditional breast-stimulating use. Little research exists on this estrogenic effect, but some authors suggest that the herb is best avoided in cases of estrogen-dependent disease and while taking the birth control pill.

Clinical Applications in Fibromyalgia
Most people today know this herb only as a male tonic for prostate enlargement. I use it in both men and women as a nutritive anabolic supplement. It is excellent for chronic debility, weakness convalescence, and loss of appetite. I combine it with other nutritive tonic herbs such as oats, kelp, fenugreek, nettles, and alfalfa to make a "superfood" supplement.

Smilax officinalis/ornata and spp. (**Sarsaparilla**)
FAMILY: *Liliaceae*
PART USED: Root
This is a large perennial vine, indigenous to Central America, that was introduced to Europe in the 1600s as a remedy for syphilis and remained popular as an alterative and blood cleanser, being especially used as a spring tonic. Smilax (sarsaparilla) is used as an antirheumatic, anti-inflammatory, antiseptic, and antipruritic. Sarsaparilla has been especially well known throughout history not only as a treatment for syphilis, but for leprosy, psoriasis, indolent ulcers, and gangrene.

Sarsaparilla contains significant amounts of steroidal saponins and a variety of phytosterols. These appear to work synergistically to give a potent anti-inflammatory effect, being most noted for arthritic and rheumatic conditions. *Smilax spp.* has been used as the starting point for the synthesis of corticosteroid drugs. There is also some liver-protective effect and an improvement of appetite and digestion. Sarsaparilla has a diuretic action and increases the urinary elimination of chlorides and uric acid.

Clinical Applications in Fibromyalgia
This is a warming, stimulating, anabolic, energizing herb. It is used for adrenal support and as an anti-inflammatory and adaptogenic tonic. I use it in cases of weakness, debility, chilliness, poor appetite, muscular and joint stiffness.

Tabebuia avellanedae/impetigunosa/ cassinoides
(Taheebo/Lapacho/Pau d'arco)
FAMILY: *Bignoniaceae*
PART USED: Inner bark
This large tree is native to Brazil. Much confusion exists in commerce over the preferred species and probably several species are active. It has an extensive folk history as a cancer remedy and to treat a variety of other conditions including leprosy, dysentery, snake bite, syphilis, diarrhea, bed-wetting, boils, pharyngitis, and wounds. Modern research has confirmed the anticancer activity, specifically against solid tumors, and it also

provides some pain relief for cancer patients.

The principal active ingredients are anthrone derivatives including lapachol, a powerful antifungal with a spectrum of activity comparable to the prescription medication ketaconazole (Nizoral). This makes taheebo an excellent remedy against *Candida albicans* overgrowth. Lapachol has demonstrated significant antibacterial activity against gram-positive bacteria, and has also shown antiviral activity including marked activity against the polio, herpes, and influenza viruses. The whole plant extract has significant anti-inflammatory activity.

Clinical Applications in Fibromyalgia
This plant is especially helpful in treating *Candida albicans* overgrowth that can lead to or aggravate food allergies and irritable bowel syndrome. It makes a pleasant-tasting tea that can be drunk freely and can also be used locally as a douche for vaginal *Candida* and as an enema for rectal and bowel application. It combines well with calendula for this purpose.

Tanacetum parthenium (Feverfew)
FAMILY: *Asteraceae*
PART USED: Leaves
This is a common garden and windowsill plant and is best used fresh for preservation of the active constituents. For storage over the winter

a tincture of the fresh plant may be used, or the herb may be freeze-dried and taken in capsules.

The leaves are very bitter and cooling and the herb was traditionally used for fevers, hence the common name. The leaves are rich in pyrethrin compounds, and as a strong tea may be used as an effective insect repellent, safe for plants, animals, and humans. Topical applications of the chopped fresh leaf will reduce the pain of insect bites and daily drinking of the tea is said to repel insects.

Extracts of feverfew have been shown to inhibit platelet aggregation and immune responses in white blood cells, which may account for its traditional use in treating allergies as well as the widely accepted effect on migraines. This is aided by the inhibition of histamine release from mast cells. In inflamed joints, feverfew inhibits the release of cytokines from white blood cells and this provides significant relief in arthritis. Feverfew is probably best known for its preventive effect in migraines, specifically the type that cause throbbing, hot headaches.

The best way to use feverfew is to grow it and eat three to five leaves daily, in a sandwich or a salad. It can take several months of continuous use for noticeable improvement to occur. If there is any oral sensitivity, then take it as a capsule or tincture. Feverfew is a known uterine stimulant with emmenagogue effects and should be avoided during pregnancy.

Clinical Applications in Fibromyalgia
This herb is beneficial in treating arthritic conditions where there is heat and redness of the joint or surrounding tissues. It is markedly cooling, which is generally not recommended in FMS for long-term use, so other anti-inflammatory and antiarthritic herbs may be preferable. Feverfew is the best remedy for migraines where there is sensation of heat, cravings for cool compresses and iced drinks, redness of the face, throbbing headache, or dilated temporal arteries. It should not be used when the headache is gripping, constrictive, or crushing, or when the person feels chilled and craves hot drinks or heat applications.

Trigonella foenum-graecum
(**Fenugreek**)
FAMILY: *Leguminoseae*
PART USED: Seeds
This small annual plant, similar in appearance to lucerne or alfalfa, is indigenous to the Mediterranean but has been cultivated widely for hundreds of years for its seeds, which are used as a medicine and a cooking spice.

The major constituents of the seeds are mucilage and protein. Soaking the seeds in water yields a slippery, demulcent mass much like psyllium, slippery elm, or flaxseed.

This may be taken as a gruel for debility, convalescence, digestive weakness, gastrointestinal ulceration or inflammation, neurasthenia, wasting, and chronic diarrhea. It is well known as a nourishing, building food. It is also widely used in animal feed and is said to give a lustrous coat.

Steroidal saponins are probably responsible for the marked anti-inflammatory effects, the whole plant extract having an action similar to cortisone and being useful for arthritis and eczema.

Hypoglycemic and cholesterol-reducing activity has been reported and there is a slight uterine-stimulating effect.

Clinical Applications in Fibromyalgia
This herb can be taken as a tincture, decoction, or gruel, but can also be included in the diet in the form of ground seeds used in curry, or by eating the fresh leaves. It is warming and nourishing, and especially useful in treating debility and convalescence, where there is loss of appetite and weight loss.

Ulmus rubra (Slippery Elm)
FAMILY: *Ulmaceae*
PART USED: Inner bark
This tree is indigenous to North America and has recently been adversely affected by a viral disease; this, coupled with persistent overharvesting of the bark, has contributed to its decline in the wild. Some is now being cultivated commercially, but the tree is slow growing and the medicinal properties are greater in older trees. The bark is usually sold in a powder, creamy reddish in color and strongly aromatic. Large cells in the inner bark are filled with mucilaginous material that is readily extracted into water. The herb is usually taken like a gruel, a heaping teaspoon being stirred into a little cold water, two cups of hot water stirred in, and flavored if desired with honey, lemon juice, or cinnamon. It should be eaten quickly because the mucilage absorbs water, swells, and gels.

The mucilage exerts a powerful demulcent effect, soothing the digestive tract from throat to rectum. It is useful for indigestion, heartburn, peptic ulcers, inflammatory bowel disease, diverticulosis, diarrhea, and constipation. Slippery elm powder is rich in complex sugars (fructo-oligosacchandes) that are the preferred food of the beneficial bowel flora. This makes it a useful remedy where there is chronic diarrhea, bowel infection, and leaky gut syndrome, and after the use of antibiotics. Slippery elm is very nutritious and makes an excellent food for infants and invalids. It is a soothing expectorant that thins and loosens thick or sticky mucus in the lungs. It can also be used topically as an emollient for sore, itchy, and irritated skin conditions.

Clinical Applications in Fibromyalgia
This herb is useful when treating the symptoms of irritable bowel syndrome. It is soothing and reduces spasms and pain while also regulating the form and consistency of the bowel movement and making it easier to pass. It combines well with psyllium seed, cramp bark, and the carminatives. By promoting growth of beneficial flora, slippery elm is helpful in treating leaky gut syndrome. Slippery elm gruel has long been known as an ideal food for invalids, being nourishing and easy to digest.

Urtica dioica (Nettle)
FAMILY: *Urticaceae*
PART USED: Leaves and root
This is a common weed, growing on disturbed soil and now naturalized around the world. The aerial parts are gathered just before flowering and may be juiced and preserved with alcohol or glycerine, or they may be dried for use in tincture or tea. The sting is neutralized by alcohol, heat, and drying, so do not ingest the fresh juice without heating it first. The roots are dug in the fall.

Nettle was used in the past as a source of fiber for spinning and weaving, and the tender spring greens can be cooked like spinach and eaten. Nettle has long been recognized as a strong styptic to stop bleeding and is used in folk medicine as a blood puri-fier or alterative with a tissue specificity for skin and joints. Topical applications of fresh nettles were traditionally used as a counterirritant treatment for arthritis.

In clinical studies, nettle is mostly recognized as being an excellent diuretic, especially for cardiac edema, venous insufficiency, and where there is excessive uric acid building up in the tissues. It is also recommended for its astringent and toning properties, especially in the urinary tract. The tiny amount of histamine in the sting of the nettle acts in an almost homeopathic way to desensitize the body, thereby reducing allergic and inflammatory situations. It can be used to treat hives, asthma, and other allergic reactions, as well as chronic inflammations such as arthritis.

Minerals, including high amounts of potassium, calcium, and silicic acid, and high amounts of chlorophyll and carotenoids contribute to the long tradition of using nettles as an alterative for arthritis, rheumatism, cancer, and eruptive skin conditions. Nettle root can also significantly benefit benign enlargement of the prostate gland.

Clinical Applications in Fibromyalgia
This is a very useful and deservedly popular herb in folk medicine. It is a very nutritious plant and can be cooked and eaten freely. The spring

growth is preferred because later in the season calcium crystals start to form in the leaves and these can cause accumulation of calcium oxalates in the kidneys and aggravate kidney stones. I often prescribe it in the form of a tincture to treat arthritis, rheumatism, gout, and FMS. It is anti- inflammatory, alterative, and energizing to the whole body.

Vaccinium myrtillus (Bilberry/Blueberry)

FAMILY: *Ericaceae*
PART USED: Leaves and fruit
This small, shrubby bush with slightly bell-shaped drooping flowers, leathery leaves, and dark purple-blue berries is indigenous to the temperate north, growing in acidic, rocky soil. The deep purple color of the fruit is imparted by a large and complex group of pigments called the anthocyanidins. Additionally, there are tannins, flavonoids, and phenolic acids that are structurally related and have supportive and adjunctive properties.

In the literature and in clinical practice the leaves and flowers seem to be interchangeable, although more research needs to be done to determine the relative strength of the two parts. The sum effect of the constituents is to enhance the structural integrity of the collagen matrix of the body. Blueberry is one of the very best connective tissue tonics. It gives increased tensile strength and

improved repair ability to connective tissue, including the capillary and vein walls, the heart valves, tendons, ligaments, fascia, muscle, and cartilage.

By improving functional disturbances of capillary beds and veins, bilberry is one of the best treatments for diabetic microcirculatory damage. Anthocyanidins have a tissue specificity for the pigmented epithelium at the back of the eye and hasten the regeneration of rhodopsin, one of the visual pigments. Bilberry is used to treat diabetic retinopathy as well as poor night vision, glaucoma, and cataracts.

The antioxidant effect of bilberry is also significant. Bilberry is helpful for varicose veins, hemorrhoids, edema, blood clots, and easy bruising. Extract of bilberry has long been known to possess insulin-like properties that lower blood sugar. The fruits have significant amounts of vitamin C, making them useful as a nutritive supplement. The high level of tannins in the fruits provide a mildly antibacterial and astringent effect, useful for treating mild to moderate diarrhea, colitis, diverticulosis, and gastroenteritis, as well as giving an antigalactogogue effect. Weiss suggests that the anthocyanidin pigments also enter the intestinal mucosa and form a protective layer that reduces mucosal abrasions and irritations. He recommends bilberry for dystrophy and erosion of the intestinal lining such as occurs in inflammatory bowel diseases. The fresh fruits, being rich in cellulose, tend to act as a mild laxative for persistent, low-grade constipation. The leaves can be used as a douche for *Candida,* leucorrhoea, and vaginitis, and as a mouthwash for leukoplakia and periodontal disease.

Clinical Applications in Fibromyalgia
For those people who enjoy the idea of eating their medicine, a cup of blueberries daily is easy to prescribe. I use them, fresh or frozen, to treat many conditions. Bilberries have the added advantage of being a collagen/connective tissue tonic. This means they are also beneficial for arthritic joint damage, cartilage damage, and brittleness, and for improving the tensile strength of fascia. Due to their connective tissue tonic properties, bilberries can also be used to treat mitral valve prolapse.

Valeriana officinalis (Valerian)
FAMILY: *Valerianceae*
PART USED: Root
This plant has a long history of use, being mentioned by Hippocrates, Theophrastus, Dioscorides, Pliny, and Galen. By the sixteenth century in Europe it was highly regarded as a strengthening tonic for the nerves, being recommended for epilepsy, hysteria, convulsions, overexcitement, and "the vapors."

Valerian has a tranquilizing effect, reducing sensitivity in the nervous system and inducing drowsiness. It has traditionally been used to promote deep and restful sleep. Unlike prescription sleeping drugs, valerian does not suppress REM (rapid eye movement) sleep and thus does not leave the person groggy and hungover the next day unless very high doses are used. Valerian is an excellent remedy for chronic insomnia, as it seems to put the person into a drowsy twilight zone from which it is easy to fall asleep. It is also useful for sleep-onset insomnia due to excitement or fear and for sleep-maintenance insomnia.

Valerian has also been shown to have antispasmodic activity, with a focus of action in the digestive organs, heart, and circulatory system. Thus valerian may be used to relax the blood vessels and balance the blood pressure, as well as to reduce abdominal cramping and colic.

Because of the relaxing effect of valerian in the central nervous system it can be used effectively for fits, seizures, and convulsions, as well as for nervous palpitations. In fact, valerian is particularly effective in nervous tension and anxiety states, including nervous headaches and nervous exhaustion.

Clinical Application in Fibromyalgia
Valerian is well known as a relaxing agent for symptoms of stress, tension, anxiety, worry, and inability to relax. It is particularly indicated where there

is sleep-onset or sleep-maintenance insomnia, or nighttime motor activity, including restless leg syndrome, inner restlessness, and tension. It may be helpful in stress headaches, depression, muscle tension, and skeletal or smooth-muscle cramping. I have used it with excellent results where there is a lot of digestive spasms and cramping, in combination with cramp bark and the sedative carminatives such as chamomile or lemon balm. I have used it to reduce the spasms of interstitial cystitis in combination with cramp bark, yarrow, ginger, and demulcents such as couch grass or corn silk. For sleep disorders it can be combined with passionflower or skullcap. The tincture is more effective than the tea because it will better extract the volatile constituents; the tea is also less appealing due to its very strong and somewhat disagreeable smell.

Verbena officinalis/hastata (Blue Vervain)

FAMILY: *Verbenaceae*
PART USED: Aerial parts

The *officinalis* species, indigenous to Europe, is a small, weedy perennial with inconspicuous foliage and small lilac flowers. Its cousin, the American *V. hastato* species, is much taller, reaching 4 or 5 feet high, and topped with dramatic spikes of intense purple flowers. Related genuses include *Lippia,* from which comes lemon verbena, and *Vitex,* from which comes chaste berry. This herb was sacred to the ancient Greeks and the Druids, and old folk names for it include "herb of grace" and "sacred herb." The name *Verbena* was the ancient Roman name for altar plants in general. *Vervain* is reputed to be the herb that was used to staunch the wounds of Christ on Mount Calvary. Both species are noted as traditional tonic nervines. Traditional American Indian uses include expectorant, diaphoretic, sweat inducing, antispasmodic, and tonic applications.

Verbena (vervain) contains a volatile oil rich in monoterpenes that tend to be sedative, antispasmodic, and anti-inflammatory. Interestingly, it appears to be most effective in very small doses, with larger doses actually reducing efficacy. It also has some antiviral properties. Commercial *verbena* volatile oil is usually made from lemon verbena and the true *V. officinalis* volatile oil is incredibly expensive.

Vervain also contains a bitter that provides a gentle but persuasive stimulating effect to the entire digestive tract, promoting mucus, enzyme, and acid secretion; smooth peristaltic action; and increased hepatic and biliary action. It eases digestive cramping and colic, and reduces chronic gastritis and dyspepsia.

Vervain is reputed to regulate hormone balance by virtue of promoting adequate hepatic clearance. Traditionally, vervain has also been used as a general endocrine normalizer, balancing pituitary, thyroid, pancreatic, ovarian, testicular, and adrenal function. Recent research has shown that vervain has a luteinizing action, similar to though weaker than *vitex.* It has been used traditionally to treat dysmenorrhoea and as a galactogogue to stimulate milk production. *Verbena* has been shown to suppress thyroid hormone production by reducing TSH (thyroid-stimulating hormone) from the anterior pituitary.

The effects of vervain are dose dependant: More vervain is sedating, while small doses are stimulating and tonic. This explains the traditional claims for its tonic action, being used as a treatment for both nervous excitability and nervous exhaustion.

Vervain is used to treat anxiety, hysteria, insomnia, fatigue, lethargy, nervous debility, depression, epilepsy, tension headaches, menstrual and reproductive organ cramping, and endocrine abnormalities and deficiencies.

Clinical Applications in Fibromyalgia
Blue vervain or *verbena* is the most commonly prescribed herb in my clinical practice and has been for years. I have never met a person who didn't benefit from taking it! As a gentle normalizer of sympathetic and parasympathetic tone, it is beneficial for all stress, anxiety, and depression conditions, all the way from total apathy and lethargy right up to hysteria and mania. By the bitter action it improves liver and digestive function and promotes overall hormone balancing. It is useful for headaches, whether from stress and tension, digestive distress, or menstrual irregularities. Its nervine properties make it helpful for improved energy in the day and improved sleep quality at night, causing it to be classified as a perfect adaptogen.

Vinca major/minor (Periwinkle)
FAMILY: *Apocynaceae*
PART USED: Leaves
This trailing evergreen perennial has a five-petaled flower of intense lilac-blue and is frequently grown as an ornamental, providing dense ground cover in shady places. It was cited by Dioscorides and Galen almost 2,000 years ago as an excellent astringent for diarrhea and dysentery and was known as a remedy for bleeding conditions, including nosebleed, hemorrhoids, gastrointestinal or pulmonary bleeding (including tuberculosis), and wounds. It was also reputed to cure muscle cramps if the fresh leaves were bound over the affected part.

Modern research has discovered the presence of the indole alkaloid vincamine, which has a pronounced effect on cerebral circulatory dynamics. Administration of *vinca* extract causes an increased consumption of glucose and oxygen by the brain cells, which is attributed to a general tonic effect on the cerebral blood vessels. *Vinca* is used to treat memory loss, loss of mental acuity and clarity, senility, Alzheimer's disease, tinnitus, dizziness, Ménière's disease, Parkinson's disease, behavior disorders, mental fatigue, vertigo, and constrictive headaches. It is especially useful after brain trauma such as stroke, brain surgery, or a severe blow to the head. Several weeks of continuous therapy may be required before clinical effects are noticed. *Vinca* is contraindicated in cases of raised intracranial pressure.

The root is used in sub-Saharan Africa to treat hypertension. Note that this plant is related to, but therapeutically quite different from, the Madagascar periwinkle from which is extracted vinblastine and vincristine, the chemotherapy agents used to treat Hodgkin's disease and leukemia.

Clinical Applications in Fibromyalgia

This is a much underused plant, and very easy to find because it is so widely grown. In fact you can probably harvest your own, provided you have access to an area that isn't sprayed. Alkaloids are partially soluble in water, so a tincture of 45 to 65 percent alcohol is recommended for optimum extraction of active compounds. I use periwinkle whenever there is severe brain fog, memory loss, confusion, dizziness, and spaciness.

Withania somnifera (Ashwagandha)

FAMILY: *Solanaceae*
PART USED: Root

This is one of the most revered tonic plants in Ayurvedic medicine. It is a member of the nightshade family and grows extensively across the Middle East and subtropical India. It is considered an excellent adaptogen and tonic, and a relaxing nervine, and is used as an anti-inflammatory and antitumor agent. It was traditionally considered to improve learning, memory, and recall.

In high doses, the isolated alkaloids exhibit a sedative and suppressive effect on the higher brain centers while at the same time lowering blood pressure, slowing the heart, and stimulating respiration. They are also spasmolytic to intestinal, uterine, bronchial, and arterial smooth muscle, with a similar mode of action to an alkaloid in opium poppy. *Withania* alkaloids are nontoxic, non-habit-forming, and nonirritating to the mucous membranes.

Saponins have antibacterial, antitumor, and anti-inflammatory actions and some protect against chemically induced liver damage. They also increase liver glycogen stores in the same way that the glucocorticoids do. The isolated saponin *withaferin a* is an immune suppressant, in contrast to the whole plant extract, which is immune stimulating.

Memory-enhancing, antidepressant, and stress-reducing properties have been demonstrated in animal studies. The seeds of *withania* have a sparing effect on stress-induced adrenal cortisol and ascorbic acid depletion, and an adrenal protective effect. An anabolic effect at oral doses of 100 mg/kg of body weight has been demonstrated. In children, *withania* extract has demonstrated increased body weight, total plasma proteins, mean corpuscular hemoglobin, and hand grip. In middle-aged adults, *withania* extract has demonstrated significant improvement in hemoglobin and red blood cell count, hair melanin (color), cholesterol levels, sexual function, and calcification of the nails.

Clinical Applications in Fibromyalgia
This is an herb I have been using more and more. It is sometimes (inaccurately) known as "Indian ginseng" because of its remarkable adaptogenic properties. It modulates adrenal function, including energy conservation and management during times of stress, as well as glucocorticoid-induced anti-inflammatory and antiproliferative effects. It is a mild sedative, used to improve sleep quality

and duration. It is a tonic used to promote good energy production. It is used for chronic inflammations and immune dysregulation. It is especially well known for treating weakness, debility, convalescence, neurasthenia (reduction in vital force), impotence, anemia, aging, and senility. Ashwagandha combines very well with other adaptogenic and tonic herbs, including ginseng (Korean or Siberian), licorice, devil's club, and blue vervain.

Yucca bacata/glauca/brevifolia and spp. (Yucca)
FAMILY: *Liliaceae/Agavaceae*
PART USED: Whole plant
This plant has traditionally been used as a valuable food item by the Plains Indians and is currently approved in the United States for food use.

Various saponins that have been isolated from different yucca species appear to act in a similar way to those found in sarsaparilla, being anti-inflammatory, especially to the joints. There appears to be a range of responsiveness, varying from days to weeks among individuals. The saponins are also considered to be responsible for the notable hypotensive, cholesterol-, and triglyceride-reducing effect of the extract.

Clinical Applications in Fibromyalgia
I use this herb when treating symptoms of arthritis, including swelling,

pain, and stiffness. It is especially indicated in cases where there is also elevated blood pressure or cholesterol. It is best taken as a tincture for optimal extraction of the saponins, which are not water soluble.

Zanthoxylum clava-herculis/ americanum (Prickly Ash)
FAMILY: *Rutaceae*
PART USED: Root bark/berry

This plant was much esteemed by American Indians and was called toothache plant by the early settlers because its root bark was considered to relieve toothaches. Prickly ash is part of the traditional Hoxsey cancer formula because of its stimulating, tonic, alterative properties.

Its alkaloids are structurally related to the alkaloids of opium poppy, corydalis, goldenseal, and barberry, as well as to curare (arrow poison in the Amazon). Studies have demonstrated a reversible neuromuscular blocking effect, notably affecting smooth muscle and leading to vasodilation and an hypotensive action. There is also a significant anti-inflammatory action, and it can potentiate the analgesic effect of morphine, prolonging barbiturate-induced sleep. Thus prickly ash may be helpful to reduce requirements of sleeping aids. There are also significant antibacterial effects, notably against gram-positive bacteria but not against gram-negative ones.

Prickly ash is known to induce copious salivation, along with a sensation of warmth in the stomach, an increased flow of digestive juices, and biliary and hepatic activity. The heart rate increases slightly, causing renal function and urine production to become slightly increased. It is somewhat diaphoretic, as a result of vasodilation. It is considered to be a warming, stimulating digestive tonic. The bark is considered to be an alterative and has more tonic properties, while the berries are more aromatic and hence more antispasmodic and stimulating.

Taken internally, prickly ash berries are used for muscle cramps (both skeletal and smooth), asthma, colic, menstrual cramps, arthritis, and rheumatism. Prickly ash is also excellent for circulatory insufficiency, including Raynaud's disease and chilled extremities. The bark is used internally for weak and insufficient digestive functions.

Clinical Applications in Fibromyalgia
I use prickly ash for chilly patients who have muscular weakness, stiffness, and aching. It is especially good for Raynaud's. I also find it helpful where there is digestive bloating, belching, bad breath, feeling of heaviness in the stomach, and atonic constipation.

Zingiber officinalis (Ginger)
FAMILY: *Zingiberaceae*
PART USED: Rhizome

Ginger is widely used as a kitchen spice, for which purpose it is usually sold dried and powdered, which causes the loss of much of the valuable volatile oils. The fresh root of ginger is readily available and is infinitely preferable, both for cooking and for medicinal use. Fresh ginger has a very pungent flavor and leaves a hot sensation in the mouth; this reflects its warming and stimulating properties.

Ginger exerts a calming influence on the heart, slowing the rate and regulating the rhythm. It slows the breathing rate, reduces blood pressure and cholesterol, and has cardiotonic properties.

Ginger especially stimulates the blood supply to the hands and feet and is therefore very useful in conditions involving poor circulation to these areas. Chilblains, cramps, pins and needles, and cold hands and feet can all be helped by drinking ginger tea. It is also useful for cramps of the digestive system, painful menstruation, or for cramps of the large intestine, especially where there is associated flatulence. Recent research into ginger has focused on its ability to reduce nausea. Trials carried out on airline pilots and stewards have shown that ginger gave more effective and long-lasting relief from travel sickness than did over-the-counter pills, and did not cause any drowsiness.

Clinical Applications in Fibromyalgia
Ginger is warming and tonifying. It can be easily added to any herbal tea or tincture to improve peripheral and abdominal circulation and reduce queasiness, nausea, gas, or cramps. It is considered an adjuvant to other herbs, improving their absorption and assimilation. I use ginger for patients who feel chilly; have digestive cramps, gas, or poor peripheral circulation; or simply those in need of a warming, stimulating tonic.

INDEX

guaifenesin, 33, 69, 80, 89–93, 172
  contraindications, 91
  effective dosages, 91–92
  guidelines for taking, 92–93
  salicylates and, 91
guided visualization, 203

hair problems. *See* skin, hair, and nail
  problems
head injuries. *See* closed head injuries
headaches, 9, 15, 32–33
  natural remedies, 33
healing, diet and, 148–50
herbal remedies, 155–89
  advantages of, 159, 160
  for FMS, 165–89
  in holistic context, 161–62
  materia medica, 235–309
  most effective formulas, 164–65
  to treat FMS, 162
histamine, 85
history of FMS, 6
holistic medicine, 160–61
  on causal chain of disease, 163–64
  defined, 160
  herbal remedies and, 161–62
  methods and approach of, 163–65
  premise and focus of, 162–63
  principles of, 161
  therapeutic approaches, self-care, 192
holistic therapy, 97–216
homeostatic balance mechanisms,
  144–45
homogenization, 109, 111
hormones, 109
  significant in FMS, 62–63
hunter-gatherers, 100–104, 110, 123
hypoglycemia, 35, 39–40, 146–48

hypothalamic-pituitary-adrenal axis,
  53–55
hypothyroidism, 42

ibuprofen, 89, 93
immune response, 57, 212
inflammation, 172–73. *See also*
  anti-inflammatories, herbal
  arachidonic acid and, 105
injuries
  as causative agent, 73–74, 75
  whiplash, 74–75, 76
inositol, 132
insulin levels, 40
interleukin 2, 57
Internet resources, 4
interstitial cystitis, 26–27, 144
irritable bowel syndrome, 24–25, 38

kava, 88
kynurenine, 64–65

lactic acid, 18, 48, 71, 72
Lactobacillus bacteria, 125
leaky gut syndrome, 25, 111
lecithin, 138
lectins, 112–13
legumes, 107, 152–53
  recommended, 153
lifestyle, 7, 9
  balanced, need for, 9, 10–12
  change of, 9
  disharmonious, and FMS, 10–12
  drugs and, 80–81
  holistic medicine and, 163
light therapy, 198–200
linoleic acid, 119, 120, 121, 123
linolenic acid, 119, 122